MODEL LAW ENFORCEMENT CONTRACT: A LABOR PERSPECTIVE

(Third Edition)

By
Will Aitchison

 For information, please write: The Labor Relations Information System, 3021 N.E. Broadway, Portland, OR 97232-1810. (503) 282-5440.

Aitchison, William Bruce, 1951 -

ISBN 1-880607-14-X
Model Law Enforcement Contract: A Labor Perspective
(Third Edition)

1. Police Officers
2. Law and Procedures

ACKNOWLEDGMENTS

As usual, putting together this book was a group effort. I owe thanks to them all, and in particular to the three individuals who contributed mightily to the effort.

Marc Fuller waded through the hundreds of contracts we gathered to collate and reproduce the contract clauses contained in this book. Marc was also responsible for the lion's share of the process of collecting the contracts from around the country that we used as the basis for our Model Contract. Marc helped us prove that, yes indeed, some things are better the second time around.

Debbie Frields did her usual stellar job managing the production of the book, typesetting it, reading it and rereading it, and ensuring that we all met our deadlines. Debbie also had the unenviable task of converting the hundreds of contract articles we selected into a coherently organized and numbered model contract, a task that was daunting indeed.

Carol Green proofread the final text of this book until her eyes glazed over, doing her usual great job of catching things that I miss. Carol also orchestrated the rest of my work life so that I would have the time necessary to put together this book.

ABOUT THE AUTHOR

Will Aitchison is a Portland, Oregon attorney who has, over the course of his career, represented over 100 law enforcement and firefighter labor organizations in five western states.

Aitchison graduated from the University of Oregon (Honors College) in 1973, and received his Doctor of Jurisprudence Degree from Georgetown University Law Center in Washington, D.C. in 1976. After two years of clerking for the chief justice of the Oregon Court of Appeals, Aitchison entered private practice and has been representing labor organizations since that time. In addition to his private practice, Aitchison has served as both an arbitrator and a pro tem district court judge, and has contributed numerous articles to various periodicals.

Aitchison is the author of *The Rights of Law Enforcement Officers (Third Edition)*, *The Rights of Firefighters (Second Edition)*, *Model Firefighter's Contract: A Labor Perspective*, and *Factfinding and Arbitration*, all published by the Labor Relations Information System. He has lectured on numerous occasions throughout the country on FLSA issues and topics concerning public sector collective bargaining, and has served as an expert witness and consultant on matters pertaining to the rights of law enforcement and fire protection personnel.

Aitchison resides in Portland, Oregon.

INTRODUCTION

Over the years, I have represented approximately 90 law enforcement labor organizations in six states. As part of my practice, I have regularly negotiated collective bargaining agreements on behalf of our firm's clients, who include city police, county sheriff, and state police associations.

While wage and health insurance issues seem to dominate law enforcement collective bargaining these days, virtually every contract negotiation also involves numerous so-called "language" issues. Language issues are the nuts and bolts of a collective bargaining agreement, covering topics which range from disciplinary standards to overtime clauses, from bills of rights to seniority provisions, and from vacation and holiday accruals to the requirements for off duty work permits.

In drafting contract language, it is almost impossible to anticipate every possible circumstance in which the contract clause which is being written will be applied. Who could anticipate, for example, that a police officer on his way home from a court appearance on his regular day off would intervene in a burglary in progress he happened to see on his way home, and would later ask for two callback minimum payments for his activities that day? Or who could anticipate that a police employer would mistakenly assume that the health insurance clause in a contract required it to provide coverage for radial keratotomy eye surgery, and would later attempt to correct its mistake?

The reason I compiled this book was to allow those who negotiate law enforcement labor agreements to profit by the experience of others. All of the clauses in the Model Contract are taken from actual law enforcement labor agreements in existence in different parts of the country. In each case, there is a history behind how the contract clause came into being and has been applied, and perhaps even an arbitrator's interpretation of the clause. Rather than creating a contract out of a vacuum, the reader can use the contract language in this book as a guide in crafting language that can be applied in a variety of circumstances.

The Model Contract is derived from the more than 1,000 law enforcement collective bargaining agreements in our files. It is a "model" contract only from the standpoint of a law enforcement labor organization – representatives of management may find it a better example of what to avoid in a collective bargaining agreement.

To avoid confusion, the "legal" numbering style is used in the Model Contract. The various clauses in the contract provisions are given different numbers at the second level of the numbering system. For example, under Article 2 (Recognition), the clause covering the definition of the bargaining unit is numbered 2.1, while the clause covering the creation of new job classifications is numbered 2.2.

Different examples of contract language covering the same topic are given different numbers at the third level of the numbering system. For example, Article 9.2 covers the topic of when negotiations for a new contract commence. Articles 9.2.1 and 9.2.2 give examples from separate jurisdictions of contract language covering the same issue.

This third edition of the Model Contract is significantly different from its predecessors. It is much expanded, including a variety of new topics for negotiations such as deferred compensation "matches," combined leave accounts, and a wide variety of patrol work schedules reflecting the fact that the 5/8 shift is now used only by a minority of law enforcement agencies. It also contains many more examples of different ways to approach the same underlying contract issue.

Will Aitchison
Aitchison & Vick
Portland, Oregon
January 1, 1999

Table Of Contents

CHAPTER 1

GENERAL PROVISIONS

The articles contained in this chapter are the general introductory provisions found in most law enforcement collective bargaining agreements. Though introductory clauses are frequently given little attention in bargaining, their impact can be significant, and can determine how other clauses in a law enforcement collective bargaining agreement are interpreted.

Included in this chapter are examples of the following basic clauses in a law enforcement collective bargaining agreement:

- Recognition
- Union Security/Dues
- Strike Prohibitions
- Management Rights
- Existing Conditions/Maintenance of Benefits
- New Work Rules

The importance of general provisions to a collective bargaining agreement can hardly be overstated. For example, the strength or weakness of Management Rights and Maintenance of Benefits clauses can control whether an employer has the obligation to bargain over a whole host of changes in working conditions during the term of the contract, or whether a labor organization will be construed to have waived its rights to bargain.

From the standpoint of a labor organization, the most important of the introductory clauses is likely to be a "maintenance of benefits" clause. Such clauses "freeze" into the collective bargaining agreement all wages, hours, and mandatorily negotiable terms and conditions of employment which are not directly specified in the contract. Maintenance of benefits clauses are close cousins to contract clauses which require an employer to collectively bargain before making any changes in a mandatory subject of bargaining. However, where such "duty to bargain" clauses preserve the obligation to bargain, they are not as strong as maintenance of benefits clauses, which forbid an employer from making a change even if the employer is willing to bargain over the matter.

ARTICLE 1

INTRODUCTORY CLAUSES

1.1 Preamble.

1.1.1 This agreement is entered into between the Employer and the Association. It is the intent and purpose of this Agreement to assure sound and mutually beneficial working and economic relationships between the parties hereto, to provide an orderly and peaceful means of resolving any misunderstandings or differences which may arise, and to set forth herein the basic and full agreement between the parties concerning rates of pay, wages, hours of employment and other conditions of employment.[1]

1.2 Purpose.

1.2.1 The purpose of this Agreement is to provide a procedure for orderly collective bargaining between the parties, to secure prompt and fair disposition of grievances or complaints, to set forth the basic principles concerning hours of employment, wages, fringe benefits, and working conditions and to establish a basis for the cooperative solution of problems by responsible parties to the end that a spirit of peace and cooperation be maintained.[2]

1.3 Incorporation of Civil Service Rules.

1.3.1 For the purpose of this Agreement, the rules and regulations of the Merit Commission, and any written rules, regulations or policies of the Department which are not in conflict

[1] ***City of Reno, Nevada and Reno Police Protective Association.***

[2] ***City of Fort Wayne, Indiana and the Fraternal Order of Police, Lodge #14.***

with this Agreement are by this reference made a part of this Agreement. No employee shall suffer any loss of wages, hours or conditions of employment by reason of signing this Agreement.[1]

ARTICLE 2

RECOGNITION

2.1 Definition of Bargaining Unit.

2.1.1 Recognition.

2.1.1.1 The Employer hereby recognizes the Association as the sole and exclusive collective bargaining agent for the unit consisting of all sworn Police Officers, except the Chief.[2]

2.2 New and/or Changed Classifications.

2.2.1 If new classifications are established by the Employer and added to the bargaining unit or if the duties of existing classifications are substantially changed, a proposed wage scale shall be assigned thereto, and the Employer shall forward the new or changed class and proposed wage to the Association for review. The contract will then be subject to reopening for the sole purpose of negotiating a wage for the class, and only if so requested by the Association. If the parties cannot agree to the pay range after negotiations and mediation, the matter shall be submitted to binding arbitration. The Arbitrator shall establish a fair and equitable pay scale for the new or changed classification.[3]

[1] ***Lancaster County, Nebraska and Lancaster County Deputy Sheriffs' Association, Fraternal Order of Police, Lodge 29.***

[2] ***City of San Antonio, Texas and San Antonio Police Officers' Association.***

[3] ***State of Oregon and Oregon State Police Officers Association.***

2.3 Classifications Added to the Bargaining Unit.

2.3.1 Whenever the Employer establishes a new classification in the bargaining unit, it shall notify the Association in writing of the new classification specification and the provisional salary range. Within ten (10) calendar days of the receipt of such Employer notice, the Association shall notify the Employer in writing of its agreement or disagreement with the Employer's provisional salary range, it and the Employer shall negotiate that issue under the terms of state law. The Employer shall have the right to employ persons at its provisional salary range during the term of negotiations and arbitration, subject to full retroactive payment to all affected employees upon the conclusion of negotiation and arbitration.[1]

ARTICLE 3

ASSOCIATION SECURITY

3.1 Union Shop.

3.1.1 Union Dues.

3.1.1.1 It shall be a condition of employment that all employees covered by this Agreement who are members of the Association in good standing on the effective date of this Agreement shall remain members in good standing. It shall also be a condition of employment that all employees covered by this Agreement and hired on or after its effective date shall, on or before the thirty-first (31st) day following the beginning of such employment, become and remain members in good standing of the Association.

[1] ***City of Salem, Oregon and Salem Police Employees' Union.***

3.1.1.2 All employees covered by this Agreement, except new employees during the first thirty-one (31) days of their employment, shall be required to be and remain members in good standing of the Association.

3.1.1.3 The Employer shall discharge any employee as to whom the Association, through its authorized representative, delivers to the Employer a written notice that such employee is not in good standing in conformity with this Article. Upon receipt of a notice requesting termination of an employee who has not become or remained a member in good standing of the Association, the Employer shall immediately notify such employee that if he has not complied with the Association membership requirements of this Agreement within fifteen (15) days, his employment shall automatically be terminated. The Association agrees to withdraw any letter of termination if the employee, in respect to whom such letter has been served, shall complete his membership requirements within the time limit specified heretofore.

3.1.1.4 Pursuant to state law, the foregoing provisions of this Article shall not apply to employees who are bona fide members of a church or religious body whose religious tenets or teachings prohibit membership in employee associations. However, every such employee shall pay an amount of money equivalent to regular Association dues and initiation fees to a non-religious charity or to another charitable organization mutually agreed upon by the employee affected and the Association. The employee shall furnish written proof that such payment has been made.[1]

[1] ***Yakima, Washington and Yakima Police Patrolman's Association.***

3.2 Fair Share.

3.2.1 Any present officer who is not a member of the Association shall, as a condition of employment, be required to pay a fair share (not to exceed the amount of Association dues) of the cost of the collective bargaining process, contract administration in pursuing matters affecting wages, hours, and other conditions of employment, but not to exceed the amount of dues uniformly required of members. All officers hired on or after the effective date of this Agreement and who have not made application for membership shall, on or after the thirtieth (30th) day of their hire, also be required to pay a fair share as defined above.

3.2.1.1 With respect to any officer on whose behalf the Employer has not received a written authorization as provided for above, the Employer shall deduct from the wages of the officer the fair share financial obligation including any retroactive amount due and owing, and shall forward said amount to the Association on the tenth (10th) day of the month following the month in which the deduction is made, subject only to the following:

3.2.1.2 The Association has certified to the Employer that the affected officer has been delinquent in his obligations for at least thirty (30) days;

3.2.1.3 The Association has certified to the Employer that the affected officer has been notified in writing of the obligation and the requirement for each provision of this Article and that the employee has been advised by the Association of his obligations pursuant to this Article and of the manner in which the Association has calculated the fair share fee;

3.2.1.4 The Association has certified to the Employer that the affected officer has been given a reasonable opportunity to prepare and submit any objections to the payment and has been afforded an opportunity to have said objections adjudicated before an impartial arbitrator assigned by the employee and the Association for the purpose of determining and resolving any objections the officer may have to the fair share fee.

3.2.1.5 Objection On Other Grounds – Any non-member making a fair share payment may object to the amount of his fair share payments on the grounds that all or part of such payments have been expended by the Association for political activities or causes not germane to the collective bargaining process, contract administration and matters affecting employee wages, hours and conditions of employment.

3.2.1.6 Any such employee with any such objection shall process his/her objection in accordance with the notice and objection procedure established by the Association, which procedure shall be consistent with the requirements of the law.

3.2.1.7 Indemnification – The Association agrees to indemnify and save the Employer harmless against any claims, demands, suits or other form of liability which may arise by reason of any action taken or omitted by the Association or Employer in complying with the provisions of this Article.[1]

3.3 Lockout.

3.3.1 The Employer agrees that it will not lock out any bargaining unit employees.[2]

3.4 Discrimination on the Basis of Association Activity.

3.4.1 There shall be no discrimination, interference, restraint, or coercion by the Employer or any Employer represen-

[1] ***City of Des Plaines, Illinois and Combined Counties Police Association.***

[2] ***City of Racine, Wisconsin and Racine Police Association.***

tative against any member because of Association membership or because of any activity permissible under the State law and this Agreement.[1]

3.4.2 It is agreed that neither the Commission, nor the Department will:

3.4.2.1 1. Dominate or interfere in the formation or administration of the Association;

3.4.2.2 2. Discriminate in the hire, tenure, or the terms and conditions of employment of employees, for the purpose of encouraging or discouraging membership in the Association;

3.4.2.3. 3. Discharge, suspend, discipline, or otherwise discriminate against any employee because the employee has filed a complaint, affidavit, or petition, or given information or testimony on a grievance;

3.4.2.4 4. Restrain, coerce, or otherwise interfere with the Association in the exercise of rights granted by statute or this Agreement.[2]

3.5 Aid to Other Associations.

3.5.1 The Employer agrees there will be no aid, promotion or financing of any other labor organizations which purport to represent the employees in this bargaining unit and that any such activities on the part of the Employer or its agents is prohibited.[3]

[1] ***State of New York and Police Benevolent Association.***

[2] ***Nashua, New Hampshire Police Commission and International Brotherhood of Police Officers.***

[3] ***Monroe County and Monroe County Deputy Sheriffs' Association, Inc.***

ARTICLE 4

EMPLOYER SECURITY

4.1 Strikes.

4.1.1 Neither the Association nor an employee may strike, slowdown, picket, boycott, or otherwise interrupt work during the term of this contract. The Employer may not lock out employees during the term of this contract, but the Employer need not provide work during a labor dispute where the number of employees reporting for work is insufficient, in the Employer's judgment, to warrant continuing operation.

4.1.1.1 If a strike, slowdown, picketing, boycott, or other interruption of work occurs, the Employer shall notify the Association of the existence of that activity and ask the Association whether it has authorized that activity. The Association shall respond immediately in writing to the Employer's request.

4.1.1.2 Upon receiving notice of such activity, whether authorized or not, the Association shall take all reasonable steps to terminate the activity and induce the participating employees to return to work.

4.1.1.3 An employee who participates in a strike, slowdown, picket, boycott, or other interruption of work in violation of this Article may be disciplined, up to and including discharge.

4.1.1.4 Actions for monetary damages arising from alleged violations of this Article are not subject to the grievance procedure of this contract. This Article may be enforced in a court of competent jurisdiction. The Association shall not be liable for actions of individual employees, provided it has taken reasonable steps to prevent violations of this Article.[1]

[1] ***Eugene, Oregon and Eugene Police Employees' Association.***

4.1.2 The service performed by the employees covered by this Agreement are essential to the public health, safety, and welfare. There shall be no interruption of the work for any cause whatsoever, nor shall there be any work slow down or other interference with the public service.

4.1.2.1 In the event that any employee in the bargaining unit is engaged in any violation of this section, the Association shall, upon notification of the Employer, immediately order such employees to resume normal work activities and shall publicly denounce any such violations. If the Association carries out its obligations under this section in good faith, and has neither authorized nor ratified the action, it shall have no liability for any such action.[1]

ARTICLE 5

MANAGEMENT RIGHTS

5.1 General.

5.1.1 The Association recognizes the right of the Employer to operate and manage its affairs in all respects in accordance with applicable law and regulations of appropriate authorities. All rights and authority which the Employer has not officially abridged, delegated or modified by this Agreement are retained by the Employer.[2]

[1] ***City of Euclid, Ohio and Fraternal Order of Police, Lodge 18.***

[2] ***Minneapolis, Minnesota and Police Officers' Federation of Minneapolis.***

ARTICLE 6

PRODUCTIVITY

6.1 General.

6.1.1 The delivery of essential services in the most efficient and effective manner is of paramount importance and interest to both the Employer and the Association. Maximized service to the community is recognized to be a mutual desire of both parties within their respective roles and responsibilities. Work procedures, schedules, and assignments for improving services shall be established and revised from time to time in accordance with management rights under this agreement so long as no other right guaranteed under this agreement is violated. The parties agree to confer at mutually convenient times to discuss means of increasing departmental effectiveness.[1]

6.1.2 The Association recognizes the need for cooperative effort with the Employer in obtaining maximum efficiency in the operation of the police department.[2]

6.2 Cooperation.

6.2.1 The Employer and the Association each agrees to use its best efforts to serve the citizens of the Employer and the public in general; to achieve better understanding between the Employer, the Association and the employees represented by the Association; to assure the proper and uninterrupted functions of the services of the Employer; and to promote mutual respect and fair dealing among the Employer, the Association and the employees represented by the Association.[3]

[1] ***Eugene, Oregon and Eugene Police Employees' Association.***

[2] ***City of Niagara Falls and the Niagara Falls Police Club.***

[3] ***City of Kettering, Ohio and Fraternal Order of Police.***

ARTICLE 7

WORK RULES - EXISTING BENEFITS

7.1 Maintenance of Benefits.

7.1.1 All conditions or provisions beneficial to employees now in effect which are not specifically provided for in this Agreement or which have not been replaced by provisions of this Agreement shall remain in effect for the duration of this Agreement, unless mutually agreed otherwise between the Employer and the Association.[1]

7.2 Proposed Mid-Term Changes.

7.2.1 The parties recognize that circumstances change from time to time during the term of labor agreements that give rise to a need to discuss changes in hours or working conditions (including the scope of bargaining unit work). In order to provide a convenient forum to discuss these issues, the parties agree to the following procedure.

7.2.1.1 This Agreement may be amended within the scope of this Article provided both parties concur. Supplemental agreements may be completed through negotiations between the parties at any time during the life of this Agreement. A joint committee comprised of the negotiating teams of the two parties will meet upon the request of either party to discuss proposals related to work hours or changes in working conditions, including the scope of bargaining unit work. Should either party desire to negotiate a matter of this kind, it shall notify the other party in writing of its desire to negotiate. Supplemental agreements thus completed will be signed by the responsible Association and Employer officials.

[1] ***Buffalo, New York and Buffalo Police Benevolent Association.***

7.2.1.2 Should either party, having been notified of the proposed supplemental language, not respond by requesting a meeting of the joint committee within thirty (30) days, the proposed language shall be considered acceptable and shall be forwarded to the other party for signature. Supplemental agreements thus completed shall become a part of this Agreement.

7.2.1.3 In those cases where the parties cannot agree, the parties agree to waive mediation and, upon the request of either party, expeditiously proceed directly to interest arbitration on the issue as is provided in state law. The parties agree to waive the appointment of partisan arbitrators and that the matter will be heard by an arbitrator selected in the same manner as is provided in the grievance procedure. Neither party may be required to arbitrate a proposal which, if granted, would require the Arbiter to change an express term of this Agreement.

7.2.1.4 In agreeing to the above procedure, neither party waives any right, claim, or defense that it may have pursuant to state law, apart from the right to demand mediation; the procedure for certifying issues to interest arbitration; and the arbitration panel selection procedure. Moreover, the Employer reserves the right to implement changes that are not mandatory subjects of bargaining, or those which have otherwise been reserved to the Employer by the express terms of this Agreement.[1]

7.3 Primacy of Contract.

7.3.1 The terms and conditions of this Contract shall supersede ordinances and resolutions wherein there is a conflict with the terms of this Contract.[2]

[1] ***City of Spokane and Spokane Police Guild.***

[2] ***Madison, Wisconsin and Madison Professional Police Officers' Association.***

7.4 Notice of New Work Rules.

7.4.1 Requirements.

7.4.1.1 The Employer agrees to furnish the Association with a written notice of the Employer's intention to make changes in departmental rules, policies or procedures that would affect the working conditions of employees or equipment peculiar to police work. If the Association does not respond in writing within seven (7) working days of the date of receipt of such written notice, the Employer may assume the Association does not wish to meet and confer on the proposed changes.

7.4.1.2 Should the Association respond within seven (7) working days from the date of receipt of such written notice, the Employer agrees to meet and confer with the Association in order to freely exchange information, opinions and proposals relating specifically to the proposed changes prior to their enactment. The Employer shall furnish the Association and the respective chapter chairperson with a copy of such changes and inform them of the proposed implementation plans. Upon request, the Employer shall at its option provide the Association with or access to available resource materials, studies or data relating to the merits of the proposed changes prior to said meeting with Employer. However, such materials shall remain the property of the Employer until such time as the Employer may choose to relinquish its right thereto.[1]

7.5 Fair Application of Rules.

7.5.1 Work rules, policies, orders, and directives are to be interpreted and applied fairly to all employees.[2]

[1] ***State of Hawaii and Hawaii Organization of Police Officers.***

[2] ***Greene County, Ohio and Fraternal Order of Police, Ohio Labor Council, Inc.***

CHAPTER 2

ASSOCIATION RIGHTS

This chapter contains contract clauses which govern the business of the labor organization, and the circumstances under which employer time and resources can be used in the pursuit of that business. The variety of clauses contained in this article include:

- Leave for Association Business
- Association Leave Banks
- Contract Negotiations
- Use of Employer Facilities

An increasing feature of law enforcement collective bargaining agreements are clauses which allow the labor organization to use the employer's facilities. Such clauses have taken a variety of forms, including language which gives a labor organization access to the employer's electronic mail system, the right to use recreational facilities, the right to hold union meetings on the employer's premises, the right to use the employer's telephone system, and the ability to use a variety of other employer-owned equipment or facilities.

Perhaps the most significant of the clauses dealing with the relationship between the labor organization and the employer concerns the amount of paid leave members of the labor organization receive to deal with union business. It is extremely common for such paid leave to be allowed for the time spent in the negotiation process. Clauses granting paid union leave for the adjustment of grievances and to attend union meetings are also fairly common. Less common are clauses which grant to a union officer full-time release time.

The laws vary from state to state as to the legality of clauses in collective bargaining agreements which allow a labor organization access to the employer's facilities or to receive paid leave to conduct union business. In some states, such clauses may be considered an impermissible gift of public funds, or may be construed to be "unlawful assistance" to a particular labor organization. As such, the law in a particular state should be carefully checked before such clauses are negotiated into a collective bargaining agreement.

ARTICLE 8

ASSOCIATION BUSINESS AND MEETINGS

8.1 Leave for Association Representatives.

8.1.1 Monthly Association Meeting. The general Association Meeting may be held on Employer time each month, not to exceed one (1) hour, unless additional time is approved by the Employer. If such meeting is not held, the one (1) hour of Employer time allowed for this activity will lapse. No overtime or compensatory time will be paid for this meeting.[1]

8.2 Granting of Leave.

8.2.1 Members of the bargaining unit selected to serve as authorized representatives of the Association shall be certified in writing to the Employer. Each representative will be expected to perform his duties as a representative of the Association on his own time. However, it is recognized that from time to time it will be necessary for Association activities to be carried on during working hours; for example, investigation and processing of complaints, disputes, and grievances, and attendance at executive board and general meetings (not to exceed sixteen (16) hours per month with a maximum yearly allowance of ninety-six (96) hours per board member). It is further recognized that there are reasonable limited deviations from this policy, such as posting of Association notices and distribution of association literature, which do not require substantial periods of time. Where such activities are necessarily or reasonably to be performed during working hours, they may be done without loss of pay to the representative involved, provided the representative notifies his on-duty

[1] ***Thurston County, Washington and Thurston County Deputy Sheriff's Association.***

supervisor, whenever possible, prior to taking time from duty to engage in Association business that exceeds one hour. All Association activity will be reported on an appropriate time reporting form provided by Management.

8.2.1.1 Upon sufficient notification, the Employer shall place officers or representatives of the Association on Special Duty for the purpose of attending as official delegates, association conventions or conferences to the extent that such Special Duty does not interfere with the reasonable needs of the Employer. However, the total time for all such leaves will not exceed three hundred and twenty (320) hours per contract year. The Association will reimburse the Employer for such time the members spend on Special Duty.

8.2.1.2 Recognizing that it is mutually advantageous to the Employer and the Association to maintain continuity of Association representatives, the Employer agrees not to transfer such representatives except in cases of promotion or necessity.[1]

8.2.2 The Secretary and Treasurer of the Association shall be allowed time off with pay and without requirements to make up said time for attendance at the regular monthly meetings and special meetings of the Association. The immediate past President of the Association shall be allowed time off with pay and without the requirement to make up said time for attendance at the first four (4) meetings (regular or special) after his successor has been elected. Time off with pay shall be no longer than three (3) hours. A special meeting shall last no longer than two (2) hours and shall be limited to time off with pay to two (2) per year. In the event the President is unable to attend the regular monthly meetings or special meetings, the Vice President shall be then

[1] ***Portland, Oregon and Portland Police Association.***

allowed time off in accordance with the provisions of this section. The Chief may call back to duty any of the above Association officials who have been allowed time off with pay in an emergency situation.[1]

8.3 Association Leave Bank.

8.3.1 There is hereby created an Association Leave Bank for the sole and exclusive use of the Association.

8.3.1.1 Any member desiring to may donate leave to the Association leave bank; said leave will be transferred from the member's annual leave accrual by signed authorization by the member.

8.3.1.2 All leave donations will be in hourly increments.

8.3.1.3 When leave is used from the Association's leave account, the person's time card will reflect the hours as regular time and be sent to payroll for processing. This particular time card will be signed by the employee and authorized by the department head.

8.3.1.4 A copy of the time card and a memorandum authorizing the leave deduction from the Association's leave account will be sent to the finance director. This memorandum will indicate the date of usage of annual leave and number of hours.

8.3.1.5 The Association's leave bank account will not be a payroll function. Copies of the Association's leave bank account may be obtained from the finance director upon written request from the Association's president, or his designee.

8.3.1.6 Requests by the Association for use of leave from the Association's leave account for absences from duty for

[1] ***City of Pawtucket, Rhode Island and Fraternal Order of Police, Lodge #4.***

Association's business leave shall be made to the department head by the president of the Association. Requests for absences for Association business shall not be unreasonably denied.

8.3.1.7 In the event that the Association is dissolved and the Association Leave Bank is terminated, any remaining business leave is not eligible for transfer or reimbursement.[1]

8.4 Management-Labor Meetings.

8.4.1 The Police Chief and Director of Personnel shall meet bi-monthly with representatives of the Association. The purpose of said meetings is to informally discuss matters of concern and/or interest to either party. On-duty time shall be provided for three (3) Association representatives, and may be increased if both parties mutually agree.[2]

8.4.2 When requested, the Chief of Police shall meet once a month with no more than five representatives of the Association to discuss matters of mutual concern. The agenda of each meeting is to be submitted five days prior to said meeting. All department notices and directives shall be sent to the President of the Association, or his designee, prior to issuance, and consultation shall be held on those requested by the Association President or his designee.[3]

8.5 Internal Association Matters.

8.5.1 The Employer recognizes the right of the Association to govern its internal affairs.[4]

[1] ***Fairbanks, Alaska and Fairbanks Police Department Employees Association.***

[2] ***Glendale, California and Glendale Police Officers' Association.***

[3] ***City of Erie, Pennsylvania and Hass Memorial Lodge #7, Fraternal Order of Police.***

[4] ***Carlsbad, California and Carlsbad Police Officers Association.***

8.6 Attendance at Hearings.

8.6.1 Leave of absence with pay may be granted to officers of the Association, not to exceed three (3) officers, to attend grievance and arbitration hearings, and hearings before the Legislature and State agencies concerning matters of importance to the Association. Such leave will require prior approval of the Employer.[1]

8.7 Leave For State and National Meetings.

8.7.1 Any employee who is a member of the state Executive Board or who is a state trustee shall be allowed time off with pay to attend all state meetings provided there is sufficient manpower to satisfy the minimum manning requirements of this contract. Not more than four (4) delegates shall be allowed time off with pay for attendance at national conventions of the Association and not more than seven (7) delegates per day shall be allowed time off with pay for attendance at state conventions of the Association.[2]

8.7.2 Association officials may be granted time off without loss of pay or benefits to attend a reasonable amount of labor oriented training sessions or seminars subject to approval of the Employer. Approval by the Employer shall not be unreasonably withheld. The Association will be responsible for the payment of travel expenses and training fees.[3]

[1] ***Commonwealth of Massachusetts and State Police Association of Massachusetts.***

[2] ***City of Pawtucket, Rhode Island and Fraternal Order of Police, Lodge #4.***

[3] ***City of Beaumont, Texas and Beaumont Police Officers Association.***

8.8 Presentations at Roll Call.

8.8.1 After the conclusion of roll call, and provided that reasonable advance notice is given to the Watch Commander by an Association officer and further that the Watch Commander consents, any such local Association officer may discuss Association business at the station with any other officer, so long as all police officers are at their respective posts of duty promptly at the beginning of their shift. It is understood and agreed that the required consent of the Watch Commander will not be withheld unreasonably by him.

8.8.1.1 Notwithstanding anything herein to the contrary, no such discussion shall be allowed and any discussion in progress may be ordered terminated if, in the reasonable judgment of the Watch Commander, a police emergency exists.[1]

8.9 Legislative Activities.

8.9.1 The Association may appoint a committee from its membership to attend the Legislature when in session. Upon proper application and notice in writing of not less than thirty (30) days, the Employer shall grant not more than six (6) members of the Association leave without pay in order to attend such sessions for Association business provided, however, not more than two (2) such members from the same section performing the same duties shall be so named. One member of the six (6) allowed the Association shall be eligible to attend the regular session of the Legislature, with pay, on straight-time basis only, when in session.[2]

[1] ***City of Des Plaines, Illinois and Combined Counties Police Association.***

[2] ***City of Louisville, Kentucky and Fraternal Order of Police, Lodge #6.***

ARTICLE 9

NEGOTIATIONS

9.1 Negotiating Team.

9.1.1 Not more than five (5) members of the Association's negotiating team shall be allowed to attend and travel to and from collective bargaining negotiations for a successor to this Agreement on on-duty status. During such travel and negotiations, the bargaining team members shall not receive per diem costs or the use of a Department vehicle. If a negotiations session is scheduled on the regular workday of a member, the member shall be entitled to his/her regular compensation payments regardless of the duration of the negotiations session or travel. If a negotiations session or travel is scheduled on the regular day off of a member, the member shall be entitled to straight-time compensatory time off not to exceed eight (8) hours. No penalty payments accrue for any changes of schedules due to collective bargaining.[1]

9.2 Commencement of Negotiations.

9.2.1 It is mutually agreed that the first meeting will be held no later than 20 calendar days after the Employer or Association receives such notification. At this meeting, each side shall set forth the sections to be revised and the proposed revisions thereto. It is mutually agreed by both Parties hereto that in the event of such notice each Article of this Agreement not referred to in such notice shall remain in full force and effect throughout the subsequent Agreement year(s).[2]

[1] ***State of Oregon and Oregon State Police Officers' Association.***

[2] ***Minneapolis, Minnesota and Police Officers' Federation of Minneapolis.***

9.2.2 It is further agreed that negotiations for future contracts shall commence on a date so that they may be completed by October 31, ____.[1]

ARTICLE 10

ASSOCIATION PRESIDENT

10.1 Paid Release Time.

10.1.1 Association President.

10.1.1.1 The Employer agrees to grant, if requested, Presidential Leave with pay and without loss of any benefits provided by the Memorandum of Understanding except as provided below to the President of Association for the term of this Memorandum of Understanding provided that:

10.1.1.2 Association promptly reimburses the Employer for all Association President salary expenses incurred during the Presidential Leave.

10.1.1.3 Association promptly reimburses the Employer for all Association President retirement, insurance and P.O.S.T. benefit expenses incurred during the Presidential Leave of Absence.

10.1.1.4 Expenses include only those which the Employer would have to pay out of pocket for payroll-related wages and benefits and do not include administrative overhead expenses.

10.1.1.5 The employee shall continue to participate in weapons qualification and any legally-mandated training.

[1] ***Calaveras County, State of California and Calaveras County Sheriff's Association.***

10.1.1.6 The employee shall continue to conform to Employer rules, regulations and grooming standards that are not inconsistent with Presidential Leave.

10.1.1.7 Vacation and Sick Leave accrual rates will apply to the employee as though he or she were on on-duty status.

10.1.1.8 Vacation and Sick Leave accrued during Presidential Leave and unused at the conclusion of the Leave must either be paid off by Association or lost.

10.1.1.9 The merit increase eligibility date, if applicable, shall be extended a number of calendar days equal to the Presidential Leave. This extended merit increase eligibility date will be effective the first day of the pay period after said date.

10.1.1.10 The probation period, if applicable, shall be extended by the length of the Presidential Leave. If the employee is on promotional probation, the extended probation period shall end on the first day of the pay period following said extended date.

10.1.1.11 The employee's eligibility for promotional examinations shall not be affected by Presidential Leave.

10.1.1.12 Layoff points shall not be affected by Presidential Leave.

10.1.1.13 In the event emergency recall of the employee becomes necessary, Presidential Leave may be suspended or canceled during the course of the emergency. Association shall not be obligated for reimbursement costs listed in this article for the period that Presidential Leave is suspended or canceled. Provisions of this article above shall be suspended during said emergency recall.

10.1.1.14 Not more than one (1) employee in the combined Peace Officer and Supervising Peace Officer Units shall be eligible for Presidential Leave at any one (1) time.[1]

10.2 Daily Leave for President.

10.2.1 The President of the Association or his designee shall be allowed time off with pay for official Association business with respect to grievances, grievance hearings and the preparation thereof. The President of the Association shall be allowed time off with pay for attendance at Association meetings, state and national conventions of the Association.[2]

10.3 Release From Duty.

10.3.1 The President and one (1) designee of the Association shall be granted reasonable leave from duty with pay whenever necessary for the performance of the duties of their respective offices, provided such leave does not interfere with the efficient operation of the Employer and advance request of no less than forty-eight (48) hours is made to the Chief for the same.

10.3.1.1 The duly appointed and elected Association delegate and the President of the Association shall be granted leave from duty with pay to attend monthly Association meetings, provided forty-eight (48) hours' written notice is given to the Chief for the same.[3]

[1] ***Orange County, California and Association of Orange County Deputy Sheriffs.***

[2] ***City of Pawtucket, Rhode Island and Fraternal Order of Police, Lodge #4.***

[3] ***East Orange, New Jersey and Policemen's Benevolent Association.***

10.4 Shift Assignment of Association President.

10.4.1 To assist the Employer, during the term of the M.O.U., the Association President shall be assigned to a normal shift with Saturdays and Sundays off if a 5/8 schedule is in effect. Should a 4/10 schedule be in effect, the Association President shall be assigned to a normal day shift with Fridays, Saturdays and Sundays off.[1]

10.5 Job Assignment of Association President.

10.5.1 A position has been placed in the Administrative and Community Services Bureau for the assignment of the current Association president or by mutual agreement, a designee. The emphasis in duties shall be placed on the Departmental support of the Employer's Human Rights Commission.[2]

ARTICLE 11

ACCESS TO EMPLOYER FACILITIES AND INFORMATION

11.1 Access by Non-Employee Association Representatives.

11.1.1 Authorized non-employee Association representatives will be given access to work locations during working hours to investigate and process grievances or post bulletins on the bulletin board(s) without unreasonable interference with employee work. The Association shall give the department head and the Employee Relations Manager a written list of such authorized Association Representatives. Only those

[1] ***City of Peoria and Peoria Police Officers Association.***

[2] ***Contra Costa County, California and the Deputy Sheriffs' Association.***

people whose names appear on the current list shall be granted access under this provision.[1]

11.2 Access to Recruits.

11.2.1 The Employer shall make available a period of one (1) hour to the Association in each recruit class with an end toward education of each employee of the rights and benefits under the collective bargaining agreement, as well as other Association benefits, and the responsibilities of the employee and the organization of the Association with an end toward having an employee who would become a better Association member and a better employee.[2]

11.3 Access to Employer Information.

11.3.1 Duty to Furnish Information.

11.3.1.1 The Employer shall make available to the Association, upon its reasonable request, any information, statistics and records relevant to negotiations or necessary for proper enforcement of the terms of this agreement.

11.3.1.2 The parties agree that they will furnish sufficient information as to the relevancy of their request to negotiations or enforcement of the Agreement.

11.3.1.3 The parties agree to pay the cost incurred in the compilation of information they request, if applicable.

11.3.1.4 The Employer agrees to furnish the Association one (1) copy of all future amendments and revisions to Departmental General Orders, or the revised District Personnel Manual, inclusive of all amendments once finalized and printed.[3]

[1] ***Sonoma County, California and Sonoma County Sheriff's Office Employees Association.***

[2] ***State of Hawaii and Hawaii Organization of Police Officers.***

[3] ***District of Columbia and Fraternal Order of Police.***

11.3.2 The Employer will provide the Association with copies of all Personnel Actions ten days after they are issued. As used in this section, "Personnel Actions" shall be defined as all written notices of actual disciplinary actions, notices of intent to take disciplinary actions, transfer notices, promotion notices and termination notices.[1]

11.4 Access to Employer Communications System.

11.4.1 The Employer's interdepartmental messenger service may be used for individual business-oriented communication between employees who are represented by the Association and between the paid staff of the Association and such employees, provided that paid staff of the Association shall pick up and deliver all written communications outside the Employer's normal distribution route. Association understands that the continuance or discontinuance of the interdepartmental messenger service is a matter within the sole discretion of the Employer.[2]

11.5 Notice of Employer Governing Body Meetings.

11.5.1 The Employer will arrange to transmit or make available to the Association President, or designee, a copy each week of the Board of Supervisors' regular public meeting agenda in advance of the regular Board meeting. The Employer will also continue to transmit or make available to the Association President, or designee, a copy of the regular Civil Service

[1] ***Montgomery County, Ohio and Fraternal Order of Police, Lodge 104.***

[2] ***Sonoma County, California and Sonoma County Sheriff's Office Employees Association.***

Commission agenda and classification studies scheduled on that agenda pertaining to classifications represented by the Association in advance of the Commission meeting.[1]

11.6 Ballot Boxes.

11.6.1 The Association shall be permitted, with the prior notification to the Chief of Police, to place ballot boxes at Police Headquarters and at a minimum of four (4) substations of the Association's choice for the purpose of collecting members' ballots on all Association issues subjected to ballot, except ballots regarding job actions. Such boxes shall be the property of the Association and neither the ballot boxes nor the ballots shall be subjected to the Employer's review.[2]

11.6.2 Association shall have access to all bulletin boards, voice mail and electronic mail channels of communications within the Police Department for information from either the Association Executive Board or the Bargaining Committee.[3]

11.7 Access to Mailboxes.

11.7.1 The Employer agrees to provide a mailbox for each employee of the bargaining unit. Associaton material to be placed in mailboxes of Association members shall be non-inflammatory and shall be placed in the mailboxes by off-duty officers of the Association, and, further shall be placed only in the mailboxes of Association members. Management and the Employer shall be held harmless by this Association activity.[4]

[1] ***Sonoma County, California and Sonoma County Sheriff's Office Employees Association.***

[2] ***Eau Claire, Wisconsin and Eau Claire Professional Police Association.***

[3] ***City of Bloomington, Indiana and Fraternal Order of Police, Lodge 88.***

[4] ***Lincoln, Nebraska and Lincoln Police Union, Local No. 544, International Brotherhood of Police Officers.***

11.8 Access to Recreation Space.

11.8.1 The Employer will allow members of the bargaining unit the use of Employer recreational facilities during regular business hours at no charge to the employee. This will include the weight room, jacuzzi, and sauna at the Recreation Center and the swimming pool during lap swimming and general public swim. Employees will comply with all registration requirements and rules and regulations of the facilities used. Employees will utilize these Employer facilities only during their time off work.[1]

11.8.2 The Employer agrees to provide recreation space which is available and not needed for Employer functions and activities for the Association. The location and size of such recreation space shall continue to be designated by the Employer and may be changed by the Employer upon prior notification to the Association. The Association therefore agrees that Employer maintains the right of continual access to recreation space in order to inspect maintenance of condition and make necessary repairs. Furthermore, employees of the Police Division shall be allowed continual access to this space for the purpose of utilizing any piece of recreation equipment located herein.[2]

11.8.3 The Employer agrees to waive the required residence for use of Employer owned and operated recreational facilities.[3]

[1] ***Lompoc, California and Lompoc Police Officers' Association.***

[2] ***Glendale, California and Glendale Police Officers' Association.***

[3] ***City of Southfield and Southfield Police Officers Association.***

11.9 Gymnasium and Recreation Equipment.

11.9.1 The Employer shall maintain present gymnasium equipment, replacing expendable items as needed, for the use of bargaining unit members on their off-duty time.[1]

11.10 Access to Physical Fitness Space.

11.10.1 The Employer agrees to provide building space, which is available and not needed for Employer functions and activities for Association to install or locate physical fitness exercising equipment. The location and size of such space shall continue to be designated by the Employer and may be changed by the Employer upon prior notification to the Association.

11.10.1.1 The Association therefore agrees in addition to the Employer's right of continual access to ensure building maintenance and repair, that before any new type or style of equipment is installed or placed in this space, prior written agreement from the Police Chief shall be obtained. Furthermore, employees of the Association shall be allowed continual access to this space for the purpose of utilizing any physical fitness equipment located therein.[2]

11.11 Sports Uniforms.

11.11.1 The Employer shall continue to provide sports uniforms for members of Employer recreational league basketball, softball, football and track teams. Uniforms will be replaced once every three years.[3]

[1] ***City of Tallahassee, Florida and the Big Bend Benevolent Association, Inc.***

[2] ***City of Westminster, California and Westminster Police Association.***

[3] ***City of Tallahassee, Florida and the Big Bend Benevolent Association, Inc.***

11.12 Association Liability Waiver.

11.12.1 In lieu of charging a rental fee for consideration of any space, equipment, or structure granted to the Association by the Employer per terms of this Agreement, the Association hereby agrees not to hold the Employer liable for any damages to any equipment, furniture, floor coverings, or other personal property not owned by the Employer.[1]

ARTICLE 12

BULLETIN BOARDS

12.1 General.

12.1.1 The Employer agrees to furnish glass enclosed bulletin boards with locks at all separate Police facilities where requested for the use of the Association to post notices relative to Association affairs.

12.1.1.1 Articles posted on the Association bulletin boards shall not be removed or tampered with by the Employer.

12.1.1.2 Bulletin board placement shall be mutually agreed upon.[2]

[1] ***City of Westminster, California and Westminster Police Association.***

[2] ***City of Toledo, Ohio and Toledo Police Patrolman's Association.***

ARTICLE 13

OFFICE SPACE

13.1 General.

13.1.1 The Employer agrees to provide office space which is available and not needed for Employer functions and activities for the Association.

13.1.1.1 The location and size of such office space shall continue to be designated by the Employer and may be changed by the Employer upon prior notification to the Association.

13.1.1.2 The Association therefore agrees that the Employer maintains the right of access without notice under emergency conditions and has the right to periodically inspect this space for maintenance of condition provided that a 24-hour prior notice is given to a Board member and the Association has the opportunity to have a representative in attendance during inspection. Failure to exercise this right after notification hereby constitutes a waiver.

13.1.1.3 The Association agrees to provide, maintain, and pay for all telephone costs charged to their office telephone.

13.1.1.4 The Association agrees to conform to all other rules, regulations, policies, and procedures set forth by the Employer concerning the use of Employer facilities.[1]

[1] ***City of Glendale and Glendale Police Officers' Association.***

ARTICLE 14

ASSOCIATION REPRESENTATION

14.1 Shop Stewards.

14.1.1 Shop Stewards shall be appointed from among the employees of the Municipality at any given point by the Association, at the Association's discretion, and in a layoff situation shall be the last members laid off. The Shop Stewards and Association Officers shall be allowed to handle complaints and grievances arising under this Agreement and Association Officers shall be allowed to attend to Association business during their normal working hours without loss of compensation for time spent in the pursuit of their duties. The Shop Stewards or Association Officers shall attempt to notify their immediate supervisors prior to leaving his duties to attend to Association business. In the event the immediate supervisor is not available, the Shop Steward shall notify Dispatch. The maximum number of Shop Stewards shall not exceed sixteen (16), including a Chief Shop Steward, but not including the President, Vice President, Treasurer, and Recording Secretary, during the term of this Agreement. For purposes of this Agreement, Association business shall not include union conferences or union training sessions, which shall be taken as leave time under the terms of this Agreement.[1]

[1] ***Municipality of Anchorage and Anchorage Police Department Employees Association.***

CHAPTER 3

DISCIPLINARY PROCEDURES AND STANDARDS

Certainly the most common type of grievance filed under a law enforcement collective bargaining agreement is one which challenges discipline. Most of these grievances challenge the fairness of the disciplinary punishment which was imposed by the employer, but an increasing number challenge the procedures used by the employer to impose the discipline.

This chapter contains examples of contract clauses which govern both disciplinary procedures and disciplinary standards. Included in the chapter are the following topics:

- Disciplinary Standards
- Bills of Rights
- Disciplinary Appeals Boards
- Performance Evaluations
- Civilian Review

Virtually all law enforcement collective bargaining agreements contain a "just cause" standard for discipline. Typically, the standard means that discipline must be fair under all of the circumstances, considering the severity of the offense, the employee's work record, mitigating circumstances, the employer's track record for discipline, and a variety of other factors.

A new feature to this chapter is a lengthy article dealing with critical incidents and the use of deadly force. It has only been recently that many law enforcement labor agreements have addressed such issues. With the complicated disciplinary, criminal, and civil proceedings that may follow the use of force, both employers and labor organizations are now starting to spell out the rights and responsibilities of each in the area.

By far the lengthiest section in this chapter deals with peace officer bills of rights. Many states have statutory peace officer bills of rights; in those states, the bills of rights which appear in collective bargaining agreements typically only supplement those procedures which must be followed under state law. In jurisdictions without statewide peace officer bills of rights, it is increasingly common to find lengthy bills of rights in collective bargaining agreements, covering topics such as the procedures which must be following in internal affairs investigations, the handling of anonymous complaints, the rights of officers to bring lawsuits for false complaints, and the release of internal affairs information to the media.

ARTICLE 15

EMPLOYEE RIGHTS

15.1 Bill of Rights – Example 1.

15.1.1 **Personnel Orders**. The Employer will provide the Association with copies of all personnel orders as soon as the personnel orders are issued. As used in this section, "personnel orders" shall be defined as all written notices of actual disciplinary actions, notices of intent to take disciplinary actions, transfer notices, promotion notices, and termination notices.

15.1.1.1 **Interview Safeguards**. Any employee who will be interviewed concerning an act which, if proven, could reasonably result in disciplinary action against him or her will be afforded the following safeguards.[1]

15.1.2 **Notification of Scope of Questioning**. Whenever an employee is being investigated, the employee shall be informed of the general scope of the investigation prior to questioning. The notification shall include the name of the complainant, the date of the incident, the specific rules the Employer alleges were violated, whether the citizen has signed a complaint form, and a summary of the factual allegations against the employee sufficient to reasonably apprise the employee of the nature of the charges. The employee may agree to answer questions at that time or request that questioning be delayed for up to five (5) calendar days in order to obtain legal advice or other assistance.[2]

[1] ***State of Oregon and Oregon State Police Officers Association.***

[2] ***Washington State Patrol and Washington State Patrol Troopers Association.***

15.1.3 **Notification of Nature of Investigation**. Employees under non-criminal investigation shall be informed of the nature of that investigation and provided a copy of the written complaint, if one exists, within four (4) working days of when the complaint is received. Employees on leave status shall be notified within four (4) working days of returning to duty. Where known, employees shall be informed of all details of the investigation which are necessary to reasonably apprise the employee of the factual background of the complaint. When, in the reasonable judgment of the Chief of Police, disclosure of the complaint will seriously jeopardize an investigation of the complaint, the notice requirement under this provision shall not apply.[1]

15.1.4 **Notification of Suspicion**. The employee will be informed prior to the interview if the Employer believes the employee is a suspect in the investigation.[2]

15.1.5 **Right to Representation**. At the request of any police officer under investigation, he shall have the right to be represented by counsel or any association representative of his choice who shall be present at all times during such questioning whenever such questioning may result in disciplinary action or criminal charges against the police officer.[3]

15.1.6 **Right to an Attorney**. In situations which involve an investigation of complaints or suspected violations in which an attorney of the Employer is a participant, the member shall

[1] ***Municipality of Anchorage and Anchorage Police Department Employees Association.***

[2] ***State of Oregon and Oregon State Police Officers Association.***

[3] ***City of Fort Wayne, Indiana and the Fraternal Order of Police, Lodge #14.***

have the right to have an attorney of his choosing accompany him in such proceedings.[1]

15.1.7 **Location of Interviews**. With the exception of telephone interviews, interviews shall take place at Employer facilities, or elsewhere if mutually agreed, unless an emergency exists which requires the interview to be conducted elsewhere.

15.1.7.1 **Time of Interviews**. The Employer shall make a reasonable good faith effort to conduct these interviews during the employee's regular working hours, except for emergencies or where interviews can be conducted by telephone.

15.1.7.2 **Employee Constitutional Rights**. The employee will be required to answer any questions involving non-criminal matters under investigation and will be afforded all rights and privileges to which he or she is entitled under the laws of the State or the United States.[2]

15.1.8 **Notification of Criminal Nature of Investigation**. If the Employer questions an employee during a criminal investigation of one of its employees, it shall advise the member of the criminal nature of the investigation and whether the member is a suspect or a witness before interviewing the member. The preceding sentence shall not apply to covert or undercover investigations. Investigations of the use of deadly force by members shall be conducted pursuant to the Employer's rules.[3]

15.1.9 **Employee Rights in the Employer's Rules and Regulations**. In a criminal investigation, interview or interroga-

[1] ***Akron, Ohio and Fraternal Order of Police, Lodge #7.***

[2] ***State of Oregon and Oregon State Police Officers Association.***

[3] ***City of Portland, Oregon and Portland Police Association.***

tion, the bargaining unit member shall be provided the same constitutional and statutory safeguards afforded to all citizens.[1]

15.1.10 **Intimidation**. Interviews shall be done under circumstances devoid of intimidation, abuse, or coercion.[2]

15.1.11 **Threats**. The employee will not be threatened with transfer or any disciplinary action as a means of obtaining information. The employee cannot be subjected to abusive language or promise of reward as inducement for answering questions.[3]

15.1.12 **Polygraph Examinations**. In the course of an interrogation, no officer shall be required to submit to a polygraph test or any other test questioning by means of any chemical substance, except with the officer's written consent. Refusal to submit to such tests shall not result in any disciplinary action nor shall such refusal be made part of his or her record.[4]

15.1.13 No employee shall be ordered to submit to any device designed to measure the truth of responses during questioning; provided, however, that there shall be no restriction on the right of any employee to submit to such device on a voluntary basis.[5]

15.1.14 **Alcohol Testing**. No employee will be ordered to submit to a blood test, a breathalyzer, or any other test to deter-

[1] ***City of Cleveland, Ohio and Cleveland Police Patrolmen's Association.***

[2] ***State of Oregon and Oregon State Police Officers Association.***

[3] ***City of Orlando, Florida and Fraternal Order of Police, Florida State Lodge.***

[4] ***Sangamon County, Illinois and Illinois Fraternal Order of Police Labor Council.***

[5] ***County of Volusia, Florida and Coastal Florida Police Benevolent Association.***

mine the percentage of alcohol in the blood except as may be provided otherwise by specific statutory law. Such test may be offered by the Employer or requested by the employee.[1]

15.1.15 **Intermissions**. The employee shall be entitled to such reasonable intermissions as he shall request for personal necessities.

15.1.15.1 **Limitation of Scope of Interviews**. All interviews shall be limited in scope to activities, circumstances, events, conduct or acts which pertain to the incident which is the subject of the investigation. Nothing in this section shall prohibit the Employer from questioning the employee about information which is developed during the course of the interview.[2]

15.1.16 **Personal Disclosure**. No law enforcement officer shall be required or requested to disclose any item of his property, income, assets, source of income, debts, or personal or domestic expenditures (including those of any member of his family or household) unless such information is necessary in investigating a possible conflict of interest with respect to the performance of his official duties, or unless such disclosure is required by law.[3]

15.1.17 **Witness Status**. If an employee is questioned only as a witness but the investigator believes or reasonably should believe the employee's responses disclose his/her own possible violations of the law and/or regulations, the employee shall be advised of the possibility that his/her actions or omissions may

[1] ***City of Memphis, Tennessee and Memphis Police Association.***

[2] ***State of Oregon and Oregon State Police Officers Association.***

[3] ***Sangamon County, Illinois and Illinois Fraternal Order of Police Labor Council.***

result in an investigation or disciplinary action and of the right to seek legal advice or other assistance. After the advice is given, the questioning will cease at the request of the employee or the investigator.[1]

15.1.18 **Tape Recording**. If the Employer tape records the interview, a copy of the complete interview of the employee, noting all recess periods, shall be furnished, upon request, to the employee. If the interviewed employee is subsequently charged and any part of any recording is transcribed by the Employer, the employee shall be given a complimentary copy thereof.[2]

15.1.19 **Time Limits on Reporting Findings**. The Internal Affairs Unit shall have one-hundred twenty (120) days from the date a complainant signs his Internal Affairs complaint in an administrative investigation or the Chief assigns a Department Investigator within which to report its findings to the Chief, which findings shall be file-stamped by the Chief's office upon receipt. In the case of a complaint which is originally investigated as a criminal investigation, the Internal Affairs Unit shall have ninety (90) days from the date such complaint is converted into an administrative investigation within which to report its findings to the Chief's office, which findings shall likewise be file-stamped by the Chief's office upon receipt. The Chief shall have thirty (30) days from that date within which to render his decision as to discipline, if any. The Chief may also return the investigation to the Internal Affairs Unit for an additional thirty (30) days, after which time he must render his decision.[3]

[1] ***Washington State Patrol and Washington State Patrol Troopers Association.***

[2] ***State of Oregon and Oregon State Police Officers Association.***

[3] ***City of Kansas City, Kansas and Fraternal Order of Police, Lodge 4.***

15.1.20 **Unfounded Complaints**. When any citizen complaint (a) alleges facts which if true could not lead to a criminal charge, and (b) is filed beyond the legal time limits for filing a civil complaint on such facts, then the complaint shall be classified as unfounded or stale, and the accused police officer shall not be required to submit a written report, but he shall be notified orally or in writing of such claim.[1]

15.1.21 **Notification of Results**. The employee shall be advised of the results of the investigation and any future action to be taken on the incident.[2]

15.1.22 **Press Release of Results**. There shall be no press release by the Employer or the Association regarding the employee under investigation until the investigation is completed and employee is either cleared or charged.[3]

15.1.23 **Publicity**. The Employer shall not cause employees being questioned to be subjected to visits by the press or news media, nor shall their home address or photograph be given to the press or news media without the employee's express consent.[4]

15.1.24 **Evidence**. Evidence obtained in the course of an internal investigation through the use of administrative pressure,

[1] ***City of Erie, Pennsylvania and Hass Memorial Lodge #7, Fraternal Order of Police.***

[2] ***State of Oregon and Oregon State Police Officers Assoiation.***

[3] ***Lucas County, Ohio Sheriff's Office and District 2A Transportation, Technical, Warehouse, Industrial and Service Employees Union.***

[4] ***Washington State Patrol and Washington State Patrol Troopers Association.***

threats, coercion, or promises shall not be admissible in any subsequent criminal action or Civil Service hearing.[1]

15.2 Bill of Rights – Example 2.

15.2.1 In an effort to ensure that investigations made by Superior Officers, as designated by the Employer, are conducted in a manner which is conducive to good order and discipline, the Association shall be entitled to the protection of what shall hereafter be termed as the "Police Officers' Bill of Rights."

15.2.1.1 Every employee who becomes the subject of an internal investigation shall be advised at the time of the interview that he/she is suspected of: (a) Committing a criminal offense; (b) misconduct that would be grounds for termination, suspension, or other disciplinary action; or (c) that he/she may not be qualified for continued employment with the Employer.

15.2.1.2 Any employee who becomes the subject of a criminal investigation may have legal Counsel present during all interviews. This representation by Counsel is confined to counseling, and not actual participation in the investigation. A criminal investigation as used herein shall be interpreted as any action which could result in the filing of a criminal charge. A major investigation as used elsewhere in this article shall be interpreted as any action which could result in dismissal from the department or the filing of a criminal charge.

15.2.1.3 The employee under investigation must, at the time of an interview, be informed of the name of the officer in charge of the investigation and the name of the officer who will be conducting the interview.

[1] ***Akron, Ohio and Fraternal Order of Police, Lodge #7.***

15.2.1.4 The employee shall be informed in writing as to whether he/she is a witness or suspect before any interview commences. If the employee is a suspect, he/she shall be apprised in writing of the allegations of such complaint before any interview commences.

15.2.1.5 The interview of any employee shall be at a reasonable hour, preferably when the employee is on duty, unless the exigency of the interview dictates otherwise. Whenever possible, interviews shall be scheduled during the normal workday of the employee.

15.2.1.6 The employee or Employer may request that a major investigation interview be recorded, either mechanically or by a stenographer. There can be no "off the record" questions. Upon request, the employee under major investigation shall be provided an exact copy of any written statement he/she has signed, or of a verbatim transcript of any interview.

15.2.1.7 Interviewing shall be completed within a reasonable time and shall be done under circumstances devoid of intimidation or coercion. In all major investigation interviews, the employee shall be afforded an opportunity and facilities to contact and consult privately with an attorney of his/her own choosing, before being interviewed. The employee shall be entitled to such intermissions as he/she shall request for personal necessities, meals, telephone calls, and rest periods.

15.2.1.8 All interviewing shall be limited in scope to activities, circumstances, or events which pertain to the employee's conduct or acts which may form the basis for disciplinary action under one (1) or more of the categories contained herein.

15.2.1.9 The employee will not be threatened with dismissal or other disciplinary punishment as a guise to attempt to obtain his/her resignation, nor shall he/she be subject to abusive or offensive language or intimidation in any other manner. No promises or rewards shall be made as an inducement to answer questions.

15.2.1.10 No employee shall be required to unwillingly submit to a polygraph test or to unwillingly answer questions for which the employee might otherwise properly invoke the protections of any constitutional amendment against self-incrimination.

15.2.1.11 Should any section, sub-section, paragraph, sentence, clause or phrase in this article be declared unconstitutional or invalid, for any reason, such decision shall not affect the validity of the remaining portions of this article.[1]

15.3 Requirement for Signed Internal Complaint.

15.3.1 Before Internal Affairs interviews an employee as a direct result of a complaint by a citizen, whose identity is known, that citizen will be required to sign a sworn affidavit, clearly stating the allegation, and a copy will be provided to the employee at the time of the interview for the employee's review.[2]

15.3.2 All complaints against members of the Department by the citizenry or by individuals being served and protected by the Police Department, alleging police brutality or excessive use of force or other police misconduct shall be submitted, in writing, under oath, to the Superintendent before any action against such member of the Police Department may be taken.[3]

[1] ***Renton, Washington and Renton Police Officers Guild.***

[2] ***City of Memphis, Tennessee and Memphis Police Association.***

[3] ***City of Waterbury, Connecticut and Waterbury Police Union, Local 1237.***

15.4 Ban on Solicitation of Complaints.

15.4.1 The Employer will not solicit any formal citizen's complaints against any officer; solicitation shall not be construed to mean any follow-up of a third-party complaint or follow-up of first-party complaints.[1]

15.5 False Complaints.

15.5.1 If the individuals who made false complaints against police officers can be prosecuted without impairing the essential confidentiality of, and surrounding investigation of, the Internal Affairs and Criminal Investigation Units, the Employer shall seek to have such cases prosecuted.[2]

15.5.2 If false complaints are alleged to have been made against a member of the bargaining unit(s) that employee may choose to proceed as a complainant, in a criminal action of employee's own against the perpetrator through the court system if a prosecution can be conducted without impairing the essential confidentiality of, and surrounding investigation of, the departmental investigation and criminal investigation units. The Employer will permit the employee that time required during employee's normal on duty hours, if necessary, to confer with the appropriate prosecutor on this matter. The Employer shall not be a direct party in the prosecution of these allegations.[3]

15.6 Lawsuits by Officers.

15.6.1 The Employer shall not adopt any resolution or ordinance and the Employer shall not adopt any regulation which

[1] ***City of Omaha, Nebraska and Omaha Police Union, Local 101.***

[2] ***Kansas City, Kansas and Fraternal Order of Police, Lodge #4.***

[3] ***Montgomery County, Ohio and Fraternal Order of Police, Lodge 104.***

prohibits the right of an officer to bring suit arising out of his duties as an officer.[1]

15.7 Civil Suits Brought by Law Enforcement Officers.

15.7.1 Law Enforcement Officers shall have the right to bring civil suit against any person, group of persons, or any organization or corporation, or the heads of such organizations or corporations, for damages suffered, either pecuniary or otherwise, or for abridgement of their civil rights arising out of action legally taken in the performance of the officers' official duties.[2]

15.8 Unfounded Complaints.

15.8.1 Complaints against a bargaining unit member, when designated by the Employer to be unfounded, shall not be included in his personnel file, and shall not be used in any subsequent disciplinary proceeding or in making promotion decisions.[3]

15.9 Assignment to Internal Affairs.

15.9.1 No employee under investigation shall be loaned or reassigned to the Internal Affairs Office except when such employee is to be interviewed, and then only for such time as is reasonably necessary to conduct such interview.[4]

15.10 Failure to Comply with Bill of Rights.

15.10.1 If, during any investigation covered thereby, the Internal Affairs Division fails substantially to comply with the pro-

[1] ***Sangamon County, Illinois and Illinois Fraternal Order of Police Labor Council.***

[3] ***City of Bridgeport, Connecticut and Bridgeport Police Local 1159 and AFSCME.***

[3] ***City of Cleveland, Ohio and Cleveland Police Patrolmen's Association.***

[4] ***City of Lincoln, Nebraska and Lincoln Police Union.***

visions of this Section, no statement which the officer may have given during such interview may be introduced or alluded to by the Employer in a disciplinary appeal hearing. In the case of a dispute as to whether the Internal Affairs Division has substantially complied with this Section, the issue may be submitted to arbitration prior to an appeal hearing before the Civil Service Commission. The sole question before the arbitrator shall be whether the Internal Affairs Division has substantially complied with this Section, and, if the arbitrator finds that the Division has not substantially complied therewith, the sole remedy shall be that, in an appeal hearing, the Employer may not introduce or allude to any statement the officer may have given during such interview.[1]

15.11 Applicability of Bill of Rights to Non-Police Employer Investigations.

15.11.1 When any Employer entity outside of the Department of Public Safety initiates an investigation of a member and the Employer orders the member to participate in such investigation, the member shall have all rights which would otherwise apply to an investigation conducted by the Internal Affairs Bureau.

15.11.1.1 When any non-Employer entity initiates an investigation of a member, the Employer may order the member to appear before the investigating entity. Should such an order be issued, the member shall be provided a reasonable opportunity to meet with an Association representative prior to complying with the order.[2]

[1] ***City of El Paso, Texas and El Paso Municipal Police Officers' Association.***

[2] ***City of Columbus, Ohio and Fraternal Order of Police, Capital City Lodge 9.***

15.12 Testimony Before Non-Governmental Agencies.

15.12.1 The Employer shall not compel an officer under investigation to speak or testify before, or to be questioned by, any non-governmental agency relating to any matter or issue under investigation.[1]

15.13 Pending Criminal Charges.

15.13.1 If any employee covered by this Agreement is charged by indictment or complaint to have violated any provision of the Criminal Code of the State or any statute of the United States, he shall be entitled to his wages and other economic benefits provided for in this Agreement until such time as formal charges are filed by the Employer with the Merit Board.[2]

15.14 Insubordination Charges.

15.14.1 Before a member may be charged with insubordination or like offense for refusing to answer questions or participate in an investigation, he shall be advised that such conduct, if continued, may be made the basis for such charge.

15.14.1.1 A bargaining unit member being investigated for criminal activity shall be advised of his Constitutional Rights as provided by Law and shall be afforded those rights if he chooses to exercise them.

15.14.1.2 It is understood that no officer will be charged with insubordination once he/she is advised of his/her Constitutional Rights and the refusal to answer questions is based on the exercise of such rights.

[1] ***Sangamon County, Illinois and Illinois Fraternal Order of Police Labor Council.***

[2] ***Sangamon County, Illinois and Illinois Fraternal Order of Police Labor Council.***

15.14.1.3 If a bargaining unit member is required to submit a written report, he shall be advised of the reason for such report, and the officer shall be required to submit a detailed statement.

15.14.1.4 Once a bargaining unit member has made his initial written reply which results in a question of potential criminal activity, the officer shall not be deprived of his Constitutional Rights to remain silent and/or disciplined in the exercise of those rights.[1]

15.15 Privacy of Personal Information.

15.15.1 The State and its agencies recognize the fact that Law Enforcement bargaining unit employees' home addresses, telephone numbers, photographs, places of employment of the spouses and children and the names and locations of schools attended by the children of bargaining unit members are exempt from disclosure under the Public Records law, and shall not be released except for a legitimate governmental purpose.[2]

ARTICLE 16

LOCKER SEARCHES

16.1 General.

16.1.1 No police officer shall have his locker, desk, or other space for storage that may be assigned to him searched except by permission of the officer, or unless a valid search warrant has been obtained.[3]

[1] ***Akron, Ohio and Fraternal Order of Police, Lodge #7.***

[2] ***State of Florida and Florida Police Benevolent Association.***

[3] ***City of Fort Wayne, Indiana and the Fraternal Order of Police, Lodge #14.***

ARTICLE 17

POLITICAL ACTIVITY

17.1 General.

17.1.1 The Employer shall not prohibit a police officer from or discriminate against his engaging in political activities or campaigning while off duty, provided that the officer does not:

17.1.1.1 Wear a uniform or any part thereof which would identify the individual as a police officer, or use property (including documents or records) of the Police Department;

17.1.1.2 Display or otherwise lead others to believe he is carrying a badge, baton or gun;

17.1.1.3 Hold himself out as a police officer, except that a truthful response to a legitimate question shall not be a violation of this section;

17.1.1.4 Engage in such activities in a District(s) where he is assigned, unless the officer lives in the District, except that the Employer shall not transfer an officer into a District for the purpose of preventing him from engaging in such activities.

17.1.1.5 Any officer who runs for political office shall take a leave of absence upon the filing of the petition for office pursuant to the Employer's regular leave of absence policy.[1]

17.1.2 Except as otherwise provided by law, no police officer shall be prohibited from engaging in or be coerced or required to engage in political activity.[2]

[1] ***Chicago, Illinois and Fraternal Order of Police.***

[2] ***City of Fort Wayne, Indiana and the Fraternal Order of Police, Lodge #14.***

ARTICLE 18

DISCIPLINE AND DISCHARGE

18.1 Standards for Discipline.

18.1.1 No employee shall be reduced in pay or position, suspended, discharged, or subjected to disciplinary action except for just cause.

18.1.1.1 Discipline will be applied in a corrective, progressive, and uniform manner.

18.1.1.2 Progressive discipline shall take into account the circumstances surrounding the incident, the nature of the violations, the employee's record of discipline, and the employee's record of performance and conduct.[1]

18.2 Limitation on Suspensions.

18.2.1 For one (1) violation, there will be one (1) type of discipline. The types of discipline shall be as follows:

18.2.1.1 Assessments (accidents and/or damages or loss to Employer property).

18.2.1.2 Oral Reprimand.

18.2.1.3 Written Censure.

18.2.1.4 Suspension Without Pay up to two hundred forty (240) work hours per violation. Upon request of the employee, the forfeiture of accrued personal leave in lieu of a suspension without pay is permitted provided the violation does not involve indebtedness to the Employer. Furthermore, forfeiture of personal leave in lieu of the first sixteen (16) hours of suspension without pay is with the concurrence of the Chief of Police or his designee.

[1] ***Lorain County, Ohio Sheriff and Fraternal Order of Police Ohio Labor Council.***

18.2.1.5 Demotion.

18.2.1.6 Termination.

18.3 Progressive Discipline.

18.3.1 Discipline will be consistent and progressive for similar or substantially similar violations. An employee's history and the seriousness of the offense will be important factors in determining discipline.

18.4 Recommendations for Discipline.

18.4.1 Recommendations as to the appropriate discipline will be requested from the employee's chain of command.[1]

18.5 Bill of Rights and Grievance Procedures.

18.5.1 In all disciplinary hearings, the employee shall be presumed innocent until proven guilty. This presumption does not increase the Employer's burden to establish just cause in any disciplinary action.[2]

18.6 Tardiness and Absenteeism.

18.6.1 In the event of a personal transportation breakdown and/or severe storms in a properly and promptly documented situation which makes it impossible for employees covered by this agreement to report for work or to be tardy as a result of such circumstances, such situation will be excused from disciplinary action.[3]

[1] ***City of Orlando, Florida and Fraternal Order of Police, Florida State Lodge.***

[2] ***Municipality of Anchorage and Anchorage Police Department Employees Association.***

[3] ***Monroe County and Monroe County Deputy Sheriffs' Association, Inc.***

18.7 Written Charges.

18.7.1 The Employer agrees that before officers can be disciplined by other than verbal reprimand:

18.7.1.1 Written charges must be served upon the officer to be disciplined within ninety (90) calendar days of the infraction or within ninety (90) calendar days of when the Employer had knowledge of the infraction.

18.7.1.2 The Association must be served with the written charges within ninety-five (95) calendar days of the infraction or when the Employer had knowledge of the infraction.

18.7.1.3 The Association will be notified of any discipline given other than verbal reprimands.[1]

18.8 Disciplinary Tracking System.

18.8.1 The computerized database and disciplinary tracking system shall expunge disciplinary records in accordance with the time schedule set forth in this contract. Further, access to computerized disciplinary records which have "member identifiable information" shall be limited to personnel normally entering data and to those individuals who would normally have authorized access to the original hard copy of such disciplinary records. Although "member identifiable information" will be removed from the data base as provided, the descriptive information of the members involved and of the circumstances will be retained (including but not limited to: age, sex, and rank of the member issuing and receiving the discipline, the date, shift, and unit of the officers involved; and a description of the discipline issued and the circumstances leading thereto).

[1] ***City of Sterling Heights, Michigan and Sterling Heights Police Officers Association.***

18.8.1.1 Disciplinary records without "member identifiable information" will be retained for a period of time after the individual records are no longer subject to administrative use and after they are sealed or destroyed. Disciplinary records without "member identifiable information" will continue to be retained for a period of time determined by the Division for various administrative purposes, including but not limited to assisting the Division in Equal Employment Opportunity analysis, compliance and defense; providing Division personnel responsible for taking or recommending disciplinary action with a resource to evaluate historical patterns of discipline; assisting the Division in identifying training needs; assisting the Division in providing appropriate direction to officers charged with the responsibility of implementing or recommending disciplinary action; and providing the Division with a resource tool for issuing or revising rules and regulations related to the conduct of officers.

18.8.1.2 The Employer reserves the right to make modifications to the Disciplinary Tracking System program in order to continually improve its effectiveness in accordance with this collective bargaining contract.[1]

18.8.2 For purposes of this section alone, a one-day suspension shall be equivalent to eight (8) hours of salary, regardless of the actual hours worked in a shift.[2]

18.8.3 The unit of measurement for any suspensions which may be assessed shall be in hours.[3]

[1] ***City of Columbus, Ohio and Fraternal Order of Police, Capital City Lodge #9.***

[2] ***City of Monterey Park, California and Monterey Park Police Officers' Association.***

[3] ***City of Minneapolis, Minnesota and Police Officers' Federation of Minneapolis.***

18.9 Working Off Suspended Time.

18.9.1 Officers suspended up to a maximum of ten (10) working days may, upon the officer's request and at the Chief's discretion, forfeit vacation designated by the Chief for a period equal to the suspension. Approval of forfeited vacation time by the Chief shall not be unreasonably withheld. The provisions of this Section shall apply solely to suspensions which are agreed to by the officer and no appeal to the Commission or to arbitration may be instituted on suspensions where the officer has agreed to the suspended time.[1]

ARTICLE 19

DISCIPLINARY REVIEW BOARD

19.1 General.

19.1.1 When departmental charges are to be filed against an employee, the Chief of Police or his designee shall have the charges against the employee reduced to writing with two (2) copies of the charges to be served on the employee. The employee may request a hearing with the Chief of Police to be conducted by the Chief or his designee not sooner than seven (7) workdays and not more than fourteen (14) workdays after the written charges have been served upon the employee.

19.1.1.1 Requests for hearings shall be made in writing within five (5) days after the charges have been served on the employee. If a hearing is not requested, the Chief/designee shall render his decision without a hearing within said fourteen (14)-workday period.[2]

[1] ***City of El Paso, Texas and El Paso Municipal Police Officers' Association.***

[2] ***City of Toledo, Ohio and Toledo Police Patrolman's Association, Local 10.***

19.1.2 In the event that formal disciplinary action before the Chief of Police or the Safety Director is taken against a bargaining unit member, the bargaining unit member shall have the right to request the presence of legal counsel and/or one representative from the official recognized Association when such action is taken, and the attorney/or representative shall have the right of cross-examination, in a disciplinary hearing before the Chief of Police, the bargaining unit member may have a representative present, selected by the Association.[1]

19.2 Requirement for Board.

19.2.1 There shall be a Review Board, as set up by the Department Manual, to hear all matters which may ultimately result in some type of discipline.

19.2.1.1 Any Officer may waive his right to a Review Board Hearing and go directly to the Police Chief for review.

19.2.1.2 Accidents involving Employee vehicles will only go to the Review Board after the Police Chief investigates the accident and finds there is a question of fault.

19.2.1.3 Off-duty incidents will go to the Review Board after the Police Chief and the officer have reviewed the incident together within five (5) days of receipt of the report of the incident if it is felt by the Police Chief that the incident involved a violation of the Department Manual.[2]

19.3 Complaint Hearing Procedures.

19.3.1 When any report of violation of the Employer's rules and regulations lodged against an employee within the bargain-

[1] ***City of Cleveland, Ohio and Cleveland Police Patrolmen's Association.***

[2] ***Everett, Washington and Everett Police Officers Association.***

ing unit has been recommended as sustained, and the penalty for that infraction may result in suspension, demotion or dismissal, the Chief or his/her designee, who shall be of the rank of Captain or above, shall immediately notify the employee of such fact, together with the disciplinary recommendation and the employee's right to a complaint hearing, provided such right is exercised within five business days. In cases where an employee has been convicted of criminal charges relating to the same conduct that is the subject of the disciplinary recommendation, the employee shall not have a right to a complaint hearing. In all other cases, the Chief of Police shall notify the employee of his/her right to a complaint hearing in the event the Chief of Police recommends a sustained finding and proposes a penalty of suspension, demotion or dismissal; provided that if deemed appropriate by the Chief of Police, discipline or discharge may be implemented immediately.

19.3.1.1 The employee has five business days from the time of notification in which to waive or exercise his/her right to a complaint hearing. The employee shall notify his/her commanding officer within five business days, otherwise he/she will be deemed to have waived his/her right to a complaint hearing. At this time the waiver may not be rescinded; provided, however, that in those cases where the employee has waived his/her right to a complaint hearing, following notification of the disciplinary recommendation, the employee shall have five business days to request such a hearing, following notification of the disciplinary decision made by the Chief of Police if the penalty proposed by the Chief of Police exceeds that previously recommended. If the employee exercises his/her right to a complaint hearing, he/she shall have adequate time to prepare his/her defense after he/she has been fully informed of the nature of the charges that have been lodged against him/her.

19.3.1.2 The appropriate command will notify the Internal Investigation Section that the employee has waived his/her rights. In addition to the circumstances under which a Complaint Advisory Board is convened under paragraph (b) above, the Chief of Police may convene a Complaint Advisory Board in any case where such a review is desired before finalizing a disciplinary decision and whether or not the employee has been convicted of a crime.

19.3.1.3 The Complaint Advisory Board shall be comprised of four (4) voting members; a Chairperson, of the rank of Captain or over, provided that if the disciplinary recommendation is more serious than a ten-day suspension, the Chairperson shall, unless otherwise agreed, be an Assistant Chief; two employees of the rank of Lieutenant or higher, and one sworn employee from the bargaining unit appointed by the Association. The Department shall use its best efforts to distribute its appointments to the Complaint Advisory Board among command personnel. In cases of complaints from outside the Department, a fifth non-voting member of the Board shall be a citizen participant appointed by the Mayor. The citizen participant (1) shall certify to the Mayor in writing whether the citizen complaint received a full, fair and impartial hearing, and (2) may request the Chief of Police, in writing, to review the decision of the Board. The employee shall have the right to challenge any member of the Board for cause and will be allowed to exercise one preemptory challenge of members of the Board. The Chairperson shall have the right to challenge the employee appointed by the Association for cause. When the Board is evenly split on what its recommendation will be (i.e., there's a tie vote), both points of view will be conveyed in writing to the Chief.

19.3.1.4 The hearing shall be conducted at a mutually agreeable site. The employee will be given an opportunity to present a full and complete defense to the accusations presented at the hearing. The employee may be granted a continuance by the Chairperson for the purpose of presenting a full and complete defense. If facts are presented during the hearing that would support additional or alternative charges of misconduct that were not made prior to the convening of the Board, the Board may not render a decision on those charges until the employee has been advised of them and provided an opportunity to respond. The employee may request that the hearing be continued in order to have an adequate opportunity to prepare a response to such additional or alternative charges. The Chairperson may also continue the hearing if further investigation by the Internal Investigations Section of the facts supporting such charges is warranted.

19.3.1.5 The employee may ask any member of the Department or an attorney for assistance in the presentation of his/her case, with the exception of personnel from the Internal Investigations Section or the Police Legal Advisors.

19.3.1.6 The employee may record the proceedings at his/her own expense. Such recording may be through audio-tape or stenographic means.

19.3.1.7 The Association shall be notified whenever a complaint hearing is scheduled. The Association may assign any elected officer of the Association to sit in as an observer.

19.3.1.8 Complaint Advisory Boards are not judicial tribunals, and any evidence pertinent to the issue may be presented. The Chairperson shall decide any question of procedure or acceptability of evidence, accepting any evidence which is reasonably relevant to the present charges. No statements made by the subject employee can be used against him/her in a criminal prosecution. The Legal Advisor may be present as an advisor on procedural matters. The Complaint Advisory Board will consider the investigation reports, statements and other documents, testimony of witnesses, and such other evidence as it deems appropriate. The Chairperson, at his/her discretion, may order the employee or any other member of the Department to appear. The Complaint Advisory Board may only consider evidence which was introduced during the hearing. Members of the Complaint Advisory Board may be provided a copy of the investigatory file in advance of the hearing.

19.3.1.9 The Board will not consider the employee's work record unless it has made a prior finding that the charges against the employee are sustained. Upon conclusion of the presentation of evidence by both sides, the Board will reach a decision by secret ballot. The employee will be advised of the results of the balloting prior to implementation of any disciplinary action that may be recommended.

19.3.1.10 On the basis of its findings, the Board will recommend one of the following actions to the Chief of Police:

1. Further investigation with specific recommendations;
2. Finding a charge unfounded;
3. Finding a charge not sustained;
4. Finding a charge sustained and listing their recommendations; and
5. Exonerating the employee.

19.3.1.11 If a sustained finding is to be recommended, the Board will then consider previous disciplinary actions taken against the employee in determining appropriate action in the present case. After being informed of a sustained finding, the employee and/or his/her representative will be provided a reasonable opportunity to address the Board regarding the level of discipline the Board may recommend. If an in-person presentation cannot be scheduled in a timely manner, the Chair may request that such input be promptly submitted in writing. If an in-person presentation is scheduled, the Chair, at its discretion, will determine whether or not the testimony of witnesses regarding the disciplinary recommendation will be admitted. The Board shall not be bound by previous recommendations in determining the severity of the disciplinary action they recommend.

19.3.1.12 Except for the subject employee, an employee ordered by the Chairperson to attend a Complaint Advisory Board hearing (provided for in this Section) as a witness during his/her off-duty time shall be compensated in accordance with Section 5.4 (Overtime Pay for Court Appearances) of this Agreement. In the event all the charges in the complaint are exonerated or unfounded by the Chief of Police, the subject employee will also be entitled to the overtime provision in this Agreement, as approved by the Chairperson.

19.3.1.13 In the event that the discipline imposed includes a suspension, at the request of the employee, the Employer and the employee may agree to allow the employee to exchange accrued vacation, holiday and/or compensatory time for all or part of the suspension.[1]

[1] ***Seattle, Washington and Seattle Police Officers Guild.***

ARTICLE 20

CIVILIAN REVIEW

20.1 General.

20.1.1 The Employer may establish a Citizen's Review Board as provided for in the City Code provided, however, no such Board shall have the authority to impose or modify disciplinary actions against employees.[1]

ARTICLE 21

PROBATIONARY EMPLOYEES

21.1 General.

21.1.1 Initial Probationary Period.

21.1.1.1 Each new sworn employee and each new communication clerk shall be hired as a probationary employee until the end of a probationary period of one (1) year. Each non-sworn employee, except communications clerks, shall serve a probationary period of six (6) months. These periods may be extendible for thirty (30) day periods by mutual consent of the Association and the Employer. Officers returning from undercover work may have their probationary period extended under this provision provided employees are placed in the Police Academy or put under direct supervision of a Field Training Officer. Any employee discharged or terminated shall have the right of review by a three (3) member Committee of designated employees appointed by the Association. If the Committee deems necessary, it shall have the right to refer the matter to the Grievance Procedure as provided in the terms of this Agreement. The

[1] ***City of Orlando, Florida and Fraternal Order of Police, Florida State Lodge.***

Employer's decision to terminate a new-hire probationary employee cannot be overturned unless it is found to be arbitrary, capricious, discriminatory, or made in bad faith.[1]

21.2 Standards for Probation.

21.2.1 All new employees who enter the Employer's service designated as "lateral entry" Police Officers, and who possess a Police Officers Standards and Training (P.O.S.T.) Basic Certificate, shall serve a probationary period of twelve (12) months.

21.2.1.1 All other new employees covered under this Agreement shall serve a probationary period of eighteen (18) months.[2]

ARTICLE 22

PERFORMANCE EVALUATIONS

22.1 General.

22.1.1 Requirements For Evaluations.

22.1.1.1 The performance of each member of the bargaining unit shall be evaluated annually at a time sufficiently in advance of the effective date of step increases to permit the exhaustion of appeal processes. This evaluation, to be conducted by the employee's immediate supervisor (also known as the "rating supervisor"), shall serve both as the "service rating" and as a departmental measurement of performance. Performance evaluations shall be based on work performance. Performance evaluations shall be conducted at least once a year. These evaluations shall be considered for promotions and lateral assignments.

[1] ***Municipality of Anchorage and Anchorage Police Department Employees Association.***

[2] ***Vallejo, California and Vallejo Police Officers Association.***

22.1.1.2 Evaluations shall be conducted by a rating supervisor who has observed in a supervisory capacity the employee's performance for six months. If this is not the case, the evaluator shall note and take into account the period of observation. If the immediate supervisor has less than three months of observation, the predecessor supervisor, if available and if he has observed the employee for more than six months, shall conduct the evaluation. If the predecessor is not available, the commanding officer, in consultation with the immediate supervisor, shall conduct the evaluation. Consistent standards of evaluation shall be made known to the bargaining unit and all evaluators. Evaluators shall make a good-faith effort to apply such standards in all evaluations.

22.1.1.3 When an employee is rated unsatisfactorily in any category, the rating supervisor shall state the reason(s) for such rating and shall if practicable suggest means of improvement.

22.1.1.4 After the evaluation is made, the employee shall be given a copy. If the employee's performance has been rated unsatisfactory in one or more factors, then the rating supervisor and the employee must meet to discuss the evaluation. If no unsatisfactory ratings have been received, either the rating supervisor or the employee may require a discussion.

22.1.1.5 Anything lower than a satisfactory annual service rating may be grieved in accordance with the grievance and arbitration provisions of this Agreement. In any such arbitration, the arbitrator shall not substitute his judgment for that of the evaluator absent evidence that the evaluator exercised his judgment arbitrarily or capriciously. During the period of an annual service rating, interim performance observation reports shall be neither grievable nor arbitrable unless incorporated into a lower than satisfactory annual service rating.[1]

[1] ***State of Connecticut and Connecticut State Police Union.***

ARTICLE 23

USE OF FORCE

23.1 Use of Deadly Force.

23.1.1 Employees involved in the use of lethal force shall be immediately advised of their rights and allowed to consult with an Association representative or attorney prior to being required to give an oral or written statement about the use of lethal force. Such right to consult with a representative or with counsel shall not unduly delay the giving of the interview, and shall not take longer than forty-eight (48) hours in any case.[1]

23.1.2 Anytime a member(s) of the Association is involved in a Critical Incident, the member(s) shall receive the necessary time off to relieve the stress which has resulted from the Critical Incident. The duration of the time shall be discussed by the Chief of Police with the Employee Assistance Program Officer, but the decision shall rest solely with the Chief of Police.

32.1.2.1 A Critical Incident is defined as "any event which has emotional power to overwhelm a person's common effective abilities to cope." The Police Officer shall continue to receive his normal rate of pay for these days and they shall not be charged against sick time.[2]

23.1.3 The Employer and the Association recognize that due to the unique nature of law enforcement, the use of force is occasionally necessary and proper for the Police Department to accomplish its mission. The Association agrees that it is the sole

[1] ***Washington State Patrol and Washington State Patrol Troopers Association.***

[2] ***City of Toledo, Ohio and Toledo Police Patrolman's Association, Local 10.***

right and responsibility of the Employer to establish standards and policy regarding the use of force, balancing the safety of the community and its police with the constitutional principles of due process. In the event that the Employer determines that a significantly more restrictive policy regarding the use of deadly force is necessary, the Employer agrees to meet and negotiate the impact of such change with the Association.[1]

23.1.4 The Employer agrees to reimburse an officer for all reasonable, usual and customary legal fees charged by an attorney as a direct result of criminal charges or a criminal investigation arising out of the officer's involvement in the actions in the performance of his or her duty as a police officer.

23.1.4.1 The reimbursement shall not be made if the officer is convicted by verdict or plea, pleads no contest to criminal charges arising out of the incident, or the Employer sustains disciplinary charges on the basis of the officer's actions which formed the basis for the possible criminal liability, and the Employer's sustaining of the charges is upheld on any appeal of discipline.

23.1.4.2 Any reimbursement required shall be made only at the conclusion of all criminal and disciplinary proceedings against the officer arising out of the incident.

23.1.4.3 To receive reimbursement under this Article, the officer must select one attorney from a list of fifteen (15) which has been mutually agreed upon by the Association and the City Attorney. Neither party shall unreasonably oppose the inclusion of an attorney on the list. Within sixty (60) days of the execution of this agreement, the Association shall submit to the City Attorney the names of the attorneys it proposes for inclusion on the

[1] ***Fort Lauderdale, Florida and Fraternal Order of Police.***

list. If the City Attorney does not object to an attorney on the list within ten (10) days, the attorney shall be included on the list. The names on the list shall be reviewed every six months upon the request of either party. If no attorney on the list is available to represent an officer, the officer may obtain another attorney, and if the Association notifies the Employer of the selected attorney by the close of the next working day, the Employer shall reimburse the officer for the Attorney's fees provided all other requirements of this article are met.

23.1.4.4 Before becoming obligated under this Article, the Employer shall be presented with a sworn affidavit by the attorney listing an hourly breakdown of time spent and describing briefly the purpose of such time. If the Employer in its discretion feels the charges exceed reasonable, usual and customary fees normally charged, the Employer may submit the bill to the State Bar Association for review. The State Bar Association's determination will be final and binding for the Employer's obligation under this Article.[1]

23.2 Firearms Required/Qualifications.

23.2.1 No employee shall be required to work without a firearm except as provided below:

23.2.1.1 The Employer may require an employee to work for up to ten (10) days without a firearm in a position that does not require dealing with the public in person.

23.2.1.2 Within that ten-day period the officer will receive a psychological evaluation, at the Employer's expense, and the results of that evaluation will determine continuation of the employee's temporary assignment. Such evaluations shall be conducted in accordance with the Americans with Disabilities

[1] ***City of Portland, Oregon and Portland Police Association.***

Act (ADA). This position would not be considered to be a limited-duty assignment.

23.2.1.3 Employees will be required to qualify with their service weapon at the range as a condition of employment. If an employee fails to qualify at the range, the Employer shall provide remedial firearms training to the employee. If the employee still fails to qualify during the course of remedial training, the employee shall be allowed sixty (60) days from the conclusion of remedial training to demonstrate the ability to qualify. An employee who fails to qualify after remedial training shall be reassigned to an administrative position. The Employer shall notify the Association when an employee fails to qualify after remedial training. The employee may appeal the reassignment to the Firearms Qualification Review Board (FQRB). During this 60-day period, the employee will be provided with a reasonable amount of additional target ammunition to assist the employee to gain proficiency, and, upon request, the Employer may provide coaching from a member of the range staff.

23.2.1.4 If, at the conclusion of the 60-day period, the employee has still not qualified, the Employer may take appropriate measures with the employee. Should the employee be disabled or on sick leave during any portion of the 60-day period, the 60-day period shall be lengthened by the amount of the time the employee was disabled or on sick leave. Appropriate measures shall include, if the employee was formerly authorized to carry a revolver, affording the employee the opportunity to qualify with a revolver, which shall thereafter be the employee's service weapon until the employee qualifies with an automatic. The Employer may not institute disciplinary measures against the employee for at least ten (10) days following the expiration of the 60-day period. If at any time during the pendency of the disciplinary action the employee qualifies with his/her service weapon, the disciplinary action shall immediately be terminated with no discipline issued to the employee based upon the failure to qualify and the employee shall be returned to the assignment held prior to the remedial training.

23.2.1.5 The FQRB shall be composed of one representative of the Training Section, one member appointed by the Chief, and one Association representative. The FQRB shall meet within seven (7) days of receiving an appeal from a member and shall consider any written or oral information provided by the employee. The FQRB shall make a recommendation to the Chief concerning the reassignment of the employee and the training options available to assist the employee in qualification.[1]

[1] ***City of Seattle, Washington and Seattle Police Officers Guild.***

CHAPTER 4

SENIORITY

Seniority is typically used for a number of purposes in law enforcement collective bargaining agreements. Seniority will often determine vacation selection, selection of shifts and days off, layoff and recall order, and may have an impact on the selection of candidates for promotions.

The articles in this chapter define how seniority is determined and used. Examples of the types of definitions of seniority include overall seniority, which typically involves the total length of service with the employer, departmental seniority, which typically only involves the length of time with the individual law enforcement agency, and classification seniority, defined as the time spent in an individual classification. Seniority can be used for a variety of purposes, including layoff, shift selection, and the selection of vacation time. It is critical that collective bargaining agreements contain a specific definition of seniority as well as how ties in seniority are to be broken. Without a clear definition of seniority, grievances can arise which pit one bargaining unit member against another.

In addition to the definition and use of seniority, other portions of this chapter deal with the protection of the seniority and job security of members of a law enforcement agency by regulating the use of reserves or auxiliary police officers.

ARTICLE 24

SENIORITY

24.1 Overall Seniority.

24.1.1 "Seniority" for the purposes of vacation accrual shall be computed on the basis of total uninterrupted length of continuous service with the Employer. Such seniority shall hereinafter be defined as "Departmental Seniority."[1]

24.2 Departmental Seniority.

24.2.1 Departmental seniority is defined as an employee's most recent period of unbroken, continuous service with the Police Department. Employees shall not attain department seniority until completion of the required probationary period, at which time department seniority shall relate back to the commencement of the most recent period of continuous employment with the Police Department.[2]

24.3 Classification Seniority.

24.3.1 Classification seniority is defined as the period of most recent continuous service in the employee's classification. Employees shall not attain classification seniority until completion of the probationary period in the classification, at which time seniority classification shall relate back to the most recent date of appointment to such classification.[3]

24.4 Ties in Seniority.

24.4.1 Whenever two (2) or more employees have the same hire date, the order of seniority shall be determined by lottery

[1] ***Lorain County, Ohio Sheriff and Fraternal Order of Police, Ohio Labor Council.***

[2] ***Vallejo, California and Vallejo Police Officers Association.***

[3] ***Vallejo, California and Vallejo Police Officers Association.***

selection. The names of all employees having the same hire date will be drawn at random, one (1) name at a time until all names are drawn. The order of selection shall determine the order of seniority, with the employee whose name is drawn first having the greater seniority. Lottery selection will be made by the Sheriff or his representative in the presence of an Association representative.[1]

24.5 Forfeiture of Seniority.

24.5.1 An employee shall forfeit seniority rights only for the following reasons:

24.5.1.1 The employee resigned and has not been reinstated within two (2) years of the date of resignation;

24.5.1.2 The employee is dismissed and is not reinstated;

24.5.1.3 The employee is absent without leave for a period of five (5) scheduled working days or more. Exceptions to this may be made by the Employer on the grounds of good cause for failure to report;

24.5.1.4 The employee retires on a regular service retirement.

24.5.1.5 If following a layoff the employee fails or refuses to notify the department of his intention to return to work within fourteen (14) calendar days from the date written notice of such recall is sent, by certified mail, to his last known address on record with the department or, having notified the department of his intent to return to work, fails to report for duty on or before said fourteenth calendar day or effective day of the notice to return to work whichever is later. Exceptions to this may be made by the Employer on the grounds of good cause for failure

[1] ***Clement County, Ohio Sheriff and Fraternal Order of Police, Ohio Labor Council, Inc.***

to notify or report. The employee will be advised during layoff processing of the necessity of a current address on record with the department.[1]

24.6 Seniority Credits.

24.6.1 Determination of Seniority.

24.6.1.1 In computing seniority, credit shall be given for all classified service in the Police Department except that a resignation or discharge shall be considered a break in service and seniority credit shall not be given for any service rendered prior to that break.

24.6.1.2 Seniority credit shall be allowed only for the following types of absence from a position in the classified service: 1. Absence without pay not exceeding seven (7) calendar days; 2. Absence during authorized vacation period; 3. Absence on leave for active service in the armed forces of the State or of the United States of America; 4. Absence on leave to accept exempt employment in any department, office or bureau of the Employer, not to exceed one (1) year of credit; 5. Absence on leave to accept temporary emergency employment; 6. Absence on leave to serve the probationary period in a new class in the event the employee does not complete the probationary period due to a layoff. Seniority shall be allowed only in the new class upon subsequent completion of the probationary period in the new class; 7. Absence on leave made necessary by injuries in the line of duty. 8. Absence on leave while on loan to another agency if, in the opinion of the Employer, the service stands to benefit from the specific experience obtained from such other employment or activity.

[1] ***Detroit, Michigan and Detroit Police Officers Association.***

24.6.1.3 In computing length of service, all periods of absence without pay from the service of the Employer in excess of seven (7) calendar days, notwithstanding the reason or necessity therefor, shall be deducted and no seniority credit granted.

24.6.1.4 Seniority credits for periods of absence from one class in order to temporarily fill in another position shall be credited in the former position.

24.6.1.5 If an employee is suspended through no fault of his own and is later re-employed, he shall not lose any seniority credit for any period of actual service; if, however, he has been separated from service by resignation or discharge for cause and is again employed, he shall not receive any seniority credit for service rendered prior to his separation from service.

24.6.1.6 When two or more employees are appointed on the same date in the same classification, the order or precedence shall be determined by the order of the relative position of such employees on the eligibility list from which said employees were appointed.

24.6.1.7 Seniority credit shall be allowed upon return from absence from a position in the classified service as a result of disability retirement, not to exceed three years. This seniority credit shall be used only in the computation of shift selection, days off, annual leave selection, layoffs and seniority points on promotion.[1]

24.6.2 In the event an employee is separated from the department as a result of disciplinary action and subsequently reinstated to his position, as a result of arbitration, commission or court decisions, his seniority shall be maintained from the

[1] ***Vallejo, California and Vallejo Police Officers Association.***

original date of hire unless the arbitrator, commission or court orders otherwise.[1]

24.7 Seniority List.

24.7.1 A departmental seniority list will be furnished by the Employer to the Association and posted on the Association bulletin board on June 1 of each year and revised each thirty (30) days as necessary to keep current while this Agreement is in effect. The seniority list shall show names, job titles or rank and the date of hire of all officers in order of their seniority.

24.7.1.2 Time in grade or "rank" seniority lists shall also be furnished by the Employer to the Association on June 1 of each year and shall be revised each thirty (30) days as necessary to keep current during the term of this Agreement. This list shall reflect the names, job titles, rank of each officer and the date of rank assignment in order of their assignment within each rank.

24.7.1.3 A list of officers within each section shall be furnished by the Employer to the Association and posted on the Association bulletin board within each section on June 1 of each year and revised each thirty (30) days as necessary to keep current during the term of this Agreement. The list shall reflect the date each officer within each section was assigned to the section in order of their assignment to the section with the rank of each officer.[2]

24.7.2 In the event it becomes necessary to lay off employees for any reason, employees shall be laid off in the inverse order of their seniority by job classification.[3]

[1] ***Redford Township, Michigan and Police Officers Association of Michigan.***

[2] ***County of Shawnee, Kansas and Fraternal Order of Police, Lodge 3.***

[3] ***City of Little Rock, Arkansas and Fraternal Order of Police, Lodge #17.***

24.8 Seniority Upon Transfer.

24.8.1 In the case of voluntary transfer and/or assignment, the seniority of an officer shall apply immediately to the officer's choice concerning holidays and vacations. The transferring officer may not use seniority to bump another officer's shift or days off until 45 days from the date of the written request. The Bureau may voluntarily accommodate the shift and/or day off preferences of the transferring officer before 45 days provided it does not involuntarily bump another officer to do so.

24.8.1.2 In the case of involuntary transfer and/or assignment, the seniority of an officer shall apply immediately to the officer's choice concerning holidays and vacations. The transferring officer may not use seniority to bump another officer's shift or days off until 30 days from the date of the written request. The Employer may voluntarily accommodate the shift and/or day off preferences of the transferring officer before 30 days provided it does not involuntarily bump another officer to do so.[1]

24.9 Compensation for Failure to Follow Seniority.

24.9.1 In the event an employee is not worked in his rightful position of seniority, as set forth in this Agreement, he shall be compensated in the amount that was earned by the employee who was worked in his stead, unless otherwise mutually agreed upon by both the Association and the Employer.[2]

[1] ***City of Portland, Oregon and Portland Police Association.***

[2] ***Municipality of Anchorage and Anchorage Police Department Employees Association.***

ARTICLE 25

LAYOFFS

25.1 General.

25.1.1 Regular employees will be laid off by inverse Department seniority within a job classification.[1]

25.2 Bumping Rights.

25.2.1 A regular employee who has been notified that he or she is to be laid off may bump into a position parallel in classification to the one from which he or she is to be laid off or into a lower job classification provided he or she is higher in Department seniority than the person occupying the position to be bumped into.

25.2.1.1 No employee may bump into a higher classification.

25.2.1.2 The employee must meet the entry level qualifications for the job he or she wishes to bump into as defined by the Employer classification and pay.

25.2.1.3 Once the employee has bumped into a position, the employee will have ninety (90) days to successfully complete training in the new position.

25.2.1.4 The employee will enter the classification bumped into at the lowest position seniority but will maintain his or her Department seniority.

25.2.1.5 An employee will be allowed one bump option per lay off notice.

[1] ***Municipality of Anchorage and Anchorage Police Department Employees Association.***

25.2.1.6 An employee shall be paid in accordance with the pay range applicable to the job classification bumped into.[1]

25.3 Demotion in Lieu of Layoff.

25.3.1 In lieu of layoff employees may be demoted, at their request, by seniority. Demotion shall be through those classifications in which the employee previously held permanent status. An employee serving a probationary period shall not displace a permanent employee in a classification in which the probationary employee has not previously held permanent status.

25.3.1.1 For purposes of this section, members of this bargaining unit who were promoted into the supervisory unit will be eligible to be demoted back into this bargaining unit in lieu of layoff for a period of up to one (1) year from the promotion.[2]

25.4 Notice of Layoff.

25.4.1 Employees to be laid off indefinitely shall be given at least thirty (30) calendar days' prior notice.[3]

25.5 Notice of Recall from Layoff.

25.5.1 Employees being recalled from layoff shall be notified by certified or registered mail at their last address of record. A copy of the recall notice shall also be sent to the Association.

25.5.1.1 Recalled employees must notify the Personnel and Training Section of the Department within fourteen (14) calendar days from the last date the letter of recall was delivered to the employee's address of their decision to return to work. The

[1] ***Municipality of Anchorage and Anchorage Police Department Employees Association.***

[2] ***City of Lansing, Michigan and Fraternal Order of Police, Capitol City Lodge 141.***

[3] ***City of Lansing, Michigan and Fraternal Order of Police, Capitol City Lodge 141.***

employee shall report for duty within fourteen (14) calendar days after the date of their written notification to the Personnel and Training Section of the Police Department, or shall report at such later date as specified within the recall notice.

25.5.1.2 Employees who fail to timely respond in accordance with the above to the recall notice or timely report for duty shall forfeit their employment rights and shall be removed from the employment rolls.

25.5.1.3 If within sixty (60) days from the date of the recall notice good cause is established for the untimely response to a recall notice, an employee may be reinstated on the recall list for future recall rights.

25.5.1.4 It is the responsibility of the employee to keep the Personnel and Training Bureau of the Department notified of his/her current address.[1]

25.5.2 No new employees shall be hired into a classification until all employees, who are on a layoff status from that classification, have been offered recall.[2]

[1] ***City of Lansing, Michigan and Fraternal Order of Police, Capitol City Lodge 141.***

[2] ***City of Little Rock, Arkansas and Fraternal Order of Police, Lodge #17.***

ARTICLE 26

USE OF RESERVES AND NON-REGULAR EMPLOYEES

26.1 Restrictions.

26.1.1 In continuing its policy on police reserves, the Employer will in no event use police reserves to do normal work of bargaining unit members or to circumvent the holiday overtime and/or any other provisions of this agreement. Reserves cannot be assigned to ride with employees unless the employee consents. Reserves shall not ride with employees assigned to one-man cars except in emergencies that arise under this agreement.[1]

26.1.2 Reserve officers shall not be regularly assigned to perform police functions normally performed by a sworn officer working in a pay status (i.e., normal beat patrol, walking beats, normal detective functions, etc.). Reserve officers may be used by the Department to supplement police services, such as for additional staffing for special projects, in emergencies, for traffic or crowd control, in positions where they have been utilized previously, or in other short-term circumstances. If the Association believes that reserve officers are being utilized inappropriately, it may meet with the Chief of Police or his or her designee to discuss such disputes or disagreements and to attempt to resolve any disputes or disagreements. Disputes regarding utilization of reserve officers shall not be subject to the grievance procedure.[2]

[1] ***Detroit, Michigan and Detroit Police Officers Association.***

[2] ***Berkeley, California and Berkeley Police Association.***

26.1.3 The Employer agrees that full-time sworn Police personnel shall be given the opportunity on a minimum of forty-eight hours' notice, to volunteer for "police contract work" before such work opportunity is afforded to non-full-time City employees.[1]

26.1.4 Civilian personnel will not be hired as the result of a layoff to perform the duties of a police officer.[2]

26.2 Use of Reserves.

26.2.1 The Employer shall utilize only sworn employees for the purposes of providing security, crowd control, and other police-related activities at all Employer facilities.

For the purposes of this article, Employer facilities shall include only the following:

(1) The Convention Center Exhibit Halls and Banquet Halls

(2) The HemisFair Arena

(3) The Lila Cockrell Theater

(4) Market Square

(5) Market Square Centre de Artes Ballroom; Fiesta Room; and Farmers Market

(6) La Villita

(7) The Alamodome

(8) Municipal Auditorium[3]

[1] ***Garden Grove, California and Garden Grove Police Officers Association.***

[2] ***City of Bloomington, Indiana and Fraternal Order of Police.***

[3] ***City of San Antonio, Texas and San Antonio Police Officers' Association.***

CHAPTER 5

HOURS OF WORK, OVERTIME AND JOB ASSIGNMENTS

Apart from disciplinary appeals, the hours of work section of a law enforcement collective bargaining agreement is likely to generate more grievances than any other area of the contract. For these reasons, it is important to pay strict attention to the details of an hours of work clause, and to spend as much time as is necessary to ensure that the contract language covers a wide variety of foreseeable situations.

The contract articles in this chapter deal with a variety of hours of work topics, including the following:

- Shift Schedules
- Overtime
- Court Appearances and Callbacks
- Compensatory Time Off
- Meal and Break Periods
- Working Out of Classification
- Shift Differentials
- Job Assignments

This chapter also includes examples of the wide variety of shift schedules which are now being used in law enforcement agencies. The large number of alternative shift schedules are testament to a trend in recent years away from what used to be the predominate schedule in law enforcement agencies – five eight-hour days per week. A recent study conducted by Labor Relations Information System indicates that the 5-8 shift is now no longer used by the majority of large law enforcement agencies in the county.

This chapter also deals with the issue of light-duty assignments and an employer's obligations under the Americans With Disabilities Act. Recognizing that there may be a conflict between the seniority provisions in a contract and the need to reasonably accommodate an individual with a disability, the language selected for inclusion in this model contract contains an expedited arbitration procedure designed to resolve ADA disputes.

ARTICLE 27

HOURS OF WORK

27.1 Definition of "Working Days."

27.1.1 Working days mean scheduled workdays, but do not include scheduled days off, approved leaves, or holidays.[1]

27.2 4/8 Plan.

27.2.1 Application. On January 1, ____, the parties agreed to implement a permanent shift plan of four (4) eight (8)-hour shifts within the entire Police Department, which is based upon seniority. The parties agree that one of the purposes of this Article is intended to define the workday, week and month, for the basis of calculations and payment of overtime.

27.2.1.1 The parties recognize the right of the Employer to assign personnel, set work schedules, and to promote the efficiency of municipal government, all within the context of the various terms of this agreement.

27.2.1.2 To effectively utilize manpower levels during traditional shift changes, early car assignments for patrol will be one (1) hour before traditional reporting times.[2]

27.3 5/8 Plan.

27.3.1 The normal workday shall be eight (8) consecutive hours of work and the normal workweek, regardless of shift arrangements, shall be an average of forty (40) hours of work. Normal work shifts will be day, middle, and dog watch, on a monthly rotating basis. Permanent shifts which deviate from the normal work shift shall be filled on a voluntary basis. Normal

[1] ***City of Columbus, Ohio and Fraternal Order of Police, Capital City Lodge 9.***

[2] ***City of Aurora, Illinois and Association of Professional Police Officers, Inc.***

monthly work schedules shall be posted one (1) week prior to the month in question.[1]

27.4 5/2 – 5/3 Plan.

27.4.1 The normal workweek for shift employees covered by this Agreement shall be five (5) workdays and two (2) days off, followed by five (5) workdays and three (3) days off. A workday shall consist of eight (8) regular duty hours plus one-half (1/2) hour at the commencement of the shift which shall normally be used for training purposes except for emergency reasons. The average workweek shall be 39.7 hours.[2]

27.4.2 The normal workweek for full-time Patrol Officers will be 5 on-2 off, 5 on-3 off and the normal workday for such employees shall consist of an eight and one-third (8.33)-hour shift.[3]

27.5 4/11.5 Plan and 4/12 Plan.

27.5.1 A normal workday is either eight (8), ten (10), eleven and one-half (11 1/2), or twelve (12) hours in duration, as assigned by the Police Chief or his designee at his sole and exclusive discretion. A normal work schedule is either five (5) consecutive eight (8)-hour days on duty with two (2) consecutive days off duty; four (4) consecutive ten (10)-hour days on duty with three (3) consecutive days off duty; four (4) consecutive eleven and one-half (11 1/2)-hour days on duty with four (4) consecutive days off duty (with one (1) hour of compensatory

[1] ***Minneapolis, Minnesota and Police Officers' Federation of Minneapolis.***

[2] ***City of Janesville, Wisconsin and Janesville Police Supervisors' Association, Inc.***

[3] ***Outagamie County, Wisconsin and Outagamie County Deputy Sheriff's Association.***

time every 28-day work period which must be utilized within that work period); or four (4) consecutive twelve (12) hour days on duty with four (4) consecutive days off duty, as assigned by the Police Chief or his designee, in his sole and exclusive discretion.[1]

27.6 4/2 Plan.

27.6.1 The parties hereto mutually agree to the following:

27.6.1.1 That a 4/2 work schedule will be implemented and will pertain to patrol and traffic officers assigned to A, B, C, and D shifts.

27.6.1.2 The 4/2 work schedule will consist of the following shifts: A Shift will be the Day Shift working from 0745 hours to 1545 hours; B Shift will be the Afternoon Shift working from 1545 hours to 2345 hours; C Shift will be the Midnight Shift working from 2345 hours to 0745 hours; and D Shift will be the Street Crimes Unit working from 2000 hours to 0400 hours unless directed otherwise by the Superintendent of Police. The number of officers on each shift will be determined by management and also the number of teams per shift will be determined by management.

27.6.1.3 Seniority for Shift Bidding: Each uniformed officer of the Bargaining Unit who will be assigned to the A, B, C shifts will have his or her choice of shifts based on seniority bidding.

27.6.1.4 The only exception to the above is Military Leave personnel. The Superintendent of Police retains the right to see that Military Leave personnel are distributed throughout the various shifts. If there is even distribution of Military Leave personnel through the normal seniority process, then the Superintendent of Police will not utilize his management right.

[1] ***City of Pompano Beach, Florida and Broward County Police Benevolent Association.***

27.6.1.5 Traffic officers who will be assigned to the A, B, and C Shifts will bid for their respective shifts among themselves using total departmental seniority.

27.6.1.6 Seniority in all instances means from the date of appointment to the position of Police Officer for the Employer.

27.6.1.7 D shift — Street Crimes Unit: The Street Crimes Unit shall remain a specialized unit and assignment shall be made by the Superintendent of Police. There will be a request for volunteers. Volunteers will submit their requests in writing. However, if the Street Crimes Unit is not filled through the volunteer selection process, the Superintendent retains the right to assign to that unit. If it becomes necessary for the Superintendent to assign to the Street Crimes Unit, he will assign the most Junior officers.

27.6.1.8 The Employer may conduct an evaluation on July 1, ____. If the Employer determines that there are abuses of sick time and/or I.O.D. (Injured on Duty) resulting in insufficient manpower to properly man the various shifts, the Employer will meet and consult with the Association in an effort to correct the problem for a period of 90 days. At the conclusion of the 90-day period, if the Employer and the Association are unable to resolve the manpower problems, the parties shall immediately go into renegotiations regarding a work schedule on January 3, ____.

27.6.1.9 The Superintendent of Police will determine the proper manning levels on all shifts, including the Street Crimes Unit. If shifts need to be readjusted to arrive at acceptable manning levels, the Superintendent retains the right to transfer to accomplish the proper manning levels by assigning the least senior officer.

27.6.1.10 Bidding for the A, B and C shifts will be done during November, ____. Assignments will be posted in the first week of December, ____ for the upcoming year taking effect on January 1, ____. All bidding will be in writing. D Shift (Street Crime Unit) will be picked prior to A, B and C Shift. Once a schedule is in effect, police officers will not be allowed to indiscriminately change their shift. However, if there is a voluntary request for a change between various officers, the same will be accommodated if all seniority requirements are taken into consideration concerning the Patrol Division as a whole by posting the position five (5) days prior to assignment.

27.6.1.11 As vacancies occur within the A, B and C shifts due to retirements, death, promotion, transfer, the vacancy will be posted. Volunteers, based on seniority, will have an opportunity to fill the vacant position. It should be understood that management retains the right to first determine whether the shift vacancy will be filled. All vacancies will be posted five (5) days prior to assignment. However, management shall have the right to temporarily make assignment during the posting period.

27.6.1.12 In the event of a transfer request or otherwise from a specialized unit to the A, B, C and D Shift, the officer being transferred from the specialized unit will go to the shift from where his replacement came. Voluntary A, B and C Shift transfers can be made to accommodate the transferred officer, taking into account seniority requirements. If this is not possible, the transferred officer will have to wait for the yearly bidding process to effect his seniority. (In no event will the officer be allowed to bump through the A, B and C Shifts at the time of his initial transfer).

27.6.1.13 Since approximately one-third of all shifts will always be on Regular Days Off, unit commanders will schedule no more than three additional officers off on all shifts. Granted time off shall include vacation time, holiday time, compensatory time, military leave time and personal leave time. To accommodate a personal leave request a unit commander may allow an additional officer off. Once a unit commander allows a total of four officers off he can deny all other time off requests other than regular days off.

27.6.1.14 If an officer assigned to A, B, C or D Shifts is injured on duty and is able to perform a light-duty assignment, that assignment will be determined by the Superintendent of Police. In addition, the shift worked will be determined by the Superintendent. However, the officer will continue to receive equalized time off.

27.6.1.15 The Uniformed Patrol Division, which includes A, B, C Shifts, Street Crimes Unit, and members of Traffic Division assigned to the referenced shifts, would be the only division to go on a straight non-rotating 4/2 shift. However, equalization of time off will be given to all other members of the bargaining unit. This time off will be taken at the discretion of the various unit commanders with direction from the Superintendent of Police. Equalized time off will not be allowed to accumulate from one contract year to another. Should an officer retire during the contract year, equalized time off will be pro-rated, and in no instance will it be converted to cash.

27.6.1.16 The Employer will compensate each officer of the Uniformed Patrol Division, Traffic Division and Street Crimes Unit who are actively working 4/2 non-rotating shift schedule in the amount of two (2) hours' pay, to be paid at the straight-time hourly rate per payroll period (i.e., not to exceed fifty-two (52) hours per year). This is to include full-time police matrons currently receiving shift compensation. The additional compensation will be paid so long as the 4/2 non-rotating shift schedule remains in effect.

27.6.1.17 Any position or vacancy within the Bargaining Unit will be posted five (5) days prior to assignment.[1]

27.7 Hours of Work.

27.7.1 The regular work schedule shall be a 5 - 2, 5 - 2, 5 - 3 work schedule. The regular workweek shall be forty (40) hours per week and eight (8) hours per day in five (5) consecutive days. This provision shall include the Communication Control Center, and shall not apply to certain positions in Headquarters, including but not limited to, the Detective Bureau, the Vice and Intelligence Division and Youth Squad where schedules contrary to the above have been worked in the past.[2]

27.8 5/9 Plan.

27.8.1 The 5-9 alternative shift plan works on a 14-day work period and will allow for at least twenty-five percent (25%) of the Detectives to have an additional day off on either a Monday or a Friday, depending on unit assignments. Officers on temporary assignment to Investigative Services may be assigned to the 5-9 Plan as determined by the Chief of Police. Detectives assigned to special units outside Investigative Services may be assigned to work a shift other than the 5-9 Plan as a part of that assignment.[3]

27.9 4/10 Plan.

27.9.1 Each week of service shall consist of five (5) eight (8)-hour workdays or four (4) ten (10)-hour workdays, including

[1] ***Niagara Falls, New York and Police Club.***

[2] ***City of Waterbury, Connecticut and Waterbury Police Union, Local 1237.***

[3] ***City of Modesto, California and Modesto Police Officers Association.***

meal time, or any other arrangement agreeable to the Association and the Employer and not detrimental to the efficient rendering of police service. Each employee working five (5) eight (8)-hour workdays shall receive one hundred and four (104) furlough days per year. Each employee working four (4) ten (10)-hour workdays shall receive one hundred and fifty-six (156) furlough days per year. A furlough day is one of the two or three days per week normally scheduled as a day off.[1]

27.10 3/12 Plan.

27.10.1 Basic Work Schedule: The basic work schedule for members assigned to the patrol division shall be three 12.5-hour workdays per week and one additional 10.0-hour makeup workday every fourth week, so that in every four (4) weeks members are scheduled to work 160 hours.

27.10.1.1 Basic Work Hours: The basic work hours for patrol shifts shall be:

Day shift:	0600 - 1830
Swing shift	1430 - 0300
Midnight shift	1800 - 0630

27.10.1.2 Basic Workdays: The basic workdays for patrol shifts shall be:

Day shift:	A-Wednesday, Thursday, Friday
	B-Saturday, Sunday, Monday
Swing shift:	A-Sunday, Monday, Tuesday
	B-Monday, Tuesday, Wednesday
Relief shift:	Tuesday Day Shift
	Wednesday Swing shift
	Thursday Midnight shift

27.10.1.3 Rotation of Basic Workdays: Members assigned to the day, swing, and midnight shifts shall change workdays in the

[1] ***Bellevue, Washington and Bellevue Police Officers Guild.***

middle of each six-month bid period so that those members working the A side will change to the B side and those working the B side will change to the A side. Members working the relief shift do not change workdays.

27.10.1.4 Make-Up Workdays: Once every four weeks each member will be scheduled to work one (1) ten (10)-hour day to make up the ten hours not worked over the four-week period. This makeup day may be used for training or special projects as determined by the Chief of Police. The makeup day shall be scheduled so that it coincides with the member's workweek, meaning that it shall immediately follow the last workday or immediately precede the first workday and it shall not be on a Saturday or Sunday. Makeup workdays shall not be scheduled on holidays. A detailed calendar shall be prepared by the Employer not later than January 1 of each year showing the schedule of makeup days for the members assigned to each shift.

27.10.1.5 Compensation: Each member shall be paid 40 hours' work at the straight-time rate for each payroll week even though the member is only scheduled to work 37.5 hours. Members shall receive no additional compensation for attending the ten-hour makeup days as these days are specifically designed to repay the Employer for the compensation advanced to the employee during the four-week period. The Employer agrees that it is responsible for keeping accurate accounting of all hours worked to ensure that employees are compensated and scheduled for makeup days as necessary to carry out the objectives of this schedule.

27.10.1.6 Absences: Members absent from work shall have an hour-for-hour deduction made to their leave bank as appropriate for the type of leave being taken by the member.

On 12.5-hour days, 12.5 hours shall be deducted. On 10-hour makeup days, 10 hours shall be deducted, unless the member makes advance arrangements to otherwise make up the 10 hours. Approval of special arrangements for makeup workdays shall be at the discretion of the Chief of Police.

27.10.1.7 Overtime: All work performed in excess of regularly-scheduled work hours, whether before or after a shift or on an employee's days off, shall be considered overtime and shall be so compensated.[1]

27.11 3/12 - 4/12 Work Schedule.

27.11.1 Workday. A workday for employees assigned to 3/12 – 4/12 Work Schedule will consist of 11 hours and 30 minutes of work with 30 additional minutes for meals.

27.11.1.1 Work Period. For those employees working 11 hours and 30 minutes a day, the "work period" will consist of two consecutive weeks with 3 three shifts of 11 hours and 30 minutes in one week and 4 shifts of 11 hours and 30 minutes in the second week. The total hours for these two consecutive weeks shall be considered equaling eighty (80) hours and thirty (30) minutes.

27.11.1.2 However, the one-half hour worked beyond 80 hours of work in a two-week period shall be added to the employee's vacation time. If during the two-week period, an employee is on leave without pay, he/she will not be eligible for one-half hour (1/2) of vacation accrual. The employee, however, will be given early release to make up for the time worked beyond 80 hours.[2]

[1] ***City of Hayward, California and Hayward Police Officers' Association.***

[2] ***City of Santa Ana and Santa Ana Police Officers Association.***

27.12 4/12 Plan.

27.12.1 Schedules.

27.12.1.1 A normal workday may consist of either eight hours per day on the basis of a five-day workweek, or ten hours per day on the basis of a four-day workweek, or twelve hours per day on the basis of the 4/12-plan workweek. The eight, ten, or twelve-hour work schedule shall be at the option of the Employer. The shift hours of any work schedule may be changed with two weeks' notice after consultation with the Association.

27.12.1.2 Each employee working the 4/12 plan will be credited with nine (9) hours' compensatory time off per month as full compensation for the additional 108 hours worked yearly under this plan.

27.12.1.3 Except as required by operational necessity, employees working a 4/12 work schedule shall receive three (3) fifteen (15)-minute breaks and one (1) thirty (30)-minute break, and employees working eight (8) hours per day or ten (10) hours per day shall receive two (2) fifteen (15)-minute breaks plus one (1) thirty (30)-minute break during each shift.[1]

27.13 6/12 Hour Shifts.

27.13.1 "Employees" referred to in this section are those assigned to the following classes and assignments:

CLASS	POSITION ASSIGNMENT
Forensic Specialist I	Crime Scene Investigator
Forensic Specialist II	Crime Scene Investigator
Police Service Dispatcher	Dispatch Center
Police Communications Supervisor	Dispatch Center

[1] ***Coos Bay, Oregon and Coos Bay Police Officers' Association.***

27.13.1.2 Workday. A workday for the above stated classes and position assignments shall be either 12 hours, or eight hours with an additional 30 minutes for unpaid meal time.

27.13.1.3 Work Period, Workweek. The regular "work period" for the employees assigned to this work schedule shall be six (6) twelve (12)-hour workdays and one (1) eight (8)-hour workday in each two-week period. A thirty (30)-minute unpaid meal time shall be scheduled each workday. A workweek consisting of seven (7) consecutive calendar days and forty (40) hours shall be assigned to each employee assigned to this work schedule. Employees shall regularly work eight (8) hours in a "work period" and forty (40) hours in a seven-day workweek.

27.13.1.4 Earned Time Usage. The usage of earned leave such as holidays, vacations, sick leave, and other paid and unpaid leave will be calculated based on the "day" of the work schedule utilized as a day off. If an employee's day off is on a scheduled twelve (12)-hour day, the employee will be charged twelve (12) hours for that day. If an employee takes a day off on the eight (8)-hour workday, the employee will be charged for eight (8) hours.[1]

27.14 12½ Hour Shifts.

27.14.1 The Employer and the Association agree that the regular work schedule for regular full-time employees assigned to the Uniform Patrol Twelve Plan by the Chief of Police shall be twelve (12) twelve and one-half (12½)-hour shifts and one (1) ten (10)-hour shift or one (1) twelve and one-half (12½)-hour shift in a twenty-eight (28)-day work period. Such schedule shall be designed and implemented by Police Department management. An employee will be scheduled by management to work a regular work schedule of one hundred and sixty (160)

[1] ***City of Santa Ana and Santa Ana Police Officers Association.***

hours in each work period. The average workweek for benefit plan purposes only shall be defined as a forty (40)-hour workweek.

27.14.1.1 The workday shall consist of twelve and one-half (12½) hours or ten (10) hours of work. Two breaks and one (1) one-half (½)-hour meal period shall be paid time included in the workday. Employees who perform authorized work in excess of the regular workday as defined in this Letter of Understanding shall be compensated for such work at the rate of one and one-half (1 ½) times their regular hourly rate of pay. Such employees shall not be eligible for overtime pay for breaks and meal periods not taken due to the duties and responsibilities of the work assignment.

27.14.1.2 The Employer and the Association recognize the need for a system of adjusted hours for employees whose work schedule does not correspond to the established eighty-hour biweekly pay period for payroll purposes. The system of adjusted hours permits employees to accrue positive adjusted hours (hours worked, but not paid) or negative adjusted hours (hours paid, but not worked). The Employer and the Association agree that transfers to and from the Uniform Patrol Twelve Plan will be effective at the beginning of a twenty-eight day work period whenever feasible. The Employer and the Association agree that an employee who transfers to a job where adjusted hours are not used on a date other than the beginning of a twenty-eight day work period, or who leaves the Employer's employment, will have any adjusted hours balance adjusted to zero by paying the employee at his current rate for any positive balance or by deducting from his pay for any negative balance. Affected employees may review payroll documents.

27.14.1.3 Employees shall receive additional compensation equivalent to 1/10th of the regular biweekly compensation for each holiday listed in this Agreement. Employees shall have the option to accrue eight (8) hours' holiday time per holiday. Selection of the holiday shall be made upon implementation and on November 1st of each year thereafter.

27.14.1.4 Employees eligible for "immediate family" bereavement leave shall be granted bereavement leave with pay for up to a maximum of thirty-seven and one-half (37½) working hours. Employees eligible for "other family" bereavement leave shall be granted bereavement leave with pay for up to a maximum of twelve and one-half (12½) working hours.

27.14.1.5 Employees shall have one (1) hour deducted from their accrued sick leave, vacation, compensatory time, holiday time or industrial accident leave for each hour of leave taken. Employees with a regular workday of twelve and one-half (12½) hours shall have twelve and one-half (12½) hours deducted from their accrued sick leave, vacation, compensatory time, holiday time or industrial accident leave for each regularly-scheduled working day that they are on paid leave. Employees with a regular workday of ten (10) hours shall have ten (10) hours deducted from their accrued sick leave, vacation, compensatory time, holiday time or industrial accident leave for each regularly scheduled working day that they are on paid leave.[1]

27.15 Pay for Reporting Time.

27.15.1 It is required of every employee covered by this Agreement that he or she report to duty twenty (20) minutes before the start of his or her shift. This requirement is due to the law enforcement nature of police work, and applies not only to

[1] ***City of Anaheim and Anaheim Police Association.***

employees assigned to patrol duties but to all functions and divisions. The time is utilized for transfer and distribution of previous shift information, assignments and equipment, and also for training and in-service education.

27.15.1.1 Said reporting time has been included in the base pay at the regular straight-time hourly rate of all personnel covered by this Agreement. Payment of reporting time shall be included in each paycheck received by employees covered hereunder for the term of this Agreement.[1]

27.16 Travel to Job Site.

27.16.1 Each employee shall report for work at the employee's regularly-established headquarters and shall return thereto at the conclusion of the day's work and the time spent traveling between such headquarters and the job site shall be considered as time worked.[2]

27.17 Community Oriented Policing Work Schedule.

27.17.1 Community police officers' work shall normally be in accordance with Section 7.1. At the officer's discretion, and with unit supervisory approval, for the purposes of fulfilling the objectives of Community Oriented Policing, the officer may split his eight and one-quarter (8¼)-hour workday. If the workday is split, one-hour travel time shall be granted to the officer as part of the eight and one-quarter (8¼)-hour workday.[3]

[1] ***City of Aurora, Illinois and Association of Professional Police Officers, Inc.***

[2] ***City of Redding, California and Peace Officers Association of Redding.***

[3] ***City of Kansas City, Kansas and Fraternal Order of Police, Lodge #4.***

27.18 Cleanup Time.

27.18.1 Each employee shall, when necessary, be permitted up to fifteen (15) minutes of paid time at the end of each work shift to perform such activities as cleaning up a work area, putting away tools, personal wash-up and changing clothes.[1]

27.19 Daylight Savings Time.

27.19.1 On any weekend during which there is a change to or from Standard Time to Daylight Savings Time, the Employer may adjust work schedules so that those assigned to work do actually work the regular number of hours normally assigned to the shift.[2]

27.20 Business Calls.

27.20.1 An employee who is required by his/her supervisor or designee to conduct business telephone calls outside his/her work hours of less than 30 minutes' duration shall receive $5.00 compensation. In no event will an employee receive the benefit of this provision more than once in his/her workday. Any Unit 5 employee who performs telephone work for thirty (30) minutes or more will be compensated in accordance with the overtime provisions contained in the employee's workweek group. This section does not apply when a business call results in a call back to work because the employee will be compensated in accordance with the call back provision of this agreement. Pay for business calls will not be considered compensation for use in computing retirement allowance.[3]

[1] ***Orange County, California and Association of Orange County Deputy Sheriffs.***

[2] ***Concord, California and Concord Police Association.***

[3] ***State of California and California Association of Highway Patrolmen.***

27.21 Attendance at College.

27.21.1 Where scheduling and manpower contingencies permit, the Employer will arrange an employee's work schedule so as to permit the employee to attend college.[1]

ARTICLE 28

MEAL AND BREAK PERIODS

28.1 Paid Meal Periods.

28.1.1 Each employee covered by this agreement will be given 30 minutes for a lunch period each shift worked. This period will be free of duty calls except in cases of emergency.[2]

28.2 Scheduling of Meal Periods.

28.2.1 Employees shall not be assigned meals as a matter of practice during either the first hour and one-half or last hour and one-half of their tours. In cases of emergency this practice may be altered.[3]

28.3 Meal Allowance.

28.3.1 Employer shall provide an employee adequate meals under the following conditions:

28.3.1.1 An employee shall be provided with two (2) adequate meals if he is called out on emergency overtime work one (1) or more hours before a scheduled workday. If a meal has been earned under another section of this rule within two (2)

[1] ***City of El Paso, Texas and El Paso Municipal Police Officers' Association.***

[2] ***Olmsted County, Minnesota and Olmsted County Deputy Sheriffs' Association.***

[3] ***New York, New York and Patrolmen's Benevolent Association of the City of New York.***

hours of the scheduled workday, only one meal shall be provided under this section.

28.3.1.2 An employee will be provided one meal if he is called back to emergency overtime work within one and one-half (1½) hours after normal quitting time and works beyond two and one-half (2½) hours after normal quitting time.

28.3.1.3 An employee shall be provided an adequate meal if he works two (2) hours or more overtime beyond the normal quitting time.

28.3.1.4 An employee shall receive one meal if he is scheduled to work overtime two (2) hours or more before a regular day.

28.3.1.5 An employee shall be provided an adequate meal at four (4)-hour intervals during the performance of emergency overtime work.

28.3.1.6 Mealtime shall be compensated at the appropriate overtime rate and shall normally be limited to one-half (½) hour with a maximum limit of forty-five minutes paid mealtime.

28.3.1.7 An employee may, at his request, be compensated for meals at the rate of one-half (½) hour of overtime pay per meal.[1]

28.4 Furnished Meals.

28.4.1 The regular hours of work each day shall be consecutive and shall include a one-half (1/2)-hour paid lunch period for sworn employees and non-sworn employees assigned to a swing or graveyard shift. Non-sworn employees assigned to day shift shall receive a one-hour unpaid lunch period.

[1] ***City of Anaheim and Anaheim Police Association.***

Correctional officers may not leave their work station during the lunch period, but each correctional officer shall be provided, at no cost to the correctional officer, one (1) meal from the correctional facility kitchen during the assigned work shift.[1]

28.5 Rest Periods.

28.5.1 Except during emergency situations, employees shall be permitted to take one (1) thirty (30)-minute lunch break and two (2) fifteen (15)-minute coffee breaks or rest periods during each workday.[2]

ARTICLE 29

TRAVEL TIME

29.1 Out-of-Town Travel Time.

29.1.1 One-day Trip – Such travel time is normally considered work time. However, travel time between home and an airport or railroad station which is comparable to normal commuting time, and duty-free mealtime, shall not be counted as time worked.

29.1.1.1 Overnight Trips – An employee traveling at the behest of the employer as a passenger on a public conveyance or in an automobile is considered to be working (except for regular meal period or sleep time), to the extent the travel time occurs during any portion of the employee's "Normal Workday," whether or not the travel time occurs during normal working hours on an otherwise regular day off.[3]

[1] ***Deschutes County, Oregon and Deschutes County Sheriff's Association.***

[2] ***City of Reno, Nevada and Reno Police Protective Association.***

[3] ***City of Escondido, California and Escondido Police Association – Non-Sworn Personnel.***

ARTICLE 30

OVERTIME

30.1 Definition of Overtime.

30.1.1 Employees shall be compensated at the rate of one and one half (1-1/2) times their regular rate of pay in either cash or compensatory time off at the employee's option for overtime work under the following conditions, but in no event shall such compensation be received twice for the same hours: All assigned work in excess of eight (8) hours on any scheduled eight (8)-hour workday; and all assigned work in excess of forty (40) hours in any one (1) week.[1]

30.2 Distribution of Overtime.

30.2.1 The Employer shall make a reasonable effort to make overtime opportunities available on an equal basis to employees capable of performing the work.[2]

30.3 Extra-Duty Assignments.

30.3.1 Allocation.

30.3.1.1 The Employer shall maintain a list in order of seniority within the Police Department of all police officers willing to perform extra-duty security work at private events. After an initial sign up period of two weeks, new names shall be added to the bottom of the list in order of signing up, without regard to seniority.

30.3.1.2 When available, the Employer shall offer extra work opportunities only to police officers on the list and only in order

[1] ***Beaverton, Oregon and Beaverton Police Officers Association.***

[2] ***Orange County, California and Association of Orange County Deputy Sheriffs.***

of their appearance on the list. Offers of extra-duty work shall be made in sequential order through the list, with new opportunities being offered first to the police officer following the one who accepted the last offer. When the list is exhausted, offers shall return to the top of the list. The intention of this paragraph is to equalize opportunities for extra-duty work among all police officers on the list.

30.3.1.3 In order to keep this list current, the Employer shall strike from the list any police officer who refuses four consecutive offers of extra-duty work.[1]

30.4 Approval of Overtime.

30.4.1 Subject to approval of the supervisor, all overtime worked, except time spent in formal training, shall be paid at the rate of time and one-half, or credited as compensatory time at time and one-half. Supervisory approval of time and one-half shall not be withheld unless the overtime was made necessary by the employee's intentional neglect of customary duties. Formal training as used in this section shall not include time spent in on-the-job training of new police officers by training officers.[2]

30.5 Treatment of Paid Leave.

30.5.1 Time worked shall include paid compensatory time off, paid annual leave, paid sick leave, paid assigned holidays, paid industrial leave, paid jury service, and paid time for serving as a witness.[3]

[1] ***Niagara Falls, New York and Niagara Falls Police Club.***

[2] ***West Covina, California and West Covina Police Officers Association.***

[3] ***Ventura County, California and Ventura County Sheriff's Association.***

30.6 Time of Payment of Overtime.

30.6.1 Overtime, court time, and holiday pay shall be paid within thirty (30) days from the date earned. The Employer agrees to pay interest at an annual rate of eight percent (8%) for any amounts owed and not paid within such thirty (30)-day period.[1]

30.7 Calculation of Hours Worked.

30.7.1 For each six (6)-minute interval worked, beginning after the regular end of the shift, Patrol Officers will be paid overtime for the one-tenth of an hour at the rate of time and one-half regular pay (commencing with the end of the shift) except that any Patrol Officer required to work over eight (8) hours on any given holiday will be paid at the rate of two (2) times the regular rate.[2]

30.8 Exceptional Hours Overtime.

30.8.1 Applicability.

30.8.1.1 Any hours of duty in excess of eight (8) hours within an employee's regularly-scheduled workday shall be compensated at the following rates:

30.8.1.2 Time and one-half (1-1/2) for all hours on duty in excess of eight (8) hours.

30.8.1.3 Double time for all hours on duty in excess of twelve (12) hours.

30.8.1.4 Double time for all hours on duty in excess of eight (8) on the following holidays:

New Year's Day	Memorial Day
Independence Day	Labor Day
Thanksgiving Day	Christmas Day

[1] ***Boston, Massachusetts and Boston Police Patrolmen's Association.***

[2] ***City of Kettering, Ohio and Fraternal Order of Police, Lodge #92.***

30.8.1.5 Any employee who is compelled to perform official overtime duty during scheduled vacation shall be compensated at the rate of double (2x) time for the time actually worked.[1]

30.9 Cancellation of Day Off.

30.9.1 When the Employer cancels an officer's day off and requires the officer to work on that day over and above the officer's regularly-scheduled week, there shall be a minimum pay guarantee of eight (8) hours' pay at the officer's regular straight-time hourly rate.[2]

30.10 Supervisory Ratio.

30.10.1 All work performed outside of the regularly-scheduled workday shall be on a position seniority basis within the section concerned, then the division, providing senior employee/employees are qualified to perform the work required, unless otherwise mutually agreed upon by both the Association and the Employer. For purposes here, Traffic and Patrol shall be considered one section. For every seven (7) employees scheduled for the work described herein, one (1) supervisor shall also be assigned. These special assignments will be posted no less than four (4) days prior to the event, where possible.

30.10.1.1 Nothing in this section shall be construed to require the Employer to call in an employee on an overtime basis when the work can be done by an employee on duty who is otherwise qualified to perform the assignment.[3]

[1] ***Lakewood, Ohio and Fraternal Order of Police.***

[2] ***Evanston, Illinois and Combined Counties Police Association [Evanston Chapter].***

[3] ***Municipality of Anchorage and Anchorage Police Department Employees Association.***

30.11 Double Time Pay During Emergencies.

30.11.1 Effective December 25, ____, continuous emergency overtime that extends the regular work shift for a represented employee for more than one and one-half (1 ½) the number of hours of that shift (12 hours for 8 hour shifts and 15 hours for 10 hour shifts) will be paid at two times the represented employee's hourly rate for the regular shift. If the extended time occurs on an overtime assignment, the double-time rate will apply to the hourly rate upon which the time and one-half overtime rate is based.

30.11.1.1 Voluntary overtime which causes an employee to work continuously for more than one-half his/her shift will not qualify for the double time premium until more than one and one-half shift of continuous work, excluding any volunteer overtime, has been worked. Volunteer overtime is described as an assignment that is charged to a private business and only for those hours posted upon sign-up.

30.11.1.2 For all consecutive hours worked, including the regularly-assigned shift, overtime will be paid at 1½ times the regular hourly rate for the first half shift of overtime and double time for all overtime in excess of the first half shift of overtime. If all or a portion of a second regular shift is worked without an interruption, straight-time overtime will be paid in addition to the regular time for the hours worked on <u>that</u> shift.[1]

30.12 Medical Treatment.

30.12.1 Time spent by an officer in obtaining duty-injury medical treatment or therapy during off-duty hours shall be compensated at a rate of one and one-half (1½) times the regular hourly rate if such medical treatment is so scheduled by the

[1] ***City of Santa Clara and Santa Clara Police Officers Association.***

Employer or its contractual medical facility. Officers shall not be compensated while pursuing such medical treatment or therapy during off-duty hours if the treatment was scheduled by the employee.[1]

ARTICLE 31

COMPENSATORY TIME OFF

31.1 Accrual.

31.1.1 Overtime will be paid in cash except, at the option of the officer, compensatory time shall be granted in lieu of overtime pay.[2]

31.1.2 Each officer may accumulate 480 hours of compensatory time.[3]

31.2 Usage.

31.2.1 An officer who has requested the use of such compensatory time shall be permitted by the Employer to use such time within a reasonable period after making the request if the use of the compensatory time does not unduly disrupt the operations of the Employer.[4]

31.3 Donation to Other Employees.

31.3.1 Recovery time transfer is that system whereby an officer grants earned time off from compensatory time to another officer. Employer regulation shall limit such transfer to situations

[1] ***City of Lansing, Michigan and Fraternal Order of Police, Capitol City Lodge 141.***

[2] ***City of Portland, Oregon and Portland Police Association.***

[3] ***City of San Antonio, Texas and San Antonio Police Officers' Association.***

[4] ***City of Portland, Oregon and Portland Police Association.***

where the recipient of the transfer is, by reason of illness or injury, threatened with the loss of earnings due to his or her exhaustion of employment benefits. In no instance will there be a transfer from an officer of one rank to an officer of another rank or between sworn and non-sworn employees. All such transfers shall require the approval of the Employer or the Employer's designee.[1]

31.4 Voluntary Compensatory Time Buy Out.

31.4.1 The Employer shall budget the following amounts in each calendar year covered by this Contract for employees to cash out their accumulated compensatory time under a formula to be agreed upon between the Employer and the Association.

1995 $250,000

1996 $250,000

1997 $250,000[2]

31.4.2 Effective January 1, ____, and each calendar year thereafter, an officer may purchase up to a maximum of one-hundred and sixty (160) hours of paid leave, compensatory time, or a combination thereof.

31.4.2.1 Prior to March 31st of each calendar year, the bargaining unit member shall notify the Finance Director of the total amount of time he/she wishes to purchase and when such payment shall be made.

31.4.2.2 Payments shall be made in April or September of each calendar year.

[1] ***Berkeley, California and Berkeley Police Association.***

[2] ***City of Cleveland, Ohio and Cleveland Police Patrolmen's Association.***

31.4.2.3 All purchases are subject to the Finance Director's approval.

31.4.2.4 Payment shall be at the officer's hourly rate at the time of the pay-out.[1]

ARTICLE 32

STANDBY TIME

32.1 Fixed-Dollar System.

32.1.1 When a unit member is required and assigned to be available for immediate emergency call-out at times that the employee is not otherwise on duty and the employee complies with Departmental regulations incident thereto, the employee shall be compensated at One Dollar and Fifty Cents ($1.50) per hour up to a maximum of sixteen (16) hours on the employee's non-workdays, and a maximum of eight (8) hours on a workday.[2]

32.2 Percentage-Based System.

32.2.1 Any employee assigned to standby duty shall receive twenty-five percent (25%) of the employee's regular straight-time rate of pay for each hour of standby duty.[3]

32.2.2 Standby assignments issued by the Employer for reasons other than assignments connected with a court appearance shall be compensated at the rate of time and one-half the employee's normal rate of pay with a minimum of three (3) hours. Standby is defined as receiving instructions from

[1] ***Akron, Ohio and Fraternal Order of Police, Lodge #7.***

[2] ***Phoenix, Arizona and Phoenix Law Enforcement Union.***

[3] ***Thurston County, Washington and Thurston County Deputy Sheriff's Association.***

authorized personnel to remain at a specific location for a stated period of time.[1]

32.3 On-Call Weekend Duty.

32.3.1 Employees who are assigned to be on call during a weekend shall receive eight (8) hours of compensatory time for each day on call during that weekend.[2]

32.4 Overtime Basis.

32.4.1 Standby assignments issued by the Employer for reasons other than assignments connected with a court appearance shall be compensated at the rate of time and one-half the employee's normal rate of pay with a minimum of three (3) hours.[3]

32.5 Site-Specific Standby.

32.5.1 Any employee who, while in an on-call status, is required to remain on the Employer's premises, or at his home or other specific location to await a call when needed, is considered as being unable to use the time effectively for his own purposes and shall be considered to be working the entire time he is on call. [4]

32.6 Pager Pay.

32.6.1 In order to fulfill objectives of the Employer and to properly complete crime scene investigations in a timely manner, it is necessary that members of the Detective Division be available by telephone and/or pager on a rotating basis.

[1] ***City of Miami, Florida and the Fraternal Order of Police, Lodge #20.***

[2] ***City of Ontario, California and Ontario Police Officers Association.***

[3] ***City of Miami, Florida and the Fraternal Order of Police, Lodge #20.***

[4] ***Clement County, Ohio Sheriff and Fraternal Order of Police, Ohio Labor Council, Inc.***

32.6.1.1 Detectives Assigned to General Investigations. To compensate such employees required to periodically carry a pager, employees assigned to General Investigations within the Detective Division shall receive a salary adjustment of two percent (2%) per pay period.

32.6.1.2 Sergeants Assigned to the Detectives Division. To compensate such employees required to periodically carry a pager, any employee who is assigned as a Sergeant in the Detective Division shall receive a salary adjustment of four percent (4%) per pay period.[1]

ARTICLE 33

COURT APPEARANCES AND CALLBACKS

33.1 Callbacks.

33.1.1 If an officer who is called back to work works less than four (4) hours, the officer shall be paid at the overtime rate the lesser of: The time elapsed from the beginning of the overtime to the beginning of the shift; or the time elapsed from the end of the shift to the end of the overtime; or four (4) hours.[2]

33.1.2 Motorcycle Cleaning. The past practice of allowing overtime for the cleaning of motorcycles will be abolished. Regular, on-duty time will be allowed for this purpose, as assigned by the supervisor.[3]

[1] ***City of Boulder, Colorado and Boulder Police Benefit Association.***

[2] ***City of Portland, Oregon and Portland Police Association.***

[3] ***City of Santa Clara, California and Santa Clara Police Officers Association.***

33.2 Court Appearances.

33.2.1 Minimum Payments. When an employee is on court duty outside his regularly-scheduled shift, he shall receive court duty compensation at the appropriate overtime rate and shall be guaranteed a minimum of four (4) hours' overtime pay. In the event that more than four (4) hours are required, said employee shall be guaranteed eight (8) hours' pay at the appropriate overtime rate.

33.2.1.1 Any court time within one (1) hour of employee's duty time shall be paid at the appropriate overtime rate for the time worked. Periods of more than one (1) hour will be paid in accordance with the above.[1]

33.2.2 Short-Notice Emergency Callbacks. Emergency call-backs shall be paid at the overtime rate for a minimum of four (4) hours. Emergency call-backs with less than three (3) hours' time elapsed from the end of the shift shall be paid at the overtime rate for a minimum of five (5) hours.[2]

33.3 Morning and Afternoon Court Appearances.

33.3.1 An officer who is required to make morning and afternoon court-related overtime appearances on the same calendar day shall be compensated the lesser of:

33.3.1.1 The time elapsed from the beginning of the first court appearance to the beginning of the shift; or

33.3.1.2 The time elapsed from the end of the shift to the end of the last court appearance.[3]

[1] ***Anchorage, Alaska and Anchorage Police Department Employees Association.***

[2] ***City of Portland, Oregon and Portland Police Association.***

[3] ***City of Portland, Oregon and Portland Police Association.***

33.4 On-Call Court Time.

33.4.1 Each affected employee in an off-duty status shall receive the following straight-time compensation when in an on-call status for a court appearance.

33.4.1.1 There shall be two (2) hours of compensation for court on-call per day.

33.4.1.2 In the event an employee is in an on-call status and is called into court, he/she shall receive the two (2) hours' on-call compensation in addition to the 3 hours' minimum. If the employee reverts to an on-duty status prior to completion of the three (3)-hour minimum, he/she shall be compensated for actual court appearance time prior to his/her reversion to an on-duty status.

33.4.1.3 An employee shall be compensated for no more than one on-call subpoena in the morning or afternoon hours of the same court day.

33.4.1.4 At no time shall an employee receive on-call compensation when in an on-duty status, whether it be his/her regularly-assigned shift or a contracted overtime assignment.

33.4.1.5 Absent notification by a designated department authority, an employee in an on-call status who elects to appear in court shall not receive more than one (1) hour on-call compensation.[1]

33.5 Cancellation of Court Appearances.

33.5.1 When an employee complies with all departmental procedures on the day prior to a court appearance, and is notified on that date that the court appearance is still scheduled for the

[1] ***City of Pomona, California and Pomona Police Officers' Relief Association.***

next day, the employee shall be entitled to receive the minimum payments provided by this agreement even if the court appearance is thereafter canceled.[1]

33.6 Advance Notice of Court Appearance.

33.6.1 An officer who is required to make court-related overtime appearances on his day off without seventy-two (72) hours of advance notice shall be compensated at the overtime rate for a minimum of five (5) hours.[2]

33.7 Court Appearance Meals.

33.7.1 For any court appearance outside the City where an officer is required to remain over the lunch hours, he/she shall be entitled to one meal not to exceed $5.00 in cost.[3]

33.8 Use of Employer Vehicles.

33.8.1 For any court appearance originating from the Police Department, outside a radius of ten (10) miles, an Employer vehicle will be made available whenever possible and shall be utilized by the officer. If the officer must utilize a private vehicle, he/she will be reimbursed for his/her actual mileage according to the rates set forth for use of private vehicles. [4]

33.9 Reporting Pay.

33.9.1 Employees who report for work at a regularly-scheduled time in a regular workday and are sent home by their

[1] ***Auburn, Washington and Auburn Police Guild.***

[2] ***Portland, Oregon and Portland Police Association.***

[3] ***City of Ontario, California and Ontario Police Officers Association.***

[4] ***City of Ontario, California and Ontario Police Officers Association.***

supervisor because the work cannot be performed shall receive a minimum of four (4) hours' pay.[1]

33.10 Off-Duty Arrests.

33.10.1 Any employee who makes an off-duty felony arrest shall receive a minimum credit of four (4) hours of work or the actual amount of hours required, whichever is the greater, computed at time and one-half (1-1/2). The term "off-duty felony arrest" shall not include an arrest made while privately employed in a law enforcement capacity.[2]

33.11 Overnight Pay.

33.11.1 Any employee ordered to be away from home overnight shall receive an additional four (4) hours pay at straight time for each full night away from home.[3]

ARTICLE 34

WORKING OUT OF CLASSIFICATION

34.1 Procedures.

34.1.1 To assure the orderly performance and continuity of services, the Employer may elect to temporarily upgrade officers on an acting basis to positions of a higher rank. For the purpose of this Article, it is understood that temporary upgradings may be authorized and made in order to fill or compensate for temporary position vacancies, which may exist for any of the following reasons: A position is permanently vacant and is scheduled to be filled by a regular commissioned officer, and a

[1] ***City of Sioux City, Iowa and Sioux City Police Officers' Association.***

[2] ***Lakewood, Ohio and Fraternal Order of Police.***

[3] ***Toledo, Ohio and Toledo Police Patrolman's Association.***

short period of time is required so as to proceed with and complete the normal selection and appointment procedure, or the position is temporarily vacant, although permanently filled, because the officer currently assigned to it is on an approved leave of absence (i.e., vacation leave, sick leave, duty injury leave, military reserve leave, educational leave, maternity leave, or other type of temporary leave of absence).

34.1.1.1 It is not the intent of the Employer to circumvent or avoid the normal appointment or promotion process, and therefore the Employer agrees that it shall not use temporary upgrading for this purpose. In this same regard, the Employer shall make every possible and reasonable effort to fill position vacancies in a most expeditious manner, and to keep the need for such temporary upgradings to a minimum. However, for the purpose of this Article and this Agreement, it is understood that whether or not a position vacancy is to be temporarily filled shall be determined by and at the sole discretion of the Employer. In this same regard, nothing contained in this Article or this Agreement shall be construed or interpreted as requiring the Employer to fill a temporary position vacancy.

34.1.1.2 The various provisions of this Article shall apply to temporary position vacancies involving both the bargaining unit position classification (rank) of Police Sergeant, as well as the non-bargaining unit position classification (rank) of Police Lieutenant. The provisions of this Article shall not apply to temporary position vacancies involving any other position classifications (including both non-bargaining unit position classifications, as well as position classifications in other bargaining units), even when such temporary position vacancies are filled on a temporary upgrading basis by officers from this bargaining unit.

34.1.1.3 It is understood and agreed by the parties to this Agreement that no temporary upgrading may be required so long as at least one (1) officer of Command rank is on duty by Division, or by duty shift within the Operations Bureau. In this regard, no temporary upgrading of a Police Officer to the rank of Police Sergeant may be required if a superior officer of any rank is on duty within the Police Officer's individual chain of command.

34.1.1.4 The selection of an officer for temporary upgrading shall be made from within the same Division, or from within the same duty shift in the Operations Bureau, that the temporary position vacancy occurs. In the case of a temporary upgrading which exceeds (or is expected to exceed) two (2) weeks, however, such selection shall be made from within the entire Police Department. Such selection shall be made by and at the sole discretion of the Police Chief, taking into consideration the applicable promotional eligibility list; the knowledge, skill and ability requirements of the position to be filled; and the qualifications, job performance, and seniority of those officers eligible for the temporary upgrading.

34.1.1.5 No officer shall be temporarily upgraded more than one (1) rank, and all officers shall have the option to refuse temporary upgrading without prejudice when it is offered.

34.1.1.6 When Police Officers are temporarily upgraded to and acting in the position classification (rank) of Police Sergeant, and when Police Sergeants are temporarily upgraded to and acting in the position classification (rank) of Police Lieutenant, they shall be eligible to receive temporary upgrading pay for the total duration of their temporary upgrading assignment, provided that they are upgraded for at least a full duty shift. The temporary upgrading pay which these eligible officers shall receive, retroactive to the beginning of their temporary upgrading assignment, shall be as follows: Police Officers who are temporarily upgraded to the rank of Police Sergeant shall receive the Police Sergeant rate of pay during their temporary upgrading assignment, which rate of pay shall be in lieu of (and not in addition to) their regular Police Officer rate of pay; Police Sergeants who are temporarily upgraded to the rank of Police Lieutenant shall continue to receive their regular Police Sergeant rate of pay during their temporary upgrading assignment, plus a bonus of one dollar ($1.00) for each full hour that they are upgraded.

34.1.1.7 In accordance with the above, officers who are temporarily upgraded to and acting in the position of higher rank for less than a full duty shift shall not receive temporary upgrading pay, but rather shall continue to receive only the same rate of pay which they would normally receive in their regular position classification (rank).[1]

34.2 Acting Detective.

34.2.1 Patrolmen may be temporarily assigned to the Bureau of Investigations as Acting Detectives. Such temporary assignments shall be filled by the individual who is highest on the Detectives eligibility list, if such individual so chooses, and that individual shall receive the per diem pay of a Detective.[2]

34.3 Acting Lieutenant.

34.3.1 Detectives and sergeants on the lieutenant promotion eligibility list for each Bureau will be given an opportunity to serve as an Acting Lieutenant to fill temporary vacancies in the following manner:

[1] ***Champaign, Illinois and Champaign Policemen's Benevolent and Protective Association.***

[2] ***City of Kansas City, Kansas and Fraternal Order of Police, Lodge 4.***

34.3.1.1 Each vacancy in the department known to be temporary at the time it occurs will be filled by the individual highest on the lieutenant's eligibility list for that station and shift or unit and shift. If there is no one available on the same station and shift or same unit and shift who is listed on the lieutenant's eligibility list, then the most senior sergeant or detective, as the case may be, on that same shift and station or unit, shall fill the temporary vacancy.

34.3.1.2 Each vacancy known to be permanent at the time it occurs, shall be filled from the lieutenant's eligibility list by the highest sergeant or detective on the lieutenant's eligibility list.

34.3.1.3 Per diem pay shall commence on the first day of such service following the lieutenant's regular days off.[1]

ARTICLE 35

SHIFT TRADES

35.1 General.

35.1.1 Subject to departmental manpower requirements, police officers shall be permitted to voluntarily trade work or leave days; providing that employees scheduled to work must inform the Employer in advance of any voluntary trade of workdays or leave days and such originally-scheduled employee shall be responsible for the attendance of the scheduled officer's replacement and absences of replacements shall be charged to the originally-scheduled employee unless scheduling is changed in the scheduling book; provided further, that no employee shall

[1] ***City of Kansas City, Kansas and Fraternal Order of Police, Lodge 4.***

trade days with any other employee for the purpose of achieving any premium payments due under this contract.[1]

ARTICLE 36

SHIFT ASSIGNMENT

36.1 Seniority System.

36.1.1 Subject to manpower needs and maintaining efficiency of the Division/Detail, seniority shall be the prime factor in the selection of shifts and days off provided the officer is otherwise qualified. Seniority shall govern in the selection of vacation and holidays.[2]

36.2 Changes in Shift Assignment.

36.2.1 Involuntary changes in shifts, days off or job assignments can only be made with the joint concurrence of the Association and the Employer. Additionally, with the joint approval of the Association and the Employer, employees may change shifts and days off prior to the next scheduled posting of the monthly roster.[3]

36.2.2 An employee must be notified of a change in a normally-scheduled shift twenty-four (24) hours before the change is to take place except in cases of emergency. If an employee is required to work non-scheduled hours, the employee will be compensated at the rate of one and one-half (1-1/2) times the employee's basic hourly rate or given compensatory time off.[4]

[1] ***Dearborn Heights, Michigan and Dearborn Heights Police Officers Association.***

[2] ***Portland, Oregon and Portland Police Association.***

[3] ***Anchorage, Alaska and Anchorage Police Department Employees Association.***

[4] ***Olmsted County, Minnesota and Olmsted County Deputy Sheriffs' Association.***

36.3 Shift Changes.

36.3.1 Employer agrees to post changes in shift at least thirty (30) days in advance, except in emergencies. This Section shall not be utilized to avoid the payment of overtime or call-back premiums or to prohibit schedule changes necessary for training purposes.[1]

36.4 Shift Adjustment Premium.

36.4.1 Employees shall be paid at the rate of time and one-half (1-1/2) the employee's regular rate of pay for hours worked outside of their regularly assigned shift when said shift is temporarily adjusted in accordance with the provisions of this contract.[2]

36.5 Extra-Duty Assignments.

36.5.1 The Police Department shall maintain a list in order of seniority within the Police Department for all police officers willing to perform extra-duty seniority work at private events or traffic control. After an initial sign up period of two weeks, new names shall be added to the bottom of the list in order of signing up, without regard to seniority.

36.5.1.1 When available, the Police Department shall offer extra work opportunities only to police officers on the list and only in order of their appearance on the list. Offers of extra-duty work shall be made in sequential order through the list, with new opportunities being offered first to the police officer following the one who accepted the last offer. When the list is exhausted, officers shall return to the top of the list. The intention of this

[1] ***The City of Napa, California and Napa Police Officers' Association.***

[2] ***Madison, Wisconsin and Madison Professional Police Officers' Association.***

paragraph is to equalize opportunities for extra-duty work among all police officers on the list.

36.5.1.2 Prior to being placed on the extra-duty assignment list a police officer must have completed at least eight months of his/her initial probationary period of 12 months and upon review by the Chief, based on experience and the nature of off-duty work, on a case-by-case basis.

36.5.1.3 In order to keep this list current, the Police Department shall strike from the list any police officer who refuses three (3) consecutive offers of extra-duty work. Refusal to work a pre-arranged leave, including vacation, jury duty and funeral leave, Employer overtime assignment, or other Department-scheduled function will not be counted as refusal.[1]

36.6 Shifts for Older Employees.

36.6.1 Upon reaching the age of forty-eight (48), a police officer may exercise the option in writing of not working between midnight and 5:00 a.m., unless otherwise provided for in this memorandum.[2]

36.7 Time Off Between Shift Assignments.

36.7.1 An employee who so requests shall be off duty a minimum of eight (8) hours between the employee's scheduled work shift (excluding emergency overtime situations) and a scheduled training assignment.[3]

[1] ***City of Peoria and Peoria Police Officers Association.***

[2] ***City of Modesto, California and Modesto Police Officers Association.***

[3] ***City of Lansing, Michigan and Fraternal Order of Police, Capitol City Lodge 141.***

36.8 Preferred Job Assignments.

36.8.1 The Employer retains the right to make all assignments, but the Employer shall make preferred job assignments as set forth in this Article. Preferred job assignments shall be made as follows:

36.8.1.1 When a job opening is available for any preferred assignment, the Employer will post the opening on a bulletin board for a ten (10)-day period.

36.8.1.2 Any Employee may file a written request for the preferred job assignment.

36.8.1.3 Except as otherwise set forth herein, the filling of a preferred job opening shall be determined from the list of Employees who file written requests.

36.8.1.4 The following shall be recognized as preferred jobs:

36.8.1.5 Marine Division, Jail Information Officer, Traffic Division, Breathalyzer Operator, Crime Prevention, Youth Bureau, Scuba Diver, Identification Bureau, S.W.A.T., Evidence Technician, Circuit Court/Station Three, C.O.M.E.T., Special Enforcement Team, Court Cars, Circuit Court Officers, Warrants, Court Papers/Salvage Vehicle, Inmate Funds, WAYMAC, Detective Bureau Investigator, Classification Officer, Visiting Officer and Field Training Officer.

36.8.1.6 For the purposes of this Article, any newly-created jobs shall be subject to the procedures of this Article.

36.8.1.7 The above-described preferred jobs shall be placed in various groups, which placement shall determine the selection method and length of assignment.

36.8.1.8 Group A.

36.8.1.9 Group A jobs shall be posted annually. The Employee with the highest seniority on the list shall receive the job. Length of assignment in Group A jobs is subject only to annual bumping by a more senior Employee.

36.8.1.10 Group A jobs are specified as follows:

36.8.1.11 Circuit Court/Station Three, Court Cars.

36.8.1.12 Group B.

36.8.1.13 Group B jobs shall be posted annually to give all qualified Employees, including the incumbent jobholder, an opportunity to indicate interest. Selection of Group B jobs shall be determined from the list of Employees who sign up on the basis of qualifications, sufficient ability, and seniority.

36.8.1.14 Group B jobs are subdivided as follows:

36.8.1.15 Group B(1): Breathalyzer Operator, S.W.A.T., Evidence Technician, Scuba Diver, Marine Division [three (3) month and six (6) month job].

36.8.1.16 An Employee currently holding a Group B(1) job may continue in that job indefinitely.

36.8.1.17 Group B(2): Identification Bureau, Court Papers/ Salvage Vehicle.

36.8.1.18 An Employee currently holding a Group B(2) job may continue in that job until the next year's preferred job assignments are made, and for every two (2) years thereafter, unless bumped by a senior Employee, which bump is subject to the Sheriff's discretion. An Employee is permitted to remain in a Group B(2) job for a minimum of two (2) years before the possibility of removal through the exercise of bumping rights by a senior Employee. If a senior Employee does not bump, the incumbent Employee may remain in a Group B(2) job indefinitely.

36.8.1.19 Group B(3): Special Enforcement Team.

36.8.1.20 There is a two (2) year maximum on holding a Group B(3) job.

36.8.1.21 Group B(4): Traffic Division.

36.8.1.22 Selection of and continuation in this job is subject to State appropriation. There is no minimum or maximum time on holding a Group B(4) job.

36.8.1.23 Group B(5): C.O.M.E.T., WAYMAC.

36.8.1.24 Selection of rank to this job is dependent upon the needs of C.O.M.E.T. and WAYMAC, and the filling of the assignment shall be at the Sheriff's discretion. There is a two (2)-year maximum on holding a Group B(5) job.

36.8.1.25 Group C.

36.8.1.26 Group C jobs shall be posted annually. Selection to Group C positions shall be determined on the basis of qualifications, ability and seniority. The Association, through a designated representative, shall participate in the process of formulating recommendations to the Sheriff on the selection of applicants. It is recognized that the assessment of ability and qualifications of Group C applicants requires subjective judgment by the Department. As such, the determination of the best qualified candidate shall be made by the Sheriff at his discretion.

36.8.1.27 Group C jobs are as follows: Marine Division [twelve (12)-month job], Crime Prevention, Youth Bureau, Classification Officer, School Liaison Officer, Field Training Officer, Detective Bureau Investigator.

36.8.1.28 Group D.

36.8.1.29 Group D jobs shall be posted annually. Except as otherwise specified below, selection to Group D jobs shall be at the discretion of the Sheriff.

36.8.1.30 Group D jobs are subdivided as follows:

36.8.1.31 Group D(1): Circuit Court Officer.

36.8.1.32 A Circuit Court Officer shall be assigned at the sole discretion of the Sheriff, except that the selection shall not interfere with or abridge an Employee's right to select shift assignment. The Sheriff shall first consider those Employees volunteering for a Group D(1) job before exercising discretion in the assignment of the job. The exercise of discretion shall be limited to bargaining unit employees.

36.8.1.33 Group D(2): Warrant Officer.

36.8.1.34 Except for two (2) Warrant Officer Positions, Group D(2) jobs shall be assigned at the sole discretion of the Sheriff. Selection by the Sheriff, however, shall not interfere with or abridge an Employee's right to select shift assignment. The Sheriff shall first consider the Employees volunteering for a Group D(2) job before exercising discretion in the assignment of a job. The exercise of discretion shall be limited to bargaining unit employees. The assignment of two (2) reserved Warrant Officer positions shall be in accordance with the selection process for Group A jobs.

36.8.1.35 Group D(3): Inmate Funds.

36.8.1.36 Group D(3) jobs shall be assigned at the sole discretion of the Sheriff and offered to any employee within the Sheriff's Department.

36.8.1.37 Group D(4): Jail Information Officer.

36.8.1.38 The Employer shall maintain one (1) Corrections Officer as Jail Information Officer on each shift. The assignment of the Corrections Officers shall be in accordance with the selection process for Group B(2) jobs. Any additional assignment to the Jail Information Officer job shall be at the sole discretion of the Sheriff and may be offered to any employee within the Department.

36.8.1.39 Group D(5): Visiting Officer.

36.8.1.40 The Employee with the highest seniority signing up for the job shall receive the job. In the event that no employee signs up for the position, the Sheriff may fill the position with the least senior employee. An employee may elect to leave the position after one (1) year. If no employee submits a bid for the vacancy, the Sheriff must select the next least senior employee if the job is to remain filled.

36.8.1.41 In the event that there is no Employee applying for a specific preferred job assignment, the Employer may fill the preferred job assignment from among any Employees within the required classification, unless otherwise specified within the language of a particular group.

36.8.1.42 Substation assignments are not preferred jobs. The substation assignments, however, will be posted each November and the Employer will select available Deputies for the substation assignments.

36.8.1.43 When an Employee is reassigned from a preferred assignment back to regular duties, said Employee shall be afforded an opportunity to select a shift preference as provided in this Agreement.

36.8.1.44 All preferred jobs shall be posted in November of each year. The assignment shall then be made effective, subject to scheduling, as near January 1 as possible. The holding of any job under this Article is subject to the Employee's ability to perform satisfactorily in the assignment. In the event that an Employee is reassigned to regular duties, the Sheriff, or designated representative, will explain to the Employee the reason for the reassignment.

36.8.1.45 Probationary Employees shall not be eligible for any preferred assignment.[1]

36.9 Filling Vacant Positions.

36.9.1 Assignment of Police Officers to vacant positions within the Department will be accomplished through the procedure established herein.

36.9.1.1 Vacant positions shall be separated into three categories and assignments shall be made accordingly:

36.9.1.2 Positions which shall be exempt from the bidding procedure and will be filled at the discretion of the Chief, both in filling a vacancy and in determining tenure of the Officer position.

36.9.1.3 Positions which fall in this category are as follows:

Administrative Staff, Planning and Inspection, Intelligence, Vice-Metro Drug Unit and Property Room Management.

36.9.1.4 Positions where the seniority of the Police Officer shall be given sole preference, providing the Officer seeking assignment is capable of performing the required duties of the assignment.

[1] ***Macomb County, Georgia and Macomb County Deputy Sheriff's Association.***

36.9.1.5 Positions falling into this category are as follows:

Traffic Section, Communications Section, Records Section, License Bureau and Tax Bureau.

36.9.1.6 Positions which shall be subject to the selection process set forth herein.

36.9.1.7 For all other positions, except as otherwise stated herein and except for those in the Field Operations Bureau, bids will be accepted for assignment to the Bureau and assignment within the Bureau will be at the discretion of the Department Head.

36.9.1.8 In selecting Officers to be assigned to vacancies, a standard job description and qualification form shall be available to all Officers seeking to bid for the assignment. The Officer shall complete the standard bidding form relative to the vacancy, in advance of the interview with the Bureau Head or his designee.

36.9.1.9 The Bureau Head or his designee shall review all such applications and shall prepare a list of those meeting the minimum qualifications of the position. At least fifty (50%) of those meeting the minimum qualifications for the position shall be interviewed. Officers who do not meet the minimum qualifications of the position shall be so advised.

36.9.1.10 A prescreening process consisting of the following criteria shall be established to determine those entitled to an interview:

(1) attendance/sick leave

(2) discipline

(3) years of service

(4) education

36.9.1.11 All those applicants who meet the standards as established under the prescreening process shall be entitled to an interview. Those applicants who do not meet the standards established under the prescreening process will not be interviewed; however, they will be advised as to the area(s) of their deficiency.

36.9.1.12 The interview shall consist of a standard questioning format for all interviews. The Bureau Head or his designee shall make recommendations to the Chief of the Department, who will have the final determination as to the Officers to be selected.

36.9.1.13 Qualifications, competence and seniority shall be given fair consideration by the Chief in selecting Officers to fill these vacancies. Those assigned to Vice-Metro for three or more years shall be given special consideration upon bidding for Investigative Services Bureau vacancies. For the purpose of this section, seniority shall be defined as the employee's accumulated length of service with the Department.

36.9.1.14 When an Officer has been assigned to a vacant position under the second and third categories, the Officer will retain the assignment except where there are general changes of assignment or where there is just cause for removal. Officers assigned to the Directed Policing and Gang Units shall serve in a six (6)-month probationary period.

36.9.1.15 In the event the Chief of Police, due to general changes of assignment, removes employees and transfers them to other bureaus or sections, the employee(s) shall be removed by reverse seniority. When the affected vacancies are back-filled, the assignments shall be filled with most senior displaced employee being the first to return and all other returned employees falling in that order provided the return occurs within four (4) years of the change in assignment.[1]

36.10 Supervisory Ratio.

36.10.1 At time of the execution of this Agreement, there are ______ Police Officers, ___ Sergeants, and ____ Lieutenants. This supervisory ratio shall not be increased during the term of this agreement.[2]

36.11 Other Duties.

36.11.1 The employees will not be required to perform any janitorial, maintenance, or construction functions of any building, grounds, or vehicles, or transport animals, except by mutual agreement or in the case of unusual circumstances or emergencies.[3]

36.12 Nepotism.

36.12.1 The Employer shall not appoint to a salaried position under the Employer any person who is a relative by blood or marriage within the third degree of any one or more of the members of such City Council, nor shall the Employer or any department head or other officer having appointive power appoint any relative of his or of any Council Member within such degree to any such position.[4]

[1] ***City of Toledo, Ohio and Toledo Police Patrolman's Association, Local 10.***

[2] ***Detroit, Michigan and Detroit Police Officers Association.***

[3] ***Toledo, Ohio and Toledo Police Patrolmen's Association.***

[4] ***Anaheim, California and Anaheim Police Association.***

ARTICLE 37

TRANSFERS

37.1 Assignment to Assignment.

37.1.1 If an employee's permanent work assignment is changed from one precinct or division to another, the employee shall be sent specific written notice of the reason for the change at least ten (10) calendar days before it becomes effective.[1]

37.2 Employer Assignments/Transfers.

37.2.1 In the interest of the most efficient management by the Employer and the best utilization of its resources, involuntary transfers of personnel may at times be necessary. The Employer shall make every effort to avoid involuntary transfers.

37.2.1.1 Any employee who is involuntarily reassigned due to reorganization or reduction in size of the Employer or through other non-disciplinary involuntary transfer shall have reversionary rights at the option of the employee to assignment to the following positions:

37.2.1.2 a. To an assignment in a detachment where the employee will be able to comply with the residence requirements in this Agreement without moving his/her residence. An assignment under this provision shall supercede the transfer list; or

37.2.1.3 b. To an assignment in the geographic area where the employee was assigned immediately prior to his/her transfer into the position from which the employee is being presently transferred. An employee reassigned under this provision must comply with the residency requirements within 120 days. An assignment under this provision shall supercede the transfer list.

[1] ***Minneapolis, Minnesota and Police Officers' Federation of Minneapolis.***

37.2.1.4 c. No other employee shall be reassigned as a result of an employee's exercise of his reversionary rights.

37.2.1.5 d. Employees who transfer under this section shall be entitled to receive moving cost reimbursement in accordance with Office of Financial Management guidelines.[1]

37.3 Moving.

37.3.1 Moving costs shall be paid by the Employer for relocation of employees resulting from initial assignment from the Academy, promotion, and when the employee is transferred at the Employer's discretion. The Employer shall also pay the expense of moving household items for transfers when advertising open positions and requesting volunteers. The notice of willingness to pay shall be included when advertising for the position. Routine employee-requested transfers shall not receive moving expenses. Employees accepting Employer-requested transfers shall have the expense of moving household items paid by the Employer up to the maximum limit authorized by Office of Financial Management regulations.

37.3.1.1 Employees who are transferred shall be allowed to use accrued annual leave and/or compensatory time off in the two weeks prior and/or subsequent to the transfer.[2]

37.4 Retraining Provisions.

37.4.1 In the event of an involuntary transfer of a member from one function to another function, or a transfer due to the phasing out of a particular function, the officer will be given adequate training to become proficient in the newly-assigned function.[3]

[1] ***Washington State Patrol and Washington State Patrol Troopers Association.***

[2] ***Washington State Patrol and Washington State Patrol Troopers Association.***

[3] ***City of Portland, Oregon and Portland Police Association.***

ARTICLE 38

SHIFT DIFFERENTIAL

38.1 Percentage Based Differential.

38.1.1 Night Shift Differential.

38.1.1.1 Employees covered by this Agreement shall receive a night shift differential equal to three percent (3%) of their base pay for working swing shifts and six percent (6%) of their base pay for working mid shifts.

38.1.1.2 The day shift is any shift starting between the hours of 5:00 a.m. and 12:00 noon.

38.1.1.3 The swing shift is any shift starting between the hours of 12:00 noon and 7:00 p.m.

38.1.1.4 The mid shift is any shift starting between the hours of 7:00 p.m. and 5:00 a.m.[1]

ARTICLE 39

TEMPORARY ASSIGNMENTS

39.1 Temporary Assignments.

39.1.1 No employee shall be loaned or temporarily reassigned to a location or duty assignment if a sworn member of his department would not normally be sent to that location or would not normally be given that duty assignment under similar circumstances.[2]

[1] ***Municipality of Anchorage and Anchorage Police Department Employees Association.***

[2] ***City of San Bernardino, California and San Bernardino Police Officers' Association.***

39.2 Assignment Abolishment.

39.2.1 Prior to abolishing an assignment, the Division shall, whenever practicable, first utilize attrition. Thereafter, the Division shall thoroughly review and utilize other practicable alternatives, if any, prior to any abolishment. During such review, the Division shall consider, among other factors, the efficiency and the operational needs of the Division, and the potential disruptive effect of such alternatives on the members. In the event of an abolishment, the affected members will be given at least seventy (70) days' written notice of the abolishment and be advised to consult the Daily Bulletin for vacant assignments at the beginning of the notice period. Members failing to request and receive a requested assignment will be placed in any available, vacant assignment. If only a portion of the unit is to be abolished, the member(s) will be retained on the basis of his/her seniority.[1]

ARTICLE 40

LIGHT-DUTY WORK

40.1 General.

40.1.1 Should an employee covered by this Agreement become physically or mentally handicapped to the extent that the employee cannot perform his/her regular job, the Employer will make every reasonable effort to place the employee in a position within City employment that the employee is physically and mentally able to perform, subject to the Employer's legal or contractual obligations to other employees.[2]

[1] ***City of Columbus, Ohio and Fraternal Order of Police, Capital City Lodge 9.***

[2] ***City of Lansing, Michigan and Fraternal Order of Police, Capitol City Lodge 141.***

ARTICLE 41

THE AMERICANS WITH DISABILITIES ACT

41.1 General.

41.1.1 In the administration of this Agreement, the Employer and the Association will provide reasonable accommodations to qualified employees with a disability. The need for and extent of such accommodations shall be determined by the Employer in accordance with its interpretation of the requirements of law, even if such accommodations may be in conflict with another provision of this Agreement. Prior to making an accommodation that would conflict with the provisions of this Agreement, the Employer will notify the Association of such accommodation and discuss it with the Association upon request. If the Association does not agree to the accommodation, the matter shall be submitted to expedited arbitration as agreed upon by the Employer and the Association or to the American Arbitration Association for expedited arbitration.[1]

ARTICLE 42

TRAINING

42.1 General.

42.1.1 The Employer shall make every effort to provide a program of in-service training for employees in the bargaining unit designed to maintain a high standard of performance and to increase the skills of employees in the bargaining unit. Training courses to be attended shall have a direct bearing on the work

[1] ***City of Southfield and Southfield Police Officers Association.***

of the employee. Attendance at Training courses may be authorized by the department head. Decisions by department heads on request by employees should be based on: The effect the absence of the employee will have on the department's operations and its ability to continue to provide the services and perform the functions for which it is responsible; the relationship of the subject of the program, seminar, conference or workshop to the function performed by the employee and the department, and the employee's professional development; and the method of financing the request by the employee. There are three ways the expenses of the program might be paid: By the Employer with expenditures for travel, meals, lodging, registration and other items included annually within the Employer budget; by other public or private agencies (occasionally employees receive approval for their expenditures to be paid by grants from the State or Federal governments, from private organization or from a professional organization); and by the individual employee. Occasionally, the departmental budget may not permit trips to be paid by the Employer. The employee may feel that the trip would be of benefit to the employee's professional development and, therefore, would be willing to pay the expenses if the employee were permitted time off from work at full salary.[1]

42.1.2 A Patrol Officer working the midnight shift, 2230-0630 hours or 2300-0700 hours, will not be subject to a one (1)-day training course during this shift of duty, unless he/she voluntarily attends the training course. Any Patrol Officer on the midnight shift who attends a training course of two (2) days or more and who is required to report to duty less than eight (8)

[1] ***Sonoma County, California and Sonoma County Sheriff's Office Employees Association.***

hours between the end of the instruction day and the start of the midnight shift shall be paid time and one-half for any hours less than the eight (8) hours between assignments.[1]

[1] ***City of Des Plaines, Illinois and Combined Counties Police Association.***

CHAPTER 6

UNIFORMS, EQUIPMENT, AND SAFETY

Law enforcement agencies have adopted a variety of approaches to dealing with the clothing and equipment which is a required part of the duty uniform. Some agencies operate on a quartermaster system, furnishing each employee with the appropriate clothing. Other agencies reimburse officers for the reasonable costs of purchasing items of clothing and equipment. Yet other agencies pay a flat allowance, without regard to whether or how the employee spends the allowance.

This chapter contains contract provisions which deal with the different uniform and equipment issues which arise on a regular basis. Among the topics covered in this chapter are the following:

- Uniform and Plainclothes Allowances
- Quartermaster Systems
- Equipment Safety
- Damage to Equipment and Uniforms

An increasing trend in the area of equipment is the furnishing of home cars, which employees are allowed to use to commute to and from their residences. Home car programs not only have the advantage of providing an increased law enforcement presence in the community, but also significantly reduce maintenance and increase the life expectancy of a vehicle. Two versions of home car programs are provided in this chapter.

This article also contains "minimum manning" or staffing clauses. Laws vary significantly from state to state over whether staffing clauses are mandatory for collective bargaining. Where such clauses exist in collective bargaining agreements, they typically require a specified number of officers to be on duty at any one time, or that patrol cars be staffed by two or more individuals. It is extremely rare to find a minimum staffing clause which requires the department to actually employ a certain number of officers for every thousand individuals in the community.

One change in law enforcement contracts in recent years is usually the product of the fact that the Internal Revenue Service now treats plainclothes allowances as taxable income. This has resulted in some law enforcement agencies changing from a fixed dollar amount paid as the plainclothes allowance to a percentage of base wages. The plainclothes allowance in this book, taken from the contract in Lansing, Michigan, is such a percentage-based allowance.

ARTICLE 43

CLOTHING

43.1 Uniform Allowance.

43.1.1 The Employer agrees to pay a uniform and safety equipment allowance to each employee as a reimbursement for expenses incurred for acquisition and maintenance of uniforms and safety equipment in an amount of seventy-five dollars ($75) per month. The parties expressly agree that the payment each month of said allowance will cover the expenses of acquisition and replacement of all uniforms and safety equipment required for the various assignments of police officers and police sergeants, and that said allowance will meet any and all obligations the Employer has by law to provide, furnish, use, or provide for the said uniforms and safety equipment. Employees shall be required to buy their own required uniforms and safety equipment and to maintain and replace, when necessary, any of the said items, from moneys received from the aforestated allowance. In consideration of the Employer's agreement to pay said allowance, the Association agrees not to commence, during the effective period of this Agreement, any litigation or other proceeding in which it is contended the Employer is failing to comply with a legal obligation to provide safety equipment.[1]

43.1.2 A deputy may use up to one-half (½) of his clothing allowance per year to pay for a membership at the YMCA.[2]

[1] ***Palm Springs, California and Palm Springs Police Officers' Association.***

[2] ***Wyandotte County, Kansas and Fraternal Order of Police, Lodge 40.***

43.2 Furnished Uniforms.

43.2.1 The following shall be furnished to all sworn employees:

3 pairs of trousers	1 Sam Browne belt
2 winter shirts	1 Loop Loader
4 summer shirts	1 Smith & Wesson 357
Model 66 (2 inch)	or Magnum Model 1 (4 inch)
1 winter jacket	1 tie bar
1 pair of shoes	1 badge
1 cap	1 badge (for cap)
1 tie	1 cuff case
1 summer jacket	1 holster
1 set APD cut outs	1 protective vest
1 badge (for coat)	1 set handcuffs
2 speed loaders & 2 Belt keepers [1]	

43.2.2 All new police officers shall be issued the following clothing and equipment:

ITEMS	NUMBER
Hat (winter)	1
Hat (summer)	1
Black Tie	1
Shirt (winter gray with patch)	1
Shirts (winter blues with patch)	3
Shirts (summer blues with patch)	4
Trousers (winter)	2
Trousers (summer)	2
Black Leather Shoes	2
Blue Police Blouse (with patch)	1
Blue Reefer Gortex Coat (with patch)	1
Blue Gortex Jacket	1

[1] ***Aberdeen, Washington and Aberdeen Police Association.***

Black/Orange Rain Coat and Rain Cover for hat	1
Black Leather Gloves w/snap	1
Black two-D-Cell, break proof Flashlight with Black Leather Case	1
Handcuffs and Black Leather Case (S & W Peerless Cuffs)	1
Sam Browne Belt w/Brass Buckle	1
Leather Magazine Holder (2 clips)	1
ASP	1
ASP Holder	1
Black Leather Key Holder	1
Whistle	1
Rules and Regulations (with updates)	1
Day-Off Book	1
Hat Badge	1
Breast Badge	1
Pistol 9-mm w/3 magazines; ammunition for same	1
Identification wallet with badge and Identification card	1
Security Holster	1

43.2.2.1 Those employees assigned to non-uniformed bureaus shall not be required to maintain the above-listed items of clothing worn by the employees assigned to the uniform division; however, an employee assigned a detail is required to wear the proper uniform as designated by the Employer. Employees assigned to non-uniform bureaus who do not maintain a uniform because they choose not to work details or uniform call back shall nevertheless be required to maintain a "Police" jacket at their own expense. The Employer shall designate the type of jacket which shall be similar to the jacket worn by the Special Squad.[1]

43.2.3 All uniformed employees of the Employer shall wear a uniform prescribed by the Employer, and the Employer agrees to issue new uniform articles and apparel and replace such uniform articles and apparel as the original issue wears out. It shall be the responsibility of the Employer to determine when an article is sufficiently worn out to justify a replacement. Further, the Employer agrees to provide dry cleaning service for such uniform apparel.[2]

43.3 Plainclothes Allowance.

43.3.1 Everyone eligible for a clothing allowance (Metro, Special Operations, Detectives and Personnel Officers) shall receive a clothing allowance of two percent (2%) of their base wage to be included in their biweekly pay.[3]

43.3.2 The Employer will provide a clothing allowance for plainclothes officers of $350.00 per year. Employee shall be paid a prorated share when they are assigned to plainclothes during the fiscal year.[4]

43.4 Footwear.

43.4.1 The Employer shall provide one pair of shoes and one pair of boots that conform to Department policy. When several types of footwear are approved for wear by the

[1] ***City of Pawtucket, Rhode Island and Fraternal Order of Police, Lodge #4.***

[2] ***Stark County, Ohio Sheriff and Fraternal Order of Police, Ohio Labor Council, Inc.***

[3] ***City of Lansing, Michigan and Fraternal Order of Police, Capitol City Lodge 141.***

[4] ***Beaverton, Oregon and Beaverton Police Officers Association.***

Employer, the Officer shall be allowed to choose the type that he/she prefers under this provision. The Employer shall pay one hundred percent (100%) of the expense of repair and replacement for all footwear provided by the Employer. When footwear needs to be resoled, the Police Officer shall select any sole consistent with the rules and regulations of the Police Department.[1]

43.4.2 The Employer will select a style of winter boot and shoes for official use. Each uniformed employee will be provided, at no cost, either one (1) pair of shoes or winter boots (employee choice) each calendar year, which will be required to be worn during all working hours.[2]

43.5 Cleaning Allowance.

43.5.1 The Employer will pay for the cleaning of clothes used on the job by employees not to exceed $22 per month for uniformed employees and $18 per month for non-uniformed employees.[3]

43.6 Cleaning Furnished.

43.6.1 The Employer shall pay one hundred percent (100%) of the cost necessary to clean each employee's uniform and/or each detective's clothing through a cleaning service provided by the Employer.[4]

[1] ***Aurora, Colorado and Aurora Police Association.***

[2] ***Greene County, Ohio and Fraternal Order of Police, Ohio Labor Council, Inc.***

[3] ***Corvallis, Oregon and Corvallis Police Officers' Association.***

[4] ***Redmond, Washington and Redmond Police Officers Association.***

43.6.2 The clothing articles listed below will be cleaned at Employer expense on an as needed basis for Association members.[1]

Sworn Uniformed Men & Women and Non-Sworn Uniformed Men	Uniformed Non-Sworn Women	Non-Uniformed Men	Non-Uniformed Women
Parka (sworn only)	Shirts	Suits	Jackets
Jackets	Slacks	Ties	Skirts
Shirts	Skirts	Vests	Pantsuits
Trousers	Vests	Overcoats	Blouse/Sweaters
Hats	Ties	Shirts/Sweaters	Overcoats
Ties	Jacket	Trousers	Dresses
		Sports Coat	

43.7 Replacement of Lost/Damaged Clothing and Equipment.

43.7.1 The Employer agrees to repair or replace both personal and Employer-owned uniforms, equipment and property damaged or destroyed on duty unless gross negligence can be shown on the part of the employee. Repair or replacement of the following items shall not exceed the following costs: Watches, actual cost not to exceed $25.00; corrective lens, excluding frames, actual cost not to exceed reasonable replacement of damaged item(s); eyeglass frames not to exceed $65.00. Receipts will be required prior to payment by the

[1] ***Municipality of Anchorage and Anchorage Police Department Employees Association.***

Employer. Repair or replacement of non-listed items shall not exceed reasonable costs for only those items which are normally associated with an officer's on-duty status.[1]

43.8 Long or Short Sleeve Shirts.

43.8.1 The Employer agrees that employees assigned to uniformed work units may elect to wear long sleeve or short sleeve uniform shirts at the employee's discretion. For special events such as parades, concerts, funerals, etc., the Employer may designate the appropriate uniform to be worn.[2]

43.9 Flat Badges.

43.9.1 Subject to the limitations described in Division policies and procedures concerning the use, display, and ownership of police badges, the Employer shall furnish to any unit employee, upon request, a flat replica of the authorized chest police badge which shall be permanently affixed in a specified carrying case.[3]

ARTICLE 44

EQUIPMENT

44.1 Equipment Allowance.

44.1.1 Each uniformed officer shall receive $90.00 per year for the purchase of job-related equipment (example: batons, flashlights, gloves, etc.).[4]

[1] ***State of Oregon and Oregon State Police Officers Association.***

[2] ***Anaheim, California and Anaheim Police Association.***

[3] ***Glendale, California and Glendale Police Officers' Association.***

[4] ***Portland, Oregon and Portland Police Association.***

44.2 Protective Vests.

44.2.1 Body armor shall be issued and replaced as follows:

44.2.1.1 The Employer agrees to issue body armor to all bargaining unit members and shall repair or replace issued body armor in conformance with industry standards and manufacturer's recommendations, provided that armor in regular use over five (5) years old shall be replaced upon request of the employee. Armor not in regular use by the employee shall be replaced at the request of the employee after it has received the equivalent five (5) years' use.

44.2.1.2 The Employer shall issue body armor that is in conformance with NIJ rating as adequate for normal duty use (no less than level 2A). If an officer chooses to purchase a vest that exceeds the above requirements, the Employer will reimburse that officer for the cost of said vest, not to exceed three hundred fifty dollars ($350.00).

44.2.1.3 Those sworn employees who are assigned to the "Uniformed Bureau" of the Department are highly encouraged to wear their body armor. Wearing of body armor is mandatory when ordered by an employee in a supervising capacity. Depending upon a situational occurrence or assignment, a supervising employee will have the authority to decide when the wearing of body armor is mandatory. Whenever an employee is not wearing body armor, the employee will have the body armor immediately available in the event the employee is assigned and ordered to wear it.

44.2.1.4 Issued body armor which is damaged through improper care or use shall be subject to repair or replacement at the employee's expense.

44.2.1.5 The Employer will not permanently issue used body armor without the consent of the Association.[1]

44.2.2 The vests provided by the Employer must meet or exceed a ballistic threat level of the duty ammunition issued by the Police Bureau for day-to-day use by patrol officers.[2]

44.3 Service Weapons.

44.3.1 The Employer agrees to furnish all newly-hired employees with a duty firearm upon their date of hire.

44.3.1.1 Over the five-year period between July 1, ____ and July 1, ____, the Employer shall provide duty firearms to current employees who carry other than the approved Glock firearms. The goal of the parties shall be that 20% of the eligible current employees shall receive the replacement weapon in each year. The replacement of weapons shall occur in the following three groupings of employees:

44.3.1.2 Employees who have successfully completed Glock training but who do not currently carry the Glock as their assigned primary service weapon;

44.3.1.3 Employees who carry revolvers; and

44.3.1.4 Employees carrying semi-automatics other than Glocks.

44.3.1.5 Within each group, the weapons shall be replaced in the order of the seniority of the employees involved. Employees within five years of retirement shall be allowed to carry their current weapons.

[1] ***The City of Napa, California and Napa Police Officers' Association.***

[2] ***City of Portland, Oregon and Portland Police Association.***

44.3.1.6 Current employees who have purchased their own Glock duty firearms from the Employer and who qualified with the weapon as a primary duty weapon during the Winter qualification shall continue to carry their personally-owned weapons. The Employer shall be responsible for the maintenance and repair of the personally-owned weapons, and for the replacement of the weapons if they are lost or stolen. If an employee who carries his personally-owned weapon changes duty assignment to a position where the carrying of a different model weapon is more suitable to the assignment, the Employer shall furnish the employee with the different model weapon. Disputes as to which model weapon is suitable to an assignment shall be resolved by the Safety Committee. If the Safety Committee is unable to decide the matter, the final decision will be left to the Chief of Police or the Chief's designee.

44.3.1.7 When an employee whose duty firearm has been purchased by the Employer retires, the employee shall be allowed the option of purchasing the firearm from the Employer at the price originally paid for the firearm by the Employer.

44.3.1.8 Modification of weapons allowable under Employer rules (e.g., the addition of night sights or the installation of different magazines) shall be performed by the Employer; the employee requesting the modification shall be responsible for paying the cost of hardware used in the modification.

44.3.1.9 Employees shall have an opportunity to purchase additional weapons from the Employer at the Employer's costs pursuant to the terms set forth in the Employer's rules.[1]

[1] ***Portland, Oregon and Portland Police Association.***

44.3.2 No lieutenant or police officer shall be required to work without a firearm.[1]

44.4 Firearms Qualification.

44.4.1 The Employer shall provide firearms qualification training with range ammunition or Department-issued duty ammunition to all full-time law enforcement and correction officers no less than four (4) times a year. Each officer shall qualify no less than once per year with Department-issued duty ammunition.[2]

44.4.2 The Employer shall maintain the current practice of providing ammunition for primary weapons. In addition, the Employer shall provide ammunition for the yearly qualification for state certification of secondary weapons, up to a maximum annual cost of fifty thousand dollars ($50,000).[3]

44.5 Off-Duty Weapons.

44.5.1 Each newly-hired Patrol Officer will be issued an off-duty weapon selected by the Employer which shall remain the property of the Employer.[4]

44.6 Ammunition.

44.6.1 The Employer shall provide all ammunition which is needed and necessary for the performance of the duties. Ammunition for on-duty use shall be of high quality. Practice ammunition shall be furnished by the Employer at the rate of one box of .38 caliber shells per employee every other month, provided that such employee shows that the ammunition is being

[1] ***Bellevue, Washington and Bellevue Police Officers Guild.***

[2] ***Deschutes County, Oregon and Deschutes County Sheriff Association.***

[3] ***City of Cleveland, Ohio and Cleveland Police Patrolmen's Association.***

[4] ***Kettering, Ohio and Fraternal Order of Police.***

used for practice shooting. The above is in addition to "qualification" ammunition.[1]

44.6.2 The Employer shall make available, at its expense, 600 rounds of ammunition each year for each employee covered by this agreement who is required regularly to carry a weapon in the line of duty, for use by employees desiring to improve or maintain proficiency with their weapons.

44.6.2.1 The Employer shall provide 4800 rounds of submachine gun ammunition and 1200 rounds of ammunition for each sniper rifle in the arsenal, and an additional 600 rounds of handgun ammunition for each member of the tactical team.[2]

44.6.3 The Employer shall furnish to each employee a copy of the following:

44.6.3.1 The Police Department Rules and Regulations and General Orders;

44.6.3.2 A booklet describing benefits of employment available to City employees;

44.6.3.3 This collective bargaining agreement and any contract amendments or modifications during the term of this contract;

44.6.3.4 The Texas Penal Code;

44.6.3.5 The Texas Code of Criminal Procedure;

44.6.3.6 The Texas Motor Vehicle Laws;

44.6.3.7 The Texas Family Code;

44.6.3.8 The Texas Controlled Substances Act; and

[1] ***Sioux Falls, Iowa and General Drivers and Helpers Union.***

[2] ***City of Wichita, Kansas and Fraternal Order of Police, Lodge #5.***

44.6.3.9 A current copy of the Civil Service Rules and Regulations.[1]

44.6.4 Where the Employer requires an employee to have a telephone, the Employer shall pay the minimum monthly charge of $11.11 or $12.64, as the case may be.[2]

44.6.5 The Police Department will furnish the following to each unit member assigned to the air support detail:

2 Nomax (or equivalent in quality) flight suits
1 Flight Helmet
1 Nomax Gloves (pair)
1 Standard Headset
1 Custom Ear Protectors (ear molds) (pair).[3]

44.7 Hours for Quartermaster.
44.7.1 The quartermaster will be available to employees on Wednesday of each week from 6:00 a.m. until 2:00 p.m.[4]

ARTICLE 45

SAFETY OF EQUIPMENT

45.1 General.
45.1.1 Unsafe Equipment.

45.1.1.1 Whenever an employee believes he has been assigned to use a piece of equipment which is unsafe for its

[1] ***City of El Paso, Texas and El Paso Municipal Police Officers' Association.***

[2] ***City of Des Plaines, Illinois and Combined Counties Police Association.***

[3] ***City of Phoenix, Arizona and Phoenix Law Enforcement Association.***

[4] ***Stark County, Ohio Sheriff and Fraternal Order of Police, Ohio Labor Council, Inc.***

intended use, he shall immediately report the same to his shift commander. If the shift commander determines the equipment is safe for its intended use, the employee may submit the question to the Safety Committee who shall make an independent determination. In the event the Committee determines the piece of equipment is not safe, no employee shall be required to use the same until necessary repairs have been completed. If the Committee determines the equipment safe, its use shall be continued.

45.1.1.2 A Safety Committee shall be established composed of two (2) representatives selected by the Association, two (2) representatives selected by the Employer and one (1) neutral member selected by the others. The Association, the Employer, and neutral shall have one (1) vote each. One (1) representative from the Association and the Employer and the neutral shall constitute a quorum.

45.1.1.3 The Safety Committee shall be authorized to make recommendations to the Police Chief with regard to the adequacy of the items of equipment used by the employees.[1]

45.1.2 It is the desire of the Employer and the Association to maintain the highest standards of safety and health in the Police Department in order to eliminate, as much as possible, job-related accidents, death, injuries and illness in the police service.[2]

45.2 Safety of Vehicles.

45.2.1 No employee shall be required to operate any equipment which in his opinion he deems to be unsafe. No

[1] ***Sioux City, Iowa and Sioux City Policemen's Association.***

[2] ***North Las Vegas, Nevada and North Las Vegas Police Officers Association.***

disciplinary action or other form of discrimination shall be instituted against any employee for such action.[1]

45.3 Safety and Equipment.

45.3.1 General. The Employer shall maintain at all times an adequate quantity of modern, marked and unmarked vehicles, radios and other essential equipment in sound working condition to ensure a safe work place for each employee and to maximize the Department's prime objectives of crime prevention, suppression, and detection. Such vehicles, radios, and other essential equipment must be replaced during period of repair.

45.3.1.1 Preventive Vehicle Maintenance Program. The Employer shall ensure that all police vehicles assigned to the employees are in a safe condition and shall maintain a preventive maintenance program for police vehicles. The Chief shall assign a supervisor to the vehicle maintenance shop for the purpose of inspecting the safety of police vehicles. If, at the discretion of an employee, an assigned vehicle is not in safe condition, said employee shall notify the supervisor assigned to the vehicle maintenance shop that the vehicle is not in a safe condition. The supervisor assigned to the vehicle maintenance shop shall make the decision as to the safety of the police vehicle. In the event that the supervisor assigned to the vehicle maintenance shop deems the police vehicle to be in a safe condition, and the employee disagrees with the supervisor's decision, said employee may protest the supervisor's decision in writing. The supervisor assigned to the vehicle maintenance shop shall acknowledge the employee's protest in writing and forward all copies to the employee's division commander for final disposition.

[1] ***Anchorage, Alaska and Anchorage Police Department Employees Association.***

45.3.1.2 The Vehicle Maintenance Supervisor shall maintain records on the maintenance of all police vehicles. When a vehicle reaches the 30,000-mile odometer reading, a review of the vehicle's maintenance record will be conducted. If deemed necessary, the Vehicle Maintenance Supervisor may request an exhaustive mechanical evaluation be performed on the vehicle. Any employee may request an exhaustive mechanical evaluation of the police vehicle when the vehicle reaches the 30,000-mile mark. This inspection will be accomplished in a timely manner or another vehicle will be provided for the employee.

45.3.1.3 Marked vehicles having 60,000 miles on their odometers, and assigned to the Uniform Division, must be retired from the Uniform Division fleet. An employee will not be required to operate a marked vehicle assigned to the Uniform Division having 60,000 miles or more on its odometer. Additionally, an employee will not be subject to disciplinary action for refusing to comply with an order to a drive marked vehicle in the Uniform Division which has 60,000 miles or more on its odometer. Prior to 60,000 miles a vehicle may be retired from the Uniform Division fleet if considered unsafe by the head of the vehicle maintenance unit or a division commander. No officers in the Uniform Division may be ordered to drive a patrol vehicle which has in excess of 60,000 miles.

45.3.1.4 Any vehicle retired from use in the Uniform Division pursuant to this agreement may be used by the Department in other divisions, provided that the vehicles are sound and safe to operate.

45.3.1.5 Radios. The Employer shall provide to each employee so requesting, one (1) permanently assigned hand-held radio. A charger will be issued if necessary. These radios will be replaced in accordance with Department policies and regulations. However, in the event the radio needs to be replaced or repaired due to negligence or intentional abuse on the part of the employee to whom the radio is issued, the employee shall be required to reimburse the Employer for the costs, to be paid in no more that $100-a-month installments. The cost of said radio and charger shall be, for purposes of the Section, based upon its depreciated value at a rate of 15% per year. Negligence or intentional abuse shall be determined by the Labor Relations Committee outlined in this Agreement.

45.3.1.6 Until the Employer acquires a new radio system, employees residing outside of the County shall not be eligible to request an issued radio. The Employer shall make available to employee, working approved police functions, a radio. If no radios are available for permanent issuance, the Employer shall have three hundred and sixty-five (365) days to provide the necessary radios to conform to the request.

45.3.1.7 "Permanently issued or assigned radios" are those issued pursuant to an eligible employee requesting to have one issued to them and does not imply that the officer cannot later turn in his radio.

45.3.1.8 "Approved police functions" shall mean either an Employer function where the Employer provides security for an official function sanctioned and approved by the Chief of Police and functions for which a work permit has been issued.[1]

45.4 Electronic Locking Devices for Weapons.

45.4.1 The Employer will provide in appropriate vehicles electronic locking devices to allow for the safe storage of weapons.[2]

[1] ***City of San Antonio, Texas and San Antonio Police Officers' Association.***

[2] ***Madison, Wisconsin and Madison Professional Police Officers' Association.***

ARTICLE 46

VEHICLES

46.1 Take-Home Cars.

46.1.1 The Employer will expand the current take-home program to provide take-home vehicles to all permanent sworn officers, but they may not be taken outside of the jurisdictional limits of the Employer. Home cars shall be distributed on a position seniority basis for uniformed and non-uniformed personnel. When vehicles are given to any unit, Sergeants and then Corporals shall receive their vehicles first.[1]

46.1.2 Officer-Assigned Vehicle Program.

46.1.2.1 Participation in this program shall be totally voluntary on the part of the officer. However, the right to deny participation in this program for cause is reserved to the Employer.

46.1.2.2 An officer may be denied participation in the program regardless of his assignment if, in the judgment of the Employer, the officer's duties and responsibilities will not justify the assignment of a vehicle.

46.1.2.3 Officers volunteering to participate in this program agree to abide by all rules and regulations governing this program.

46.1.2.4 This program will be reviewed monthly and may be modified at the discretion of the Employer. If, in the opinion of the Employer, the vehicle program for the Employer, as covered by this agreement, proves unworkable in practice, the Employer shall have the option of terminating this Agreement upon sixty (60) days' written notice of intent to the Association and the

[1] ***Anchorage, Alaska and Anchorage Police Department Employees Association.***

Employer will meet and attempt to solve problems relating to the program; otherwise, said notice shall be final.

46.1.2.5 No one other than a sworn police officer will be permitted to drive the police car. Officers will not presume any special privileges with a vehicle while off duty. As an example, an officer living in an apartment complex will park the vehicle in the designated area at all times, not in a reserved or no parking area.

46.1.2.6 Unattended vehicles of off-duty officers must be locked at all times and the portable radio will be removed from the vehicle.

46.1.2.7 Officers will not operate an assigned vehicle within less than four hours after consuming any alcoholic beverages.

46.1.2.8 No officer participating in the officer-assigned vehicle program will be authorized to transport any passenger except under the following conditions: (1) Approved Ride-Along; (2) children for day care only while officer is en route to and from work; and (3) when the officer is on official on-call status.

46.1.2.9 The vehicle will not be utilized for carrying heavy or excessive loads, and will not have objects protruding from the trunk or windows.

46.1.2.10 Officers will not use the vehicle for any commercial enterprise; however, the vehicle may be driven to and from a part-time job, subject to the approval of the Employer.

46.1.2.11 During vacations of five days or more when the officer will be out of the city, or when an officer is on sick leave, or injury time for five days or more, the vehicle will be turned in at the police garage, locked up, and will not be used except in an emergency. The officer will be reassigned the vehicle upon his return to the Employer, or return to normal duty. The vehicle may, at the Employer's discretion, be parked at the substation instead of the police garage.

46.1.2.12 All officers assigned a vehicle on a personal basis will exercise good judgment in utilizing it, and will not drive or use the vehicle so as to cause unfavorable comment or reflect discredit on the Employer.

46.1.2.13 Officers, while off duty and operating a vehicle, will be appropriately attired and have in his/her possession badge, I.D., and sidearm to effectively perform a police function while, at the same time, presenting a favorable image. Officers will wear trousers (slacks or jeans) and a shirt while operating the vehicle; cut-offs, shorts, t-shirts, and tank tops will be considered inappropriate attire. Officers will not utilize vehicles outside the county except on official business.

46.1.2.14 An officer using the vehicle, while off duty, will not be required to go in and out of service, but if he/she is near a priority one call, he/she must advise the dispatcher.

46.1.2.15 The safety of passengers rests solely with the officer operating the vehicle.

46.1.2.16 When responding to a felony call with non-sworn personnel as passengers, except for approved Ride-Alongs, the officers will first deposit the passengers at a convenient location, and will then respond to the call consistent with Employer regulations.

46.1.2.17 Emergency runs will not be made while the vehicle is occupied by non-sworn passengers, except for approved Ride-Alongs.

46.1.2.18 When responding to calls involving a felony, while off duty, the officer may be required to handle the call in order to best preserve and handle evidence and maintain continuity. In such cases, the officer shall be compensated with overtime pay consistent with Employer regulations and the contract.

46.1.2.19 In minor cases encountered off duty, the officer may summon a district car to handle the call, and stand by and assist until the district car arrives. In the event immediate action is necessary, the off-duty officer will handle the situation. Officers will stop at any incident that requires police attention such as accidents, stalled cars, being flagged down by a citizen, and so forth. Overtime is not authorized for the brief time needed to handle minor calls. Officers will be paid overtime for any incident requiring over one-half hour or when ordered to assist by an on-duty supervisor.

46.1.2.20 All officers assigned a marked patrol unit will have with them when operating that unit a jacket as authorized by the Standard Operating Procedures Manual for wear while enforcing traffic laws off duty. Officers are responsible for enforcing traffic laws while operating a marked police unit off duty; this is intended to be for flagrant, dangerous violations.

46.1.2.21 The officer assigned to a vehicle shall be fully responsible for seeing that the general maintenance and proper care of the vehicle is performed (the Employer shall perform and pay for the maintenance), and shall refrain from the following: (1) Making anything but minor adjustments; (2) altering the body, general design, appearance, markings, approval, mechanical, or electrical systems. The addition of lights to a vehicle will require approval from a supervisor at the police garage. This section also prohibits the addition of bumper stickers or license plates that promote a commercial enterprise or that present a theme which may be controversial among varying segments of the community; (3) making any repairs, or having any repairs made to the vehicle, other than at the authorized Department garage; (4) using fuel, oil, lubricant, or other liquid additives in the vehicle, other than those issued at authorized motor pool fuel depots; (5) AM-FM radios may be installed at the officer's expense. Citizen band radios may be installed consistent with Department policy. The Department assumes no financial responsibility for stolen, damaged or lost personal radios.

46.1.2.22 Officers will be responsible for the appearance and cleanliness of their vehicles, both interior and exterior.

46.1.2.23 Officers will wash the vehicle at their own expense and wax it at least once every six months.

46.1.2.24 Officers will change flats, when on duty or off duty. Repairs to the tires will be made by the authorized Department garage when the tire is delivered to the garage.

46.1.2.25 Officers will be required to have all maintenance and service work, including repairs that can be scheduled, done on the vehicle that is permanently assigned for any type work unless it has been previously scheduled. The only exception to this will be minor necessary repairs.

46.1.2.26 A work order must be submitted for other than regular maintenance or service work.

46.1.2.27 All vehicles will be inspected once each month by the immediate supervisor of the vehicle operator. The inspection will include: Cleanliness – interior and exterior; maintenance – performed at the proper interval; equipment – in good working order.

46.1.2.28 Officers shall, at all times, drive the vehicle with reasonable prudence in order to maintain it at the highest degree of operating efficiency.

46.1.2.29 Willful negligence, on the part of the officer, in the care and operation of the vehicle, or failure to follow these procedures, will be cause for the vehicle to be taken away from the officer. Take-home car privileges will be revoked for 30 days upon a first infraction of any of these rules governing the plan and 180 days for any subsequent infraction. Unit Commanders retain the right to extend these time periods for serious infractions. Officers will be notified by letter of the suspension of their take-home privileges. This suspension will be grievable to the Association Executive Board whose decision will be final and subject to review and change only by the Employer.

46.1.2.30 If it becomes necessary for a permanently-assigned vehicle to be out of service for extended repairs, the officer will be assigned a pool vehicle for his use. If there is sufficient number of pool vehicles available, then the officer normally assigned a vehicle may be assigned a pool vehicle for exclusive use during the time his regular vehicle is out of service.[1]

46.2 Take-Home Motorcycles.

46.2.1 Unit employees may be allowed by the Employer to take home their assigned motorcycles, providing said following conditions are met: (1) Unit employee must reside within a fifteen (15)-mile radius of the Civic Center Garage; (2) motorcycle must be kept in a secured and covered facility at the unit employee's residence; (3) unit employee must maintain motorcycle in a clean condition. This privilege may be revoked at any time by Employer if any condition is not complied with.[2]

[1] ***Albuquerque, New Mexico and Albuquerque Police Officers' Association.***

[2] ***Glendale, California and Glendale Police Officers' Association.***

46.3 County Vehicles.

46.3.1 Vehicles should be checked and tested for safe operating conditions at least once every six (6) months.[1]

46.3.2 All vehicles will be inspected in substantial compliance with the manufacturer's recommendation standards. Records of all inspections will be available upon request, to officers to whom the vehicle is assigned and a copy will be maintained in the vehicle by the officer to whom assigned.[2]

46.4 Investigation Division Home Garaging.

46.4.1 All employees in this bargaining unit assigned to the Investigation Division will be allowed to home garage their assigned automobiles. It is understood that the Employer will establish reasonable written policy and procedures consistent with Employer policy and operational needs.[3]

46.5 Air-Conditioned Vehicles.

46.5.1 All Employer automobiles primarily utilized by Bargaining Unit members in pursuit of their assigned duties will be equipped with air conditioning.[4]

46.6 Police Cruisers.

46.6.1 All replacement cruisers shall have power windows to be operated from the driver's position. All such cars shall be equipped with power door locks and a suitable protective screen.

[1] ***Greene County, Ohio and Fraternal Order of Police, Ohio Labor Council, Inc.***

[2] ***County of Shawnee, Kansas and Fraternal Order of Police, Lodge 3.***

[3] ***Contra Costa County, California and the Deputy Sheriffs' Association.***

[4] ***Macomb County, Georgia and Macomb County Deputy Sheriff's Association.***

All replacement vehicles assigned or used by members of this bargaining unit shall be equipped with air conditioning.

46.6.1.1 The Association will be provided a copy of the specifications developed for all replacement cruisers, and may initiate a special conference.[1]

ARTICLE 47

FIRST AID FACILITIES

47.1 General.

47.1.1 The Employer will provide adequate first-aid facilities in the following manner:

47.1.1.1 First-aid kits will be placed in all vehicles used by Sheriff's Department officers.

47.1.1.2 There will be a first-aid kit accessible to all officers at the main Sheriff's office and in the Sheriff's dispatch center.

47.1.1.3 Each kit shall contain the items needed for basic first aid.[2]

ARTICLE 48

STAFFING

48.1 Manning/Staffing.

48.1.1 In the best interest of the Employer and to promote the safety of the employees, patrol cars shall be manned by two (2) officers during periods of high criminal activity and in high

[1] ***City of Lansing, Michigan and Fraternal Order of Police, Capitol City Lodge 141.***

[2] ***County of Shawnee, Kansas and Fraternal Order of Police, Lodge 3.***

crime areas. Whenever one (1)-officer units are in use, the Employer will use its best efforts to maintain sufficient staffing to provide for employees' safety.[1]

48.1.2 The parties agree that it is in their best interest to have a minimum number of police cars and/or cruisers manned by patrolmen actually covering car posts with the Employer for each tour of duty. The parties further agree that in order to achieve that goal, it may be necessary to "call back" patrolmen in order to satisfy the minimum levels established herein. In that context, the following is a schedule for the minimum number of patrol cars and/or cruisers required to actually be on the street answering calls during the following time periods:

TIME PERIODS	**NUMBER OF PATROL CARS AND/OR CRUISERS**
8:00 a.m. to 4:00 p.m.	Seven (7) district cars and two (2) two-man cruisers
4:00 p.m. to midnight	Seven (7) district cars and two (2) two-man cruisers
12:00 a.m. to 8:00 a.m.	Six (6) district cars and two (2) two-man cruisers

48.1.2.1 Whenever the above-named vehicles are not manned by virtue of lack of manpower on the shift, the Employer shall be required to call back a sufficient number of patrolmen necessary to man said vehicles. Said manning shall be filled by seniority on a rotating basis. All patrolmen shall be eligible to have their names placed on a "call-in list" for such purpose. Placement on said list shall be on a voluntary basis. All patrolmen who sign up for said list shall be properly attired and physically able to perform such patrol duty as provided in the rules and regulations of the Police Division.

[1] ***City of Beaumont, Texas and Beaumont Police Officers Association.***

48.1.2.2 Patrolmen called back to satisfy the minimum manning requirements hereunder shall report to work (a) at the beginning of the tour of duty for which they have been called back (if they have been notified at least 90 minutes prior to the start of said tour); or (b) within 90 minutes of being notified (if they have been notified after the tour of duty has commenced). In the event that a patrolman fails to report for duty within the aforesaid time limits, the Employer shall be required to call back officers in accordance with this section.

48.1.2.3 Patrolmen called back to satisfy the minimum requirements hereunder shall be paid at the rate of time and one-half his/her normal rate of pay commencing once they actually report to work.

48.1.2.4 The Employer shall be required to start seeking the necessary manpower to satisfy the provisions of this section of the Agreement as soon as it is evident that employees will have to be called back to work because other employees are out of work due to work-related injuries, vacations, and/or illness. In the event that employees who have been called back to work have not yet reported to work, in order to satisfy the minimum manning requirements set forth herein, then employees holding the rank of Patrolman shall be held over until such time that the employee that has been called back to work actually reports to work.[1]

48.1.3 The Employer and the Association agree that for reasons of safety, the minimum number of patrol officers actually in the field on any given patrol shift shall be at least 75% of the number of officers officially assigned to that shift. If, because of

[1] ***City of Pawtucket, Rhode Island and Fraternal Order of Police, Lodge #4.***

illness or other reasons, 75% of the assigned officers are not actually out in the field, the Employer or its designee shall call in enough off-duty officers to bring the strength up to the required number of men.

48.1.3.1 The Employer and Association agree that the Employer shall establish a "Standards Committee" of citizens to review and make recommendations on current patrol staffing levels of the Employer on a semi-annual basis.

48.1.3.2 The Standards Committee shall consist of five (5) members: two (2) chosen by the (Mayor) (County Representative) (Governor), one (1) chosen by the (Police Chief) (Sheriff) (State Police Chief), and two (2) appointed by the Association. One of the (Mayor) (County Representative) (Governor)'s appointees shall be the chairperson of the committee.

48.1.3.3 The committee shall meet on or near the first of March and September and shall review current patrol staffing levels and shall have available to them all relevant information and data from all departments and access to all divisions within the Employer to determine the relationship that may exist between staffing levels and the patrol division, safety of officers, impact of staffing on patrol performance, and public safety and service.

48.1.3.4 The findings of the committee and its recommendations shall be submitted within (90) days of its initial meeting for review. Employer representatives will meet with the Association to announce the action the Employer deems appropriate and economically feasible to implement in the best interest of the public as a whole and the employees of Employer and members of the Association.[1]

[1] ***Everett, Washington and Everett Police Officers Association.***

ARTICLE 49

CANINE PROGRAMS

49.1 Purchase of Dog.

49.1.1 A unit member assigned to the Canine Detail will have the option of purchasing his dog as follows:

49.1.1.1 If both the police dog and the unit member have been in the Canine Detail in excess of five (5) years, at retirement the unit member may purchase his dog for one dollar ($1.00).

49.1.1.2 If both the police dog and the unit member have been in the Canine Detail in excess of five (5) years and the unit member leaves other than for retirement, the decision to allow the purchase of his dog will be made on a case by case basis and this decision will not be arbitrary.[1]

49.2 Canine Burial.

49.2.1 In the event a canine is killed in the line of duty, the Employer shall provide for burial arrangements that meet with the Employer's approval.[2]

[1] ***City of Phoenix, Arizona and Phoenix Law Enforcement Association.***

[2] ***City of Santa Clara and Santa Clara Police Officers Association.***

CHAPTER 7

PAID LEAVE

Along with wages and insurance, one of the most frequent subjects for law enforcement collective bargaining is the amount of time off which is provided to a law enforcement officer. Since each additional day off constitutes almost one-half of one percent of the total hours of work per year, changing paid leave benefits can be difficult to accomplish.

This chapter contains contract provisions which govern the accrual and usage of paid and unpaid leave. Among the topics covered in this chapter are the following:

- Vacations
- Holidays
- Sick Leave
- Leaves of Absence
- Bereavement Leave

Increasingly, leave accruals are now specified in hours as opposed to days. This change reflects the wide variety of work shifts in law enforcement agencies, and attempts to equalize the value of leave between employees working an eight-hour day and those working some form of compressed workweek with a ten, twelve, or nine-hour day.

Another feature which appears to be increasing in popularity in law enforcement collective bargaining agreements are provisions which allow an employee to sell back accrued leave – usually sick leave or vacation time – to an employer. Some leave "sell back" provisions allow the employee to cash in virtually the entire leave accrual; others only allow for the cash in of a portion of the annual leave accrual.

A relatively new development in the area of paid leave is "time off" plans, which combine traditional vacation, holiday and sick leaves into a single form of paid time off. The advantages of a time off plan is that what would traditionally be considered sick leave is made more valuable because of a loosening of the circumstances under which the leave can be taken and the fact that paid time off can generally be converted to cash. This chapter contains a very sophisticated time-off plan from Walnut Creek, California.

ARTICLE 50

VACATIONS

50.1 Accrual Rate.

50.1.1 Upon the effective date of this collective bargaining agreement, leave accrual for regular employees hired before the ratification of this Agreement by both parties shall be as follows:

50.1.1.1 <u>Months of Service Per Pay Period</u>

(1) 1st through the 60th	8.31 hours
(2) 61st through the 120th	9.23 hours
(3) 121st and thereafter	10.15 hours

50.1.1.2 Upon the effective date of this collective bargaining agreement, leave accrual for regular employees hired after the ratification of this Agreement by both parties shall be as follows:

50.1.1.3	(1) 1st through 60th	7.70 hours
	(2) 61st through 120th	8.62 hours
	(3) 121st and thereafter	9.54 hours[1]

50.1.2 Employees having served in the Employer's service for six (6) consecutive full calendar months, shall be credited with six (6) workdays' vacation leave. Thereafter, vacation leave shall be accrued with the following:

50.1.2.1 Less than five (5) years of service, 128.4 hours per year, accrued at the rate of 10.7 hours per month. Vacation leave not to accumulate beyond 240 hours.

50.1.2.2 Five (5) to ten (10) years, but less than ten (10) years of service, 152.4 hours per year, accrued at the rate of

[1] ***Municipality of Anchorage and Anchorage Police Department Employees Association.***

12.7 hours per month. Vacation leave not to accumulate beyond 240 hours.

50.1.2.3 Ten (10) to fifteen (15) years, but less than fifteen (15) years of service, 176.4 hours per year, accrued at the rate of 14.7 hours per month. Vacation leave not to accumulate beyond 280 hours.

50.1.2.4 Fifteen (15) to twenty (20) years, but less than twenty (20) years of service, 192.0 hours per year, accrued at the rate of 16.0 hours per month. Vacation leave not to accumulate beyond 280 hours.

50.1.2.5 After twenty (20) years of service, 200.4 hours per year, accrued at the rate of 16.7 hours per month. Vacation leave not to be accumulated beyond 280 hours.[1]

50.2 Method of Selection.

50.2.1 All employees shall annually select vacation leave periods (including annual leave in lieu of holidays) during the month of December of each year on the basis of classification seniority within departmental assignment. Lieutenants may be grouped with Captains for the purpose of vacation selection. Sergeants and Officers in assignments other than field patrol forces may be placed in compatible groups for the purpose of vacation selection. Officers in the field patrol forces will be grouped for the purpose of vacation selection. In order to secure equity for all Sergeants, those in the field patrol forces may be grouped with other Sergeants so the total number in each group will be comparable.

50.2.1.1 The initial selection of vacation periods may not be divided into segments of less than eighty (80), one hundred

[1] ***Clackamas County, Oregon and Clackamas County Peace Officers Association.***

twenty (120) or one hundred sixty (160) hours, dependent upon the entitlement of the employee, without the consent of the Employer. Where an employee elects to divide a vacation entitlement such employee may exercise seniority only as to the initial vacation increment selected. Upon completion of the initial selection of all employees, those electing to divide vacations may exercise seniority in making subsequent vacation period selections.

50.2.1.2 The Employer shall, during the month of December in each year, designate the maximum number of employees who may be on vacation at any one time for each division, bureau, team, unit or specialized position.[1]

50.3 Maximum Accrual of Vacation Time.

50.3.1 An employee will not be required to take vacation leave during the year and shall also have the privilege of an unlimited accrual of annual leave. However, leaves for longer than sixty (60) calendar days may be taken only with the approval of the Municipality and the Association.[2]

50.3.2 Maximum vacation accumulations for employees with an average regular workweek of forty (40) hours shall be as follows:

50.3.2.1 For employees accruing vacation at the rate of eighty (80) hours for every twenty-six (26) complete biweekly pay periods, the maximum amount of vacation that may be accumulated shall be one hundred sixty (160) hours.

50.3.2.2 For employees accruing vacation at the rate of one hundred four (104) hours for every twenty-six (26) complete

[1] ***Vallejo, California and Vallejo Police Officers Association.***

[2] ***Municipality of Anchorage and Anchorage Police Department Employees Association.***

biweekly pay periods, the maximum amount of vacation that may be accumulated shall be two hundred eight (208) hours.

50.3.2.3 For employees accruing vacation at the rate of one hundred thirty (130) hours for every twenty-six (26) complete biweekly pay periods, the maximum amount of vacation that may be accumulated shall be two hundred sixty (260) hours.

50.3.2.4 For employees accruing vacation at the rate of one hundred fifty-six (156) hours for every twenty-six (26) complete biweekly pay periods, the maximum amount of vacation that may be accumulated shall be three hundred twelve (312) hours.

50.3.2.5 For employees accruing vacation at the rate of one hundred eighty-two (182) hours for every twenty-six (26) complete biweekly pay periods, the maximum amount of vacation that may be accumulated shall be three hundred sixty-four (364) hours.[1]

50.4 Cash-Out of Accrued Vacation.

50.4.1 Cash in lieu of accrued vacation leave may be obtained upon written request one payroll period in advance of the time of cash-in subject to cash availability and budgetary limitation. In emergency situations the required notice shall be waived and the matter handled expediently. Each member must use seven (7) days of accrued vacation leave each full calendar year.

50.4.1.1 If a member is denied the use of seven (7) days in a full calendar year, the member shall be entitled to payment for the unused portion. It is understood that, should the member take no action to schedule the seven (7) days' leave, the

[1] ***Anaheim, California and Anaheim Police Association.***

Department may direct that the member take the personal leave at any time to satisfy the seven (7)-day requirement.[1]

50.5 Recall From Vacation.

50.5.1 No employee shall be called to duty during his vacation period except for an emergency.[2]

50.5.2 When a unit employee is temporarily recalled to duty from out of state while on an authorized vacation by order of the Chief of Police, he shall be reimbursed for necessary and provable transportation expenses as determined by the Police Chief.[3]

50.5.3 In the event that an employee is required by subpoena or specifically assigned by supervisory or command personnel to appear to testify in court during an authorized vacation period including furlough days, he shall be paid a minimum equivalent of eight (8) or ten (10) hours at his straight time hourly rate, depending on his regular work hours, for every day that an appearance is required and shall have the vacation days restored which are lost due to said appearance.[4]

50.5.4 Once a vacation period has been assigned to an employee, and it has been approved, said employee may request a copy of the approved vacation slip and such copy shall be given to the employee, and no change shall be made in connection with said approved vacation except in the event of either an emergency as defined in Article IV of this Agreement or upon

[1] ***Municipality of Anchorage and Anchorage Police Department Employees Association.***

[2] ***City of Waterbury, Connecticut and Waterbury Police Union, Local 1237.***

[3] ***Phoenix, Arizona and Phoenix Law Enforcement Union.***

[4] ***Bellevue, Washington and Bellevue Police Officers Guild.***

personal request of the employee affected. Such personal request shall not make any change mandatory upon the Department.[1]

50.6 Cancellation of Vacation.

50.6.1 In the event an officer requests paid time off (vacation, compensatory time, or holiday time) not less than two weeks in advance to attend a major family or social event (wedding, birthday, etc.) and permission is granted to attend such event, the permission for time off shall not be canceled, except in event of emergency.[2]

50.7 Holidays and Sick Leave During Vacation.

50.7.1 When a holiday falls within an employee's vacation period, one additional day's vacation shall be granted. If an employee becomes ill while on vacation, the time of actual illness may be charged against accumulated sick leave, subject to sick leave requirements.[3]

50.8 Accrual While on Leave.

50.8.1 Leave shall continue to accrue during the time an employee is on approved paid leave. Such additional accrual shall be canceled, however, if the employee quits and fails to resume duty upon completion of approved leave.[4]

[1] ***City of Waterbury, Connecticut and Waterbury Police Union, Local 1237.***

[2] ***Fresno, California and Fresno Police Officers Association.***

[3] ***Marin County, California and Marin County Deputy Sheriffs' Association.***

[4] ***Municipality of Anchorage and Anchorage Police Department Employees Association.***

ARTICLE 51

HOLIDAYS

51.1 Fixed Holiday System.

51.1.1 Listed Holidays.

51.1.1.1 The following days shall be observed as holidays, and employees will be granted time off with pay unless required to be on duty:

New Year's Day	Good Friday
Memorial Day	Independence Day
Labor Day	Veteran's Day
Thanksgiving Day	Christmas Eve
Christmas Day	Employee's Birthday
Friday after Thanksgiving	

Such other days as shall be officially designated as a special holiday for all of Employer's employees.

51.1.1.2 Headquarters personnel and Division Administration personnel who are regularly assigned to work Monday through Friday with Saturday and Sunday as normal days off shall observe a designated holiday which falls on Saturday or Sunday on the preceding Friday or following Monday respectively. All other employees shall observe the designated holidays on the actual days specified in this agreement.

51.1.1.3 If an employee works on any of the holidays listed above, he/she shall be paid the following premium rate, in addition to his/her holiday pay:

51.1.1.4 For the first eight (8) hours – 1 ½ times for all hours worked.

51.1.1.5 For all hours in excess of eight (8) hours – double time for hours worked.[1]

51.1.2 Holidays on Days Off.

51.1.2.1 If the day on which a holiday is observed falls on an officer's scheduled day off, the officer will receive, in addition to his or her regular rate of pay, pay for the holiday at straight-time rate.[2]

51.1.3 Work Adjacent to Holidays.

51.1.3.1 An employee must work his regularly-scheduled workday immediately preceding and immediately following the holiday to receive holiday pay when such holiday is not worked, or to receive premium pay when such holiday is worked. An approved leave of absence with pay shall be considered as time worked; however, if Employer has reason to believe that an employee has abused or has used excessive sick leave in the past, it may, in its discretion, deny his request for sick leave for the day preceding or following the holiday.

51.1.3.2 An employee who is absent on a holiday for which such employee is scheduled to work shall be placed on leave without pay during such absence unless the absence is verified by a medical statement. If the absence is so verified, the employee will receive his regular pay for the day and will not be charged a day of sick leave for the holiday.

51.1.3.3 An employee whose employment terminates and the last day worked precedes a holiday shall not be paid for such holiday, except for employees whose retirement date coincides with a designated holiday.

[1] ***Spokane County and AFSCME Local 492.***

[2] ***City and County of Denver, Colorado and Denver Police Protective Association.***

51.1.3.4 When an employee's birthday holiday falls on one of the other recognized holidays, the employee shall receive either eight (8) hours of compensatory time or eight (8) hours of pay at straight-time rates in accordance with his election for such birthday holiday. The election of compensatory time shall be subject to the maximum accrual.

51.1.3.5 For the purposes of this Agreement, "medical statement" shall be defined as communication from a licensed medical doctor (M.D.) or Doctor of Osteopathy (D.O.) stating: (1) The date or dates the employee was seen professionally by the doctor; (2) the illness or ailment which was diagnosed or treated; (3) the treatment and recommendations prescribed; and (4) the date the employee was, or is expected to be, released to go back to work.[1]

51.2 Floating Holiday System.

51.2.1 Holiday Allowance.

51.2.1.1 Employees' regular workweek may include legal holidays. Employees scheduled to work on holidays shall work on the holiday, unless they are rescheduled not to work. Such rescheduling shall be done with the permission of the employee's supervisor. All employees shall receive an annual allowance of sixteen (16) compensatory days off for working on holidays. These compensatory days off shall be scheduled with the permission of the employee's supervisor and may be taken in full or half day increments. Compensatory days will not be assigned to an employee prior to October 1 of each calendar year, but may be assigned to facilitate scheduling between October 1 and December 31, unless the employee has scheduled all compensatory days prior to October 1 of each calendar year.

[1] ***Tulsa, Oklahoma and Fraternal Order of Police.***

51.2.1.2 A bargaining unit member may opt to "sell" compensatory days back to the Employer at a "buy-back" rate of one hundred dollars ($100.00) per day during the term of this Agreement, according to the following maximums:

1989:	3 compensatory days
1990:	3 compensatory days
1991:	3 compensatory days
1992:	3 compensatory days

51.2.1.3 The bargaining unit member may elect to sell back compensatory days at any time prior to October 1 of each calendar year.[1]

51.2.2 In lieu of holidays, all employees shall accrue eight and two-thirds (8-2/3) hours' credit for each full month worked. The employee may elect to take the credit as compensatory time off at a time mutually agreeable to the supervisor and the employee, or receive straight-time pay in lieu of time off. At the end of the fiscal year, the Employer may, at the request of the employee, pay the employee for any compensatory time which has not been used.[2]

51.3 Mixed Holiday System.

51.3.1 Personal Holiday Credit.

51.3.1.1 Any day the President of the United States and/or Governor declares a holiday for all public and private sector employees shall be recognized and observed as a paid holiday. In lieu of any other specific, recognized or observed holidays, each employee shall be credited with eleven (11) personal

[1] ***Bloomington, Indiana and Fraternal Order of Police, Lodge 88.***

[2] ***Lake Oswego, Oregon and Lake Oswego Police Officers' Association.***

holidays per year at the commencement of each fiscal year and the employee shall receive one (1) day's pay at the straight-time rate for each of the holidays selected on which he performs no work. It is recognized that one of these personal holidays is in memory of the contributions of Martin Luther King to the people of the United States. An employee hired subsequent to July 1 of a fiscal year shall be credited with 7.3 hours of personal holiday time for each full month remaining in the fiscal year.

51.3.1.2 If any employee is scheduled to work New Year's Day, Independence Day, Thanksgiving Day or Christmas Day and still has remaining personal holidays, such workday may be designated as a personal holiday and worked at the holiday overtime rate of two and one-half (2-1/2) times the regular rate.

51.3.1.3 The Employer may, upon ten (10) days' notice, however, declare New Year's Day, Independence Day, Thanksgiving Day or Christmas Day to be a holiday for all or certain non-patrol personnel.[1]

51.4 Religious Holiday Accommodation.

51.4.1 The obligation to accommodate the religious beliefs of officers covered by the Agreement is fulfilled if those officers whose religious beliefs require that they not work, but who are scheduled to work on a recognized religious holiday, are permitted, at the officer's option, one of the following choices in order to be excused from their regular tour of duty: (a) The use of a personal day; (b) the use of compensatory time; (c) voluntary change of regular day off; or (d) excused from duty, non-disciplinary. This option may be applied for certain recognized religious holidays of faiths whose tenets require abstinence from

[1] ***Multnomah County, Oregon and Multnomah County Deputy Sheriffs Association.***

work, subject to the determination of the Commanding Officer that this accommodation does not unduly interfere with operational needs.[1]

51.4.2 Good Friday. Any employee who desires leave from work to attend religious services on Good Friday may be excused by the Police Chief, or the City Manager, for not to exceed three (3) hours. This absence shall be leave without pay unless the employee chooses to use accrued vacation or in-lieu time. Unless the service of employees are required by public necessity or convenience, they shall be allowed to absent themselves as herein provided.[2]

51.5 Assignments on Holidays.

51.5.1 In filling the routine manning requirements for holidays, the required personnel shall be assigned from a roster of those police officers who have indicated a desire to work on the holiday, based upon seniority in rank within sections or division. If manning requirements cannot be met from those who volunteer, then those officers who are required to work shall be assigned on the basis of reverse order of seniority.[3]

51.6 Birthday Holidays.

51.6.1 All employees shall receive a day off on their birthday without additional holiday pay. If the birthday falls on a scheduled day off, the birthday holiday will be observed on the last scheduled day prior to the day off. If the birthday holiday falls within a vacation period, the birthday will be charged as a holiday instead

[1] ***Chicago, Illinois and Fraternal Order of Police.***

[2] ***City of Burbank and the Burbank Police Officers' Association.***

[3] ***Albuquerque, New Mexico and Albuquerque Police Officers' Association.***

of vacation. If an employee is required to work on his birthday, he shall receive pay for the birthday holiday plus time and one-half for hours worked. If an employee's birthday falls on a holiday as described in this article and he is required to work on said holiday birthday, he shall receive time and one-half for hours worked, holiday pay as provided in this article, plus pay for the birthday holiday.[1]

51.7 Payment for Unused Holidays on Termination.

51.7.1 Upon termination of employment, the employee shall be paid for any unused holidays, and shall repay the Employer any wages received for holiday compensation days taken but unearned.[2]

ARTICLE 52

PERSONAL LEAVE

52.1 General.

52.1.1 Accrual.

52.1.1.1 All employees covered by this Contract on an eight (8)-hour workday shall be granted 48 personal leave hours with pay and those on a ten (10)-hour workday shall be granted 50 personal leave hours with pay which an employee is entitled to use for the following purposes:

Time lost as a result of illness/injury to the employee or the employee's immediate family.

Attend personal business.

[1] ***Bethlehem, Pennsylvania and Fraternal Order of Police.***

[2] ***Aberdeen, Washington and Aberdeen Police Association.***

52.1.1.2 For any employee who has not used the 48 or 50 personal leave hours ending November 30 of each year or any portion thereof, the Employer will compensate said employee for the unused time at the employee's wage rate to be paid during the month of December of that year. Personal leave time shall not exceed the 48 or 50 hours as designated above nor shall it be accumulated or carried over from one year to the next. Personal leave shall be scheduled and administered under the direction of the Police Chief for personal business and leisure time.

52.1.1.3 In the event of illness/injury in which personal leave is requested, the employee shall notify his supervisor or other person designated by the supervisor at least one (1) hour prior to their scheduled reporting time.[1]

ARTICLE 53

SICK LEAVE

53.1 Unlimited Usage – No Accrual.

53.1.1 Length of Sick Leave.

53.1.1.1 A member of the Department may be permitted up to six calendar months of continual sick leave for any illness or injury not sustained in the line of duty. If unable to return to duty after this period, his case will be reviewed by the Chief and one of the following determinations will be made:

Temporary termination from the payroll with reinstatement rights at any time within one year.

Retirement from active service if so entitled.

[1] ***Englewood, Colorado and Englewood Police Benefit Association.***

Dismissal from the department.

An extension of sick leave.

53.1.1.2 Prior to making his determination, the Chief will obtain a written report from the Police Physician which shall include the report, if any, of the member's personal physician.[1]

53.2 Unlimited Accrual.

53.2.1 Rates of Accrual.

53.2.1.1 Employees shall be granted sick leave entitlements according to the following schedule and under the following procedures:

53.2.1.2 Employees shall be granted full pay during absences due to sickness or other physical disability, to the extent of the sick leave credits, upon the following terms and conditions.

53.2.1.3 Employees with less than one (1) year of service shall earn sick leave credits at the rate of eight (8) hours per calendar month of service which shall be credited on the first day of the month next following the completion of each credited month of service.

53.2.1.4 Employees with more than one (1) year of service shall earn sick leave credits at the rate of eleven (11) hours per calendar month of service which shall be credited on the first day of the month next following the completion of each credited month of service.

53.2.1.5 A credited month of service is defined as a calendar month in which an employee has been compensated for all but 3 or less shifts.[2]

[1] ***Rochester, New York and Rochester Police Locust Club.***

[2] ***Buffalo, New York and Buffalo Police Benevolent Association.***

53.2.2 The annual sick leave allowance for each employee shall be computed on the basis of five (5) workdays sick leave for each calendar quarter worked in the year, plus one (1) day sick leave for the year of service, or a total of twenty-one (21) sick days in each calendar year.[1]

53.3 Use of Sick Leave.

53.3.1 Accumulated paid sick leave credits may be used, subject to appointing authority approval, by an employee in pay status, but only in the following instances:

53.3.1.1 a. An employee may use paid sick leave credits when the employee is off work because of a temporary illness or injury.

53.3.1.2 b. Sick leave may be used by permanently disabled employees until all accruals of the employee have been exhausted or until the employee is retired by the Retirement Board subject to the conditions listed below. For the purposes of this Section, permanent disability shall mean the employee suffers from a disabling physical injury or illness and is thereby prevented from engaging in any County occupation for which he or she is qualified by reason of education, training or experience. Sick leave credits may be used under this provision only when the following requirements are met:

53.3.1.3 1. An application for retirement due to disability has been filed with the Retirement Board; and

53.3.1.4 2. Satisfactory medical evidence of such disability is received by the appointing authority within thirty (30) days of the start of use of sick leave for permanent disability. The appointing authority may review medical evidence and order further examination as he deems necessary, and may terminate use of sick leave when such further examination demonstrates

[1] ***Bethlehem, Pennsylvania and Fraternal Order of Police.***

that the employee is not disabled, or when the appointing authority determines that the medical evidence is insufficient, or where the above conditions have not been met.

53.3.1.5 c. <u>Communicable Disease</u> – An employee may use paid sick leave credits while under a physician's orders to remain secluded due to exposure to a communicable disease.

53.3.1.6 d. <u>Sick Leave Utilization for Pregnancy Disability</u> – Every female employee shall be entitled to at least four (4) months leave of absence on account of pregnancy disability and to use available sick leave or vacation pay entitlements during such leave.

53.3.1.7 1. Application for such leave must be made by the employee to the appointing authority accompanied by a written statement of disability from the employee's attending physician. The statement must address itself to the employee's general physical condition having considered the nature of the work performed by the employee, and it must indicate the date of the commencement of the disability as well as the date the physician anticipates the disability to terminate. The appointing authority retains the right to medical review of all requests for such leave.

53.3.1.8 2. If a female employee does not apply for sick leave and the appointing authority believes that the employee is not able to properly perform her work or that her general health is impaired due to disability caused or contributed to by pregnancy, miscarriage, abortion, childbirth or recovery therefrom, the employee shall be required to undergo a physical examination by a physician selected by the Employer, and the cost of such examination shall be borne by the Employer. Should the medical report so recommend, a mandatory leave shall be imposed upon the employee for the duration of the disability.

53.3.1.9 3. If all accrued sick leave has been utilized by the employee, the employee shall be considered on leave without pay. Sick leave may not be utilized after the employee has been released from the hospital unless the employee has provided the Employer with a written statement from her attending physician stating that her disability continues and the projected date of the employee's recovery from such disability.

53.3.1.10 e. Medical and Dental Appointments – An employee may use paid sick leave credits for medical and dental appointments as follows:

53.3.1.11 1. For working time used in keeping medical and dental appointments for the employee's own care; and

53.3.1.12 2. Effective the first of the month following the execution of this agreement, for working time (not over forty (40) hours in each fiscal year) used by an employee for pre-scheduled medical and dental appointments for an immediate family member living in the employee's home and for children and parents who may reside outside of the employee's home. Such use of sick leave credits shall be accounted for by the department on a fiscal year basis. Any balance of the forty (40) hours remaining at the end of the fiscal year shall not be carried over to the next year; Employers shall notify the employee if the maximum allowance is reached. Authorization to use sick leave for this purpose is contingent on availability of accumulated sick leave credits; it is not an additional allotment of sick leave which employees may change.

53.3.1.13 Emergency Care of Family – Effective the first of the month following the execution of this Agreement, an employee may use paid sick leave for working time used in cases of illness, or injury to, an immediate family member living in the employee's home, or for children and parents who may reside outside of the employee's home.

53.3.1.14 g. Death of Family Member – An employee may use said sick leave credits for absence from work because of a death in the employee's immediate family, but this shall not exceed three (3) working days plus up to two (2) days of work time for necessary travel.

53.3.1.15 h. Definition of Immediate Family – For the purposes of this Section, the immediate family shall be restricted to the spouse, son, stepson, daughter, stepdaughter, father, stepfather, mother, stepmother, brother, sister, grandparent, grandchild, father-in-law, mother-in-law, son-in-law, daughter-in-law, brother-in-law or sister-in-law, of an employee.[1]

53.4 Minimum Usage of Sick Leave.

53.4.1 Credits to and charges against sick leave are made in minimum amounts of one-tenth (1/10) hour. Unused sick leave credits accumulate from year to year. When an employee is separated, other than through retirement, accumulated sick leave credits shall be canceled, unless the separation results from layoff in which case the accumulated credits shall be restored if the employee is re-employed in a permanent position within the period of his layoff eligibility.[2]

53.5 Sick Leave While on Vacation.

53.5.1 If an employee, while on vacation, contracts an illness or injury, or experiences a death in the family which would warrant paid sick leave had the member been at work, such employee shall, upon showing proper evidence acceptable to the Employer, be allowed to charge such absence to sick leave rather than to vacation leave.[3]

[1] ***Contra Costa County, California and the Deputy Sheriffs' Association.***

[2] ***Contra Costa County, California and the Deputy Sheriffs' Association.***

[3] ***Stark County, Ohio Sheriff and Fraternal Order of Police, Ohio Labor Council, Inc.***

53.6 Vacation/Sick Leave on Holidays.

53.6.1 Whenever a sworn Police Officer who is scheduled to work on a holiday as part of his/her normal duty schedule becomes sick on a holiday, the officer shall be charged with using eight (8) hours' sick leave, and shall also be credited with earning eight (8) hours' compensatory time.[1]

53.7 Family Sick Leave.

53.7.1 Use of Sick Leave.

53.7.1.1 An employee may also be granted up to a maximum of sixty (60) hours of paid sick leave in a twelve-month period for the purpose of caring for a member of his/her immediate family. In addition, if the employee requests paid sick leave in excess of sixty (60) hours in order to care, or arrange care, for a member of his/her immediate family who is critically or terminally ill, additional sick leave is available to the employee when granted by the appointing authority upon receipt of satisfactory verification from a physician.

53.7.1.2 Immediate family includes husband, wife, child, stepchild, brother, stepbrother, sister, stepsister, parent, stepparent, or any person serving as a parent, or who has served as a parent, or any other person living in the same household as the employee.[2]

53.8 Verification of Sick Leave.

53.8.1 The Employer may, at its option, reasonably require a physician's statement of the nature and identity of the illness, the need for the employee's absence and an estimated duration of the absence for any illness which causes an employee absence

[1] ***City of Ontario, California and Ontario Police Officers Association.***

[2] ***San Diego County, California and San Diego County Deputy Sheriffs' Association.***

in excess of three (3) days or at any time if the Employer believes the employee may be abusing the sick leave privilege.[1]

53.9 Examination by Physician on Return to Work.

53.9.1 Any employee who returns to work after an absence in excess of forty-eight (48) consecutive working hours due to illness or physical incapacity may be required by his department head to undergo a medical examination.[2]

53.10 Payment for Accrued but Unused Sick Leave.

53.10.1 Rate of Payment.

53.10.1.1 An officer who has accumulated sick leave at the time of his retirement shall receive credit in an amount equal to thirty percent (30%) of the first four hundred and eighty (480) hours of such accumulated sick leave, fifty percent (50%) of the second four hundred and eighty (480) hours, and seventy percent (70%) of all accumulated sick leave in excess of nine hundred and sixty (960) hours up to a maximum of 2,064 hours. The cash value of such credit will be calculated on the basis of the officer's pay rate at the time of retirement.

53.10.1.2 Upon retirement, an officer may elect to receive his sick leave credit through one of three options as follows: Option #1: He may elect to receive a lump sum cash payment for his sick leave credit. Option #2: To the extent that credit is available or until the officer reaches age 65, the cash value of such credit may be applied toward the continuation of the officer's employee and dependent group hospital and medical insurance plan. Under

[1] ***State of Oregon and Oregon State Police Officers Association.***

[2] ***Anaheim, California and Anaheim Police Association.***

Option #2, the retired officer or his heirs or estate will receive a lump sum cash payment for any unused sick leave credit remaining when the retiree reaches age 65 or upon his death. Further, the retired officer may elect to receive a lump sum cash payment for the balance of his sick leave credit at any time after his initial election of Option #2. Option #3: He may elect to have his sick leave credit paid to him on a bi-weekly basis, with each bi-weekly payment not to exceed the officer's regular bi-weekly pay at the time of his retirement.[1]

53.11 Conversion of Sick Leave to Life Insurance Benefits.

53.11.1 The designated beneficiary of a Unit member will be paid for all accumulated sick leave hours that remain on the Employer's official file at the time of the death of the employee and payment will be based upon the employee's base hourly rate of pay at the time of death. The beneficiary shall be that person designated on the Employee Declaration of Beneficiary card on file in the Personnel Department.[2]

53.12 Conversion of Sick Leave to Retirement Benefits.

53.12.1 Upon retirement of an employee, and as provided by State law and regulations established by the retirement system, fifty percent (50%) of an employee's accumulated sick leave shall be applied in the form of increased retirement benefits.[3]

53.12.2 Upon retirement, an employee's accumulated sick leave shall be converted to retirement time on the basis of one

[1] ***Portland, Oregon and Portland Police Association.***

[2] ***Phoenix, Arizona and Phoenix Law Enforcement Union.***

[3] ***Lake Oswego, Oregon and Lake Oswego Police Officers' Association.***

(1) day of retirement service credit for each day of accumulated sick leave credit.[1]

53.13 Sick Leave Incentive Pay.

53.13.1 For each calendar quarter in which an employee records perfect attendance (exclusive of on-the-job injuries and funeral of immediate family), after the completion of six (6) months' employment, such employee shall be eligible for eight (8) hours' pay. Payment shall be made on the last payday in July. Upon request of the employee and at the discretion of the Employer, an employee may utilize time off in lieu of pay for perfect attendance. Holidays, vacation, and compensatory time off shall not count against perfect attendance.[2]

53.13.2 All employees shall have established a $150 sick leave occurrence bank. For each occurrence of charged sick leave during a payroll year, $25.00 shall be deducted from the employee's individual bank. Employees on the payroll at the end of the payroll year shall receive a voucher payment equal to the balance remaining in their individual occurrence bank.[3]

53.14 Sick Leave Time Off Incentive.

53.14.1 Bonus Days.

53.14.1.1 Each employee is entitled to five (5) sick bonus days per calendar year contingent on unused sick leave. One-half (½) day of sick leave hours shall be deducted for each day of sick leave taken. Sick leave bonus days shall be deducted as time off during the calendar year following the year in which they

[1] ***Contra Costa County, California and the Deputy Sheriffs' Association.***

[2] ***Council Bluffs, Iowa and Fraternal Order of Police.***

[3] ***Elgin, Illinois and Unit #54, Policemen's Benevolent and Protective Association.***

are earned. Sick leave bonuses shall not be carried over into the following year except with the approval of the appointing authority. Any portion of a sick day used shall be considered a full day for the purpose of this section.[1]

Months Worked	Sick Days Taken										
	0	1	2	3	4	5	6	7	8	9	10
12	5	4.5	4	3.5	3	2.5	2	1.5	1	.5	0
11	4.5	4	3.5	3	2.5	2	1.5	1	.5	0	
10	4	3.5	3	2.5	2	1.5	1	.5	0		
9	3.5	3	2.5	2	1.5	1	.5	0			
8	3	2.5	2	1.5	1	.5	0				
7	2.5	2	1.5	1	.5	0					
6	2	1.5	1	.5	0						
5	1.5	1	.5	0							
4	1	.5	0								
3	.5	0									

53.15 Sick Leave Bank.

53.15.1 It is agreed upon appointment as officer, an employee shall have available to him, or her, to provide for a loan bank of eighty (80) hours' on-duty illness/injury (renewable upon payback) leave, which an officer who is injured on duty is eligible to use to supplement salary benefits from workers' compensation. These eighty (80) hours are to be a loan charged

[1] ***Lucas County, Ohio Sheriff's Office and District 2A Transportation, Technical, Warehouse, Industrial and Service Employees Union.***

against the sick leave accrued in accordance with State, City or County Code. Any of the on-duty injury leave bank hours taken shall be deducted from accumulated sick leave after thirty-six (36) months of employment. The rate of payback shall be at the rate of eight (8) hours per month. If an employee terminates before the unearned on-duty injury leave bank hours are repaid, the hours not yet repaid shall be deducted from the final paycheck.[1]

53.16 Donation of Leave to Another Employee.

53.16.1 An employee may donate sick, vacation and/or personal leave time to another employee who has exhausted all sick leave and is in documented need of sick leave due to illness. The sick, vacation and/or personal leave time will be valued at the donating employee's current rate of pay, and then converted to the appropriate amount of time based on the donee's current rate of pay. (For example, if an employee earning $10.00 an hour donates two hours of sick leave to an employee earning $20.00 an hour, the donee will be credited with one hour of sick leave.)[2]

53.17 Conversion of Sick Leave to Other Leave.

53.17.1 Basis for Conversion.

53.17.1.1 It is mutually understood by the parties hereto that the police officer's duty is hazardous in nature, in that it is strenuous both mentally and physically, and in many instances, involves physical danger. Therefore, because of this fact, the Employer will allow sick leave to be converted to leave to be known as hazardous duty leave as follows:

[1] ***Bellevue, Washington and Bellevue Police Officers Guild.***

[2] ***State of Oregon and Oregon State Police Officers' Association.***

53.17.1.2 When an officer has accumulated and maintains a total of 360 hours of sick leave, he/she may convert any part of the sick leave accumulated over and above the 360 hours to hazardous duty leave on the basis of eight (8) hours' hazardous duty leave for 24 hours of sick leave.

53.17.1.3 When a police officer has accumulated and maintains a total of 720 hours of sick leave, the police officer may convert any sick leave accumulated over and above 720 hours to hazardous duty leave on a basis of one (1) hour hazardous duty leave for one (1) hour of sick leave.[1]

53.17.2 Employees with more than 1,200 hours of accumulated sick leave may, on February 1 of each year, convert sick leave accumulated, but unused, in the prior calendar year to compensatory time, provided the total sick leave accumulation does not fall below 1,200 hours.[2]

ARTICLE 54

LIGHT-DUTY ASSIGNMENTS

54.1 Limited Duty.

54.1.1 For any employee whose physical condition prevents him from performing his normal work assignments, the Employer agrees to make a reasonable effort to place him in a classification he can perform within the Police Department.

54.1.1.1 Employees who have been on authorized leave due to serious illness or injury, personal or work connected, may

[1] ***Albuquerque, New Mexico and Albuquerque Police Officers' Association.***

[2] ***The City of Euclid, Ohio and Euclid Fraternal Order of Police, Lodge #18.***

upon release from his or her physician and upon presentation of said release to the Chief and concurrence by the Employer physician, return to a limited-duty assignment within sworn service of the Police Department. Said assignment shall be as directed by the Chief and may result in reassignment of other sworn personnel. Said reassignment shall not be affected by time limits set forth elsewhere in this Agreement but shall be governed by the term of the limited-duty assignment.

54.1.1.2 The intent of this provision is to permit the return to work as soon as is medically possible to employees who are affected as set forth in the above paragraph. Further, the parties understand that "limited duty" refers to duty other than normal outside patrol duties and that it is not the intent that said limited duty is to be of a "make work" nature.[1]

ARTICLE 55

BEREAVEMENT LEAVE

55.1 Funeral Leave.

55.1.1 All Police officers shall be allowed five (5) working days beginning with the day of death, with full pay, in each case of death of a member of the immediate family. The term "immediate family" shall be understood to include the following: mother, father, brother, sister, son, daughter, spouse.

55.1.1.1 In other cases – grandmother, grandfather, grandson, granddaughter, son-in-law, daughter-in-law, parent-in-law or near relative who resides in the household – absence will be allowed with pay through the day of the funeral with a maximum

[1] ***Fairbanks, Alaska and Fairbanks Police Department Employees Association.***

of three (3) days. Days not scheduled as workdays will be counted but not paid.

55.1.1.2 In all cases of death of near relative – aunt, uncle, niece, nephew, brother-in-law, and sister-in-law – the officer will be paid for the absence on the full day necessary to attend the funeral.[1]

55.1.2 Pallbearers. Employees who act as pallbearers during regular work hours shall receive up to four (4) hours of funeral leave.[2]

ARTICLE 56

FAMILY AND MATERNITY LEAVE

56.1 Family and Medical Leaves.

56.1.1 Pursuant to the provisions of the federal Family and Medical Leave Act of 1993 and the regulations thereunder (which shall govern employee rights and obligations as to family and medical leaves wherever they may conflict with the provisions of this paragraph), leaves of absence of up to twelve (12) weeks in any twelve (12) months will be granted to eligible employees who request them for the following reasons:

(a) for purposes associated with the birth or adoption of a child or the placement of a child with the employee for foster care,

(b) when they are unable to perform the functions of their positions because of temporary sickness or disability, and/or

[1] ***City of Erie, Pennsylvania and Hass Memorial Lodge #7, Fraternal Order of Police.***

[2] ***City of Janesville, Wisconsin and Janesville Police Supervisors' Association, Inc.***

(c) when they must care for their parent, spouse, registered domestic partner within the City Code, child, or other dependents and/or members of their households who have a serious medical condition.

56.1.1.1 Unless an employee elects to use accumulated paid leave benefits while on family and medical leaves such leaves are without pay. The Employee's group health, dental and life insurance benefits shall, however, be continued on the same basis as if the employee had not taken the leave.

56.1.1.2 Eligibility. Employees are eligible for family and medical leaves if they have accumulated at least twelve (12) months' employment service preceding the request for the leave and they must have worked at least one thousand forty-four (1,044) hours during the twelve (12)-month period immediately preceding the leave. Eligible spouses or registered domestic partners who both work for the Employer will be granted a combined twelve (12) weeks of leave in any twelve (12) months when such leaves are for the purposes referenced in clauses (a) and (c) above.

56.1.1.3 Notice Required. Employees must give thirty (30) calendar days' notice of the need for the leave if the need is foreseeable. If the need for the leave is not foreseeable, notice must be given as soon as it is practicable to do so. Employees must confirm their verbal notices for family and medical leaves in writing. Notification requirements may be waived by the Employer for good cause shown.

56.1.1.4 Intermittent Leave. If medically necessary due to the serious medical condition of the employee, or that of the employee's spouse, child, parent, registered domestic partner within the meaning of the City Code, or other dependents and/or members of their households who have a serious medical condition, leave may be taken on an intermittent schedule. In cases of the birth, adoption or foster placement of a child, family and medical leave may be taken intermittently only when expressly approved by the Employer.

56.1.1.5 Medical Certification. The Employer may require certification from an attending health care provider on a form it provides. The Employer may also request second medical opinions provided it pays the full cost required.

56.1.1.6 Relationship Between Leave and Accrued Paid Leave. Employees may use accrued vacation, sick leave or compensatory time while on leave. The use of such paid leave benefits will not affect the maximum allowable duration of leaves under this subdivision.

56.1.1.7 Reinstatement. Upon the expiration of family and medical leaves, employees will be returned to an equivalent position within their former job classification.[1]

56.2 Maternity Leave.

56.2.1 Leave will be granted for pregnancy. The time for commencing and terminating such leave will be a medical decision certified by the attending physician. Sick leave and vacation credits may be used to cover all or part of the absence. Leave without pay for a pregnancy-related disability will be granted upon request.[2]

56.3 Parental Leave.

56.3.1 A department head or designee shall grant a female permanent employee's request for an unpaid leave of absence for purposes of pregnancy, childbirth, recovery therefrom, or

[1] ***City of Minneapolis, Minnesota and Police Officers Federation of Minneapolis.***

[2] ***Portland, Oregon and Portland Police Association.***

care for the newborn child for a period not to exceed one (1) year including any paid leave taken for said pregnancy, childbirth, recovery or care for the newborn child.

56.3.1.1 A male spouse or male parent, who is a permanent employee, shall be entitled to an unpaid leave of absence for a period not to exceed one (1) year to care for his newborn child including any paid leave taken for care for the newborn child.

56.3.1.2 A department head or designee may grant a permanent employee's request for an unpaid leave of absence for the adoption of a child for a period not to exceed one (1) year except the department shall grant said one (1) year unpaid leave of absence when the adoption agency required an adoptive parent not to work outside the home during the first year of adoption as a condition of adoption.[1]

56.4 Continuation of Insurance During Maternity Leave.

56.4.1 The Employer shall pay the employee premium for a period of thirteen (13) pay periods while the employee is on medical leave without pay or maternity leave.[2]

ARTICLE 57

TIME OFF PLAN

57.1 General Leave.

57.1.1 General Leave is compensated leave for those eligible employees who are absent from duty because of illness, death

[1] ***State of California and California Union of Safety Employees.***

[2] ***Santa Clara County, California and Santa Clara Deputy Sheriff's Association.***

in the family, medical or dental care appointments, family care, personal reasons or who utilize time off as vacation.

57.2 Applicability.

57.2.1 The General Leave Plan shall apply to regular and part-time employees in the General Management, Executive, Confidential, Professional Employees,' Peace Officers' and Non-Sworn Police Employees' Units. This Plan shall also apply to the City Manager and City Attorney.

57.2.1.1 General Leave Credits. Eligible regular full-time employees shall be entitled to the following annual accrual equivalent to an eight-hour workday.

Years of Annual General Completed Service	Leave Accrual
1 through 4	160 working hours (20 days)
5 through 9	184 working hours (23 days)
10 through 14	208 working hours (26 days)
15 or more	224 working hours (28 days)

57.2.1.2 General leave shall be earned in working hours on a monthly basis.

57.2.1.3 Eligible part-time employees shall accrue hourly general leave credits in an amount proportionate to the ratio of scheduled hours per week to the standard workweek. In no case shall the number of accrued leave days per month exceed the number of general leave days allowed based on years of service. Part-time employees working less than 20 hours a week, and temporary and emergency employees shall not earn general leave.

57.2.1.4 General leave credits are not earned during periods of unpaid leave. Absence without pay or partial month's employment (e.g. last month of employment) shall cause the monthly accrual of leave to be reduced on a pro-rated basis. Any reductions in leave accruals shall be in increments of one hour.

57.2.1.5 General Leave During First Year: Upon completion of six months of continuous active service following appointment, regular and part-time employees shall be eligible to earn general leave credits. Upon the completion of said period of service, regular employees shall be credited with eighty (80) working hours (ten days) of general leave (part-time employees shall be credited with pro-rated general leave) and shall thereafter accrue general leave at the rate provided in section (1) above.

57.2.1.6 Maximum Accumulation: General leave credits may be accumulated until a maximum of 540 hours is reached, at which time the excess of hours will be lost. An employee who has exceeded or is nearing the 540-hour maximum and who is in jeopardy of losing future hours of earned credit due to current inability to use or transfer the hours of credit, may propose a program subject to the City Manager's approval to effectively reduce the general leave balance within two years by either using the general leave credits as provided in this Agreement or converting the credits to pay or sick leave as provided in this Agreement, or have General Leave hours in excess of the 540 hour maximum thereafter accrue to the sick leave bank, or any combination of these methods. Whenever such a program has been approved by the City Manager, the City Manager may allow the employee to accumulate a maximum of 640 hours of general leave credit. Solely for the purposes of this section, any employee may establish a sick leave bank subject to City Manager approval.

57.2.1.7 Employees otherwise exempt from the Fair Labor Standards Act (FLSA) shall not have their salary reduced for General Leave use for absences of less than a day, when all General, administrative or compensatory time balances, or sick leave balance if appropriate, are exhausted. Such absences shall be shown as negative General Leave balances; the negative balance shall be reduced by the crediting of future earned leave.

57.3 General Leave Implementation.

57.3.1 When an employee who has accrued vacation and sick leave credits becomes eligible to participate in the General Leave Plan, unused leave credits shall be transitioned on the first day of General Leave Plan eligibility as follows:

57.3.1.1 <u>Vacation Leave Credits</u>: All unused vacation leave credits shall be converted to general leave credits on an hour-for-hour basis.

57.3.1.2 <u>Sick Leave Credits</u>: All unused sick leave credits shall be maintained as a bank of sick leave hours to be used in accordance with the provisions of the General Leave Plan.

57.3.1.3 During the first six months of participation in the General Leave Plan, employees who have accrued sick leave credits transferred to a sick leave bank, shall be permitted to use sick leave for absence due to his/her illness, and for medical and dental appointments. Beginning the seventh month of General Leave Plan participation, an employee may use sick leave credits in accordance with Article V of this Plan. New employees hired into classes covered by this General Leave Plan will not be eligible to establish a sick leave bank.

57.4 General Leave Conversion to Pay or Sick Leave.

57.4.1 To be eligible for General Leave Conversion, an employee must have a minimum of 22 days (176 hours) of general leave or sick leave credits (or a combination thereof) remaining after the conversion. Each year in December up to sixty-four (64) hours of general leave may be converted as follows:

57.4.1.1 Buy-Back: Upon using one-half of general leave credits accrued during the preceding 12-month period from December 1 through November 30, an employee may request to receive pay for up to sixty-four (64) hours of general leave credits at the current hourly salary rate, according to the following schedule:

Years of Service	Hours
1 – 5	40
6 – 10	48
11 – 15	56
16+	64

57.4.1.2 Sick Leave: In lieu of pay, an employee with a sick leave bank may convert up to 40 hours of general leave to the sick leave bank. General leave credits may be converted to sick leave credits on an hour-for-hour basis in order to provide security against extended illness and/or to accumulate PERS service credits.[1]

57.5 General Leave Usage.

57.5.1 1. Request and Approval: Department Directors are responsible for arranging leave schedules so that adequate personnel are available to carry on necessary City work. The use of general leave shall require approval of the Department Director or his/her designee. Whenever possible, general leave requests must be approved in advance of the days to be taken

[1] ***City of Walnut Creek, California and Walnut Creek Police Association.***

as general leave. The procedure for requesting the use of general leave shall be as follows:

57.5.1.1 a. Non-Medical Personal Leave: Any leave that can be reasonably forecast or anticipated, such as vacation, care of children, personal business, etc., shall require prior approval of the Department Director, or the employee's supervisor. The time and amount of general leave to be taken for non-medical purposes shall be determined by the Department Director with due regard for the wishes of the employee and particular regard for the needs of the City.

57.5.1.2 b. Medical Leave: An absence from work due to an employee's illness or for a medical or dental appointment shall be referred to as medical leave. The Department Director may require an employee to furnish satisfactory evidence justifying the need to be absent from work for medical reasons. The determination and final approval of general leave for medical reasons shall be made by the Department Director.

57.5.1.3 c. An employee may request general leave for an unanticipated absence from work (e.g. medical leave, car trouble, care of children, etc.) by notifying his/her supervisor within one hour after the time set for reporting to work on the first day of such leave and as often thereafter as directed by his/her supervisor. Final approval for an unanticipated, unscheduled absence shall require Department Director approval. Failure to request an unscheduled leave in the manner described may result in lost work time charged as leave without pay or unauthorized leave of absence.

57.5.1.4 d. Any employee who is absent from work on an unscheduled leave may not engage in work or other activities which will inhibit his/her ability to report for work at the earliest possible time.

57.5.1.5 e. Medical examination by the Employer's examining physician may be requested by the Department Director after prolonged, serious, or repetitious illness, injury, or major surgery. An employee's return to duty following illness or injury is subject to the approval of the Department Director Personnel Officer based upon medical information supplied by the employee's physician and/or the Employer's physician.

57.5.1.6 f. General leave may not be used to supplement long-term disability payments.

57.5.1.7 g. <u>On-The-Job Injury</u>: An employee absent from work because of a temporary disability which is defined as industrial under the Workers' Compensation Act shall be entitled to an industrial leave as follows:

57.5.1.8 (1) Non-public safety employees may continue to receive regular pay for up to sixty (60) calendar days when incapacitated for work due to an on-the-job injury or illness.

57.5.1.9 (2) Public safety employees may continue to receive regular salary for up to one year when incapacitated for work due to an on-the-job injury or illness, as provided for in the Labor Code.

57.5.1.10 h. <u>Use of General Leave When Permanently Incapacitated</u>: General leave shall not be used to continue the salary or employment of any employee after it has been determined that such employee is permanently incapacitated for a return to employment and is eligible for disability retirement.

57.5.1.11 i. <u>Disability Income Protection</u>: A disability income protection plan shall be provided for all employees covered by the General Leave Program. The disability income protection plan shall have a waiting period of thirty (30) calendar days before the benefits shall be extended to an employee. The benefits, terms and conditions are described in the Long-Term Disability Insurance Plan.

57.5.1.12 j. General Leave Advance: The City Manager may advance up to ten (10) days of general leave. Should an employee take general leave in excess of his/her accrual and subsequently terminate, the Employer shall deduct from his/her final paycheck an amount equal to the unaccrued general leave that was used.

57.5.1.13 k. Use of Sick Leave: Only employees who have unused sick leave credits earned under the Employer's sick leave plan shall be eligible to establish a sick leave bank as provided by this Plan. Credits in a sick leave bank may be used if one of the following conditions apply:

57.5.1.14 (1) With the approval of the Department Director, an employee absent due to his/her illness or injury for more than eight (8) cumulative days during any calendar year may use unused sick leave balances for absences due to further illness or injuries prior to using further general leave.

57.5.1.15 (2) With the approval of the Department Director, an employee who has exhausted all general leave credits may use any unused sick leave credits for valid medical reasons.[1]

57.6 General Leave at Termination.

57.6.1 An employee with more than six (6) months of active, continuous service whose employment with the City terminates shall be paid for each hour of unused general leave. Payment for unused general leave shall be made at the hourly rate of pay in effect for such employee at the time of separation.

[1] ***City of Walnut Creek, California and Walnut Creek Police Association.***

57.6.1.1 An employee may use up to ten (10) days of general leave to extend a termination date beyond the last day actually worked. The use of more than ten (10) days shall be allowed only with the consent of the City Manager, or in the case of employees appointed by the City Council, the consent of the City Council.

57.6.1.2 When termination is caused by the death of an employee, pay for unused general leave shall be paid to the beneficiary the employee has designated. Such designation shall be in writing, signed by the employee and filed with the Personnel Office. In the event an employee has not designated a beneficiary, the payment shall be made to the estate of the employee.[1]

ARTICLE 58

MILITARY LEAVE

58.1 Military Leave.

58.1.1 An appointing authority may grant leave without pay to regular employees for the purpose of service in the Armed Forces, or for the purpose of undergoing training duty in the Armed Forces, provided that such leave shall be with pay during the first thirty (30) days of such leave of absence during each year. Any such leaves shall be reported to the Employer.[2]

58.2 Short Term Military Leaves of Absence (Reserve or National Guard Duty) – Less Than 90 Days Per Calendar Year.

58.2.1 Subject to the terms and conditions provided in this Article, employees shall be entitled to time off with pay when

[1] ***City of Walnut Creek, California and Walnut Creek Police Association.***

[2] ***Des Moines, Iowa and Des Moines Police Bargaining Unit Association.***

they are required to take a leave of absence for: (i) military training duty and/or (ii) military duty in the State because of riot or civil disturbance.

58.2.1.1 Maximum Amount of Time Off With Pay.

58.2.1.2 Continuous Service – If either military training duty leave or military duty on account of civil disturbance is limited to a single period during the calendar year, then such leave shall be granted with pay not to exceed fifteen (15) successive calendar days (including Saturdays, Sundays and legal holidays) during a calendar year.

58.2.1.3 Intermittent Service – If either military training duty leave or military duty on account of civil disturbance is taken on an intermittent basis during the calendar year, then such leave with pay shall not exceed eighty (80) hours during the calendar year.

58.2.1.4 Combined Maximum – During each calendar year of this Agreement, the amount of time off with pay for military leaves of absence provided hereunder that is taken by an employee on a continuous service basis, together with the amount taken on an intermittent service basis, shall not exceed eighty (80) hours in aggregate for military duty in the State because of riot or civil disturbance.

58.2.1.5 All employees who, because of service in any of the wars of the United States, are eligible for veterans' preferences for employment by the City and/or as provided in the State statutes, shall receive full City pay plus all military pay for duty covered under this Article, above. In all other cases, the employee agrees to allow a payroll adjustment to his/her biweekly paycheck, deducting an amount equal to his/her military pay for such duty (up to a maximum equal to his/her City pay received under this Article, above), and to make no subsequent claim for it whatsoever. Such deduction shall be administered so as not to reduce employee pension benefits.

58.2.1.6 Return to City Employment From Short Term Military Leave – The time off with pay for short-term military leaves provided hereunder shall be granted only if the employee taking such leave reports back for City employment at the beginning of his/her next regularly scheduled eight-hour work shift after the expiration of the last calendar day necessary to travel from the place of training or civil disturbance duty to the City following such employee's release from military duty.

58.2.1.7 Long Term Military Leaves of Absence – 90 Days or Longer Per Calendar Year

58.2.1.8 Employees who enlist or are inducted or ordered into active service in the Armed Forces of the United States or the State, pursuant to an act of the Congress of the United States or the Legislature of the State or an order of the Commanders-in-Chief thereof, shall be granted a leave of absence during the period of such service.

58.2.1.9 Upon completion and release from active duty under honorable conditions and subject to the terms and conditions provided below, employees on military leaves of absence shall be reinstated into the positions they held at the time of taking such leave of absence or to a position of like seniority, status, pay and salary advancement, provided, however, that they are still qualified to perform the duties of their positions or similar positions.

58.2.1.10 The rights to reinstatement provided in this Article, above, shall be terminated unless the employee satisfies the following conditions:

58.2.1.11 Reinstatement From Military Reserve or National Guard Duty.

58.2.1.12 Initial Enlistment With At Least Three Consecutive Months Of Active Duty – An employee who is a member of the Reserve or National Guard component of the Armed Forces of the United States and is ordered to an initial period of active duty for training of not less than three consecutive months shall make application for re-employment within 31 days after: (i) such employee's release from active duty from training after satisfactory service, or (ii) at such employee's discharge from hospitalization incident to such active duty for training or one year after such employee's scheduled release from such training, whichever is earlier.

58.2.1.13 All Other Active Duty – Subject to Section 673b, Title 10, United States Code, an employee not covered under this Article, above, shall report back for work with the City: (i) at the beginning of the employee's next regularly scheduled work shift after the expiration of the last calendar day necessary to travel from the place of training to the place of employment following such employee's release from active duty, or (ii) such employee's discharge from hospitalization incident to such active duty for training or one year after such employee's scheduled release from such training, whichever is earlier.

58.2.1.14 For purposes of interpretation and construction of the provisions of this subsection, full-time training or any full-time duty performed by a member of the Reserve or National Guard component of the Armed Forces of the United States shall be considered active duty training.

58.2.1.15 Other Military Service With Active Duty Of At Least 90 Consecutive Days – An employee inducted or enlisted into active duty with the Armed Forces of the United States for a period of at least 90 consecutive days, where such active duty is not covered above, shall, upon satisfactory completion of military service, make application for reemployment within 90 days after: (i) such employee's release from active duty, or (ii) such employee's discharge from hospitalization incident to such active duty or one year after such employee's scheduled release from active duty, whichever is earlier.

58.2.1.16 Exclusions From Reinstatement Benefits – In the event an individual granted a leave of absence for military service under this Article fails to meet the requirements provided in this Article, above, or the employee's military service is not covered under these two subsections, the Employer shall be under no obligation or requirement to reinstate such individual to City employment.

58.2.1.17 Military Funeral Leave of Absence – Employees shall be allowed to attend military funerals of veterans without loss of pay when a request for the leave is made by a proper veterans' organization that the service of such officer or employee is desired for the proper conduct of a military funeral.

58.2.1.18 Induction Examinations – Employees shall be entitled to time off with pay for time spent taking physical or mental examinations to determine their eligibility for induction or service in the Armed Forces of the United States; such time off with pay shall be granted only for examinations conducted by a United States military agency.

58.2.1.19 Administration – The Chief of Police shall have the authority to establish such rules and procedures that he deems necessary to administer the military leave benefits provided by this Article. These rules and procedures shall cover, but not be limited to, requirements that employees provide the Chief of Police with reasonable advance notice of any contemplated military leave and the appropriate military orders and papers that fully document such military leave.[1]

58.2.2 Any full-time and non-temporary employee who enters active service of the Armed Forces of the United States shall receive a military leave without pay for a period of his initial enlistment or induction not to exceed more than four (4) years plus one (1) additional year for voluntary extension if this service is at the request and for the convenience of the Government plus any involuntary service. An employee returning from military service shall be re-employed in accordance with the applicable Federal and State statutes and shall be entitled to any other benefits set forth in this Agreement, provided the employee satisfies the eligibility requirements set forth in this Agreement. Application for military leave of absence shall be made to the Employer in writing as soon as the employee is notified of acceptance or induction into military service and in any event not less than two (2) weeks prior to the employee's separation of employment with the Employer. All benefits such as insurance, vacation or personal days shall cease immediately upon the employee's separation from employment.

58.2.2.1 An employee shall not lose seniority while on active military leave if provisions in this section are met. The time counted in computing seniority shall include employment with the Employer prior to induction into the military service, a reasonable period between leaving his job and entering military service, not to exceed thirty (30) days, the entire period of his military service, and the period between his release from service and his return to work.

[1] ***City of Milwaukee, Wisconsin and Milwaukee Police Association, Local 21.***

58.2.2.2 Employees who return from active military leave shall commence to accrue benefits at the levels they would have received had they not entered service provided they meet all the provisions contained herein. In no case shall employees continue to accrue benefits while on active military leave.[1]

58.3 Effect of Extended Military Leave.

58.3.1 An employee who is granted a military leave of absence exceeding 180 calendar days may request payment for that part of general leave accumulation that remains as of the date the leave commences.[2]

ARTICLE 59

DISASTER TIME BANK

59.1 General.

59.1.1 The Disaster Time Bank shall continue in operation with the administration of such bank under the control of the Association. The purpose of the Disaster Time Bank is to provide the employees covered herein, in the event of a natural disaster or severe personal crisis, with a program whereby the employee may be afforded the opportunity to have other employees fulfill the responsibilities to the Employer in terms of working for the employee for a period not to exceed ten (10) days per request. All other time off must be exhausted: vacation days, bonus days, discretionary vacation days and compensatory time. This is to exclude all sick time.[3]

[1] ***Genesee County, Michigan and AFSCME Council 25.***

[2] ***City of Walnut Creek, California and Walnut Creek Police Association.***

[3] ***Toledo, Ohio and Toledo Police Patrolmens' Association.***

ARTICLE 60

JURY DUTY

60.1 General.

60.1.1 In the event any full-time employee is duly summoned to any court for the purpose of performing jury duty, he shall receive his regular compensation for any regularly-scheduled working hours spent in actual performance of such service.[1]

ARTICLE 61

OTHER LEAVES OF ABSENCE

61.1 Blood Donor Leave.

61.1.1 Employees covered by this Agreement who volunteer as blood donors to contribute to Employer-supported Blood Donor Organizations will be authorized the absence necessary to accomplish this purpose. The Blood Donor Organization's personnel will determine what amount of time the donor will need from the point of donation till they are released to go back to work.[2]

61.1.2 All officers who donate blood to Employer-approved Blood Drives shall receive four (4) hours of compensation time.[3]

61.2 Bone Marrow Donor Leave.

61.2.1 Pursuant to applicable statutes, employees who work twenty (20) or more hours per week shall, upon advance

[1] ***Anaheim, California and Anaheim Police Association.***

[2] ***Miami, Florida and Fraternal Order of Police.***

[3] ***Township of Middletown, New Jersey and Middletown Township Policemen's Benevolent Association, Inc., Local 124.***

notification to their immediate supervisor and approval by the Employer, be granted a paid leave of absence at the time they undergo medical procedures to donate bone marrow. At the time such employees request leave, they shall provide to their immediate supervisor written verification by a physician of the purpose and length of the required leave. The combined length of leaves for this purpose may not exceed forty (40) hours unless agreed to by the Employer in its sole discretion.[1]

61.3 Health Appointments.

61.3.1 Employees shall be entitled to reasonable time off with pay for necessary medical and dental appointments which cannot, with reasonable practicality, be scheduled outside of the normal workday. Except in the case of emergencies, the employee shall, in writing, inform the Chief of the time and day, at least five (5) days prior to such appointments. In the case of emergencies, the employee shall inform the Chief as soon as the appointment is made or completed, whichever is more medically practical. The scheduling of such time off shall be subject to the reasonable needs of the Employer.[2]

61.4 Pre-Induction Physical Examinations.

61.4.1 With the approval of his immediate supervisor, a full-time employee shall be excused from work, with pay, if he is ordered to report for a physical examination before compulsory induction into the military service. Such time off shall be for a period no longer than is necessary.[3]

[1] ***City of Minneapolis, Minnesota and Police Officers Federation of Minneapolis.***

[2] ***Greenwich, Connecticut and Silver Shield Association.***

[3] ***Genesee County, Michigan and AFSCME Council 25.***

61.5 Paid Educational Leave.

61.5.1 Employees selected by the Employer, with application through the chain of command, shall be granted leaves of absence for education purposes to attend conferences, seminars, briefing sessions, or other functions of a similar nature that are intended to improve or upgrade the individual's skill or professional ability in his police service. Employees who voluntarily attend college to upgrade their skills as professional law enforcement officers shall receive paid leaves of absence to take examinations, during assigned duty hours, subject to approval of the Employer.[1]

61.6 School Conference and Activities Leave.

61.6.1 Leaves of absence without pay of up to a total of sixteen (16) hours during a school year for the purpose of attending school conferences and classroom activities of the employee's child, provided that such conferences and classroom activities cannot be scheduled during non-work hours. When the need for the leave is foreseeable, the employee shall provide reasonable prior notice of the leave to their immediate supervisor and shall make a reasonable effort to schedule the leave so as not to disrupt the operations of the Employer. Employees may use accumulated vacation benefits or accumulated compensatory time for the duration of such leaves.[2]

61.6.2 Employees who are members of the Ohio National Guard will be granted emergency leave for mob, riot, flood, civil defense, or similar duties when so ordered by the Governor to assist civil authorities. Such leave will be <u>without pay</u> if it exceeds

[1] ***Aurora, Illinois and Association of Professional Police Officers.***

[2] ***City of Minneapolis, Minnesota and Police Officers Federation of Minneapolis.***

authorized paid military leave for the year. The leave will cover the official period of the emergency.[1]

61.7 Release Time for Civil Service Examinations.

61.7.1 Upon giving 48-hours' notice to his/her immediate supervisor, an Officer otherwise qualified shall be permitted to participate in a State Civil Service examination during the Officer's work hours if said examination is scheduled during that period.[2]

61.8 Voting Leave.

61.8.1 When an employee's actual work schedule prevents the employee from voting in any State, County or general election, then the employee may be granted paid time off duty to vote.[3]

61.9 Leaves for Personal Purposes.

61.9.1 A department head may authorize an employee to be absent without pay for personal reasons for a period or periods not to exceed a total of ten (10) working days in any calendar year; or five (5) working days in any one instance.[4]

61.10 Unpaid Leaves of Absence.

61.10.1 Criteria and Procedure. Subject to its reasonable operating needs and priorities, the Employer shall make a reasonable good faith effort to grant an application for leave of absence without pay not to exceed six (6) calendar months. Such leave shall not be approved for an employee for the purpose

[1] ***Stark County, Ohio Sheriff and Fraternal Order of Police, Ohio Labor Council, Inc.***

[2] ***State of California and California Association of Highway Patrolmen.***

[3] ***Sonoma County, California and Sonoma County Sheriff's Office Employees Association.***

[4] ***Cedar Rapids, Iowa and Chauffeurs, Teamsters and Helpers Local No. 238.***

of accepting employment outside the service of the Employer; and proof that the employee has accepted employment or entered into business may be accepted by the Employer as a resignation.[1]

61.11 Leaves of Absence Without Pay.

61.11.1 Leaves of absence without pay to serve in an appointive-unclassified City position or as a State Legislator or full-time elective officer in a City or County of the State shall be granted pursuant to applicable State statutes.[2]

61.12 Olympic Competition Leave.

61.12.1 Pursuant to applicable State statutes, employees are entitled to leaves of absence with pay to engage in athletic competition as a qualified member of the United States team for competition on the Olympic level, provided that the period of such leave will not exceed the period of the official training camp and competition combined or ninety (90) calendar days per year, whichever is less.[3]

[1] *State of Oregon and Oregon State Police Officers Association.*

[2] *City of Minneapolis, Minnesota and Police Officers Federation of Minneapolis.*

[3] *City of Minneapolis, Minnesota and Police Officers Federation of Minneapolis.*

CHAPTER 8

INSURANCE AND RETIREMENT

The increasing costs for health and other types of insurance have led to a greater focus on insurance issues during collective bargaining. With insurance costs approaching 25% of wage costs in some areas, both employers and labor organizations are looking for better ways of providing health care coverage for employees.

The focus of this chapter is on health insurance and the various and sundry other types of insurance that are commonly contained in a law enforcement collective bargaining agreement. The types of insurance covered by this chapter include the following:

- Health Insurance
- Dental, Disability and Life Insurance
- Retiree Health Insurance
- Tort Claim Insurance
- Retirement Benefits
- Retirement Counseling
- Workers' Compensation Benefits
- Employee Assistance Programs

An additional topic treated in this chapter is retirement pickup. Under the retirement pickup mechanism, the employer pays or "picks up" the employee's required retirement contribution, as well as paying its own required contribution. Because this leaves all retirement contributions paid with pre-tax dollars, the net benefit of retirement pickup to the employee is greater than the cost of the pickup to the employer. This "win-win" nature of retirement pickup has led to its frequent use where it is allowed by state law.

A relatively new feature of law enforcement collective bargaining agreements calls for an employer to match an employee's contributions to a deferred compensation account. Such payments, which are usually in lieu of all or part of a scheduled wage increase, are often designed to compensate for the employer's lack of participation in the Social Security system.

An increasing number of law enforcement collective bargaining agreements contain clauses which require the employer to pay for the costs of an attorney to defend an officer against job-related criminal charges. This development is the product of the fact that prosecutors more aggressively consider filing criminal charges against police officers for on-the-job conduct. Where an employer is required to pay for the cost of criminal defense, it is almost always the case that the contract language calls for the employer to reimburse the employee only after the employee has been cleared of the underlying criminal charges.

ARTICLE 62

HEALTH AND DENTAL INSURANCE

62.1 Health Insurance.

62.1.1 On the first day of the month following employment, every member of the unit shall be provided during the life of this contract with medical and hospitalization insurance under Blue Cross – Blue Shield, Series 2000, or its equivalent. The Employer shall pay the full premium for family plan and for single plan. The Employer may from time to time change the insurance carrier and/or self fund its health care program if it elects to do so, if such change provides equivalent coverage.[1]

62.1.2. HMO Alternative. Effective August 1, ____, members of the Bargaining Unit will have the option of selecting, as an alternative to traditional Blue Cross/Blue Shield coverage, Community Blue No. 1 Health Maintenance Organization (HMO) coverage as well as the previously available Independent Health HMO. The Employer will pay the full premium for this coverage up to the total premium cost of traditional Blue Cross/Blue Shield coverage with each enrolled officer responsible for any additional premium cost in excess of the premium cost for aforementioned traditional coverage.[2]

62.2 Dental Insurance.

62.2.1 During the life of this Agreement, the Employer shall provide each employee with fully paid family dental insurance at the current benefit level.[3]

[1] ***City of Racine, Wisconsin and Racine Police Association.***

[2] ***City of Niagara Falls, New York and the Niagara Falls Police Club, Inc.***

[3] ***Bend, Oregon and Bend City Police Association.***

62.2.2 The Employer agrees to provide a family dental plan. The plan shall provide for 70/30% insurance with incentives. It shall include orthodontia with a 12-month waiting period.[1]

62.3 Paid Insurance for Retirees.

62.3.1 Represented employees who retire from City service shall be eligible, after retirement, for continuation of medical insurance at the same level as active employees in accordance with Section XI.A under this Agreement; vision coverage of $200 per person biannually; life insurance to $35,000 with a monthly premium not to exceed $19.10 per month; and contribution to dental insurance benefits not to exceed $240 annually.[2]

62.4 Unpaid Insurance for Retirees.

62.4.1 The Employer shall allow retired employees to be eligible for group health insurance coverage under provisions of law or the applicable insurance contract.[3]

62.4.2 The Employer shall continue a Section 125 program for pre-tax deductions for the employee share of health, dental and vision insurance premiums and for dependent care costs.[4]

62.4.3 The benefits provided for herein shall be provided through a self-insured plan or under group insurance policy or policies issued by an insurance company or insurance companies selected by the Employer. "Insurance Companies" include

[1] ***Portland, Oregon and Portland Police Association.***

[2] ***City of Westminster, California and Westminster Police Association.***

[3] ***Brownsville, Texas and Brownsville Police Officers' Association.***

[4] ***City of Modesto, California and the Modesto Police Management Association.***

regular line insurance companies and non-profit organizations providing hospital, surgical, medical, optical or dental benefits. If these benefits are insured by an insurance company, all benefits are subject to the provisions of the policies between the Employer and the insurance company. Notwithstanding any such changes, the level of benefits shall remain substantially the same.[1]

62.5 Bill Review Incentive.

62.5.1 Employees finding errors in their hospital bills which result in overcharges to the Employer's insurance carrier shall be granted ten percent (10%) of any such error up to a maximum of one thousand dollars ($1,000.00) per hospital stay. Payment shall be made to the employee only after the Employer verifies the error and receives copies of the original and corrected billings directly from the hospital and/or insurance carrier.[2]

62.6 Opt-Out.

62.6.1 At the time of open enrollment for health care selection, the Employer will allow up to thirty (30) members of the bargaining unit who are currently enrolled in an Employer medical insurance plan or who received a payment under this section in the current year to opt-out of the Employer's Health Care Plan, provided each employee provides proof of coverage from another source other than an Employer-provided medical insurance plan, exclusive of coverage provided through an Employer plan available to a spouse who is a current or retired City employee. Re-enrollment of an employee into an available plan, at a time other than the regular enrollment period, shall only be

[1] ***Municipality of Penn Hills, Pennsylvania and Police Bargaining Unit.***

[2] ***Municipality of Penn Hills, Pennsylvania and Police Bargaining Unit.***

allowed upon loss of alternative coverage and shall be at the earliest date permitted by the vendor (i.e., the employee shall not have to wait until open enrollment).

62.6.1.1 Payment. Any employee who opts out of the Employer's health care plan will be eligible to receive $1,500 in any year in which they opted out under this section. Such payment shall not be eligible to be considered in the calculation of the employee's final average compensation. In addition, such payments shall be made twice a year, by separate check, following the period of time during which the employee waived coverage by the Employer's group health insurance plan.

62.6.1.2 Procedures. The parties will meet and mutually agree to a written procedure for implementation of the terms of the opt-out program.[1]

62.7 Inoculations and Immunization.

62.7.1 If an employee, while carrying out his/her duties, is exposed to a contagious disease, the Employer agrees to pay the expense for inoculation and immunization for members of the officer's family. The Employer further agrees to reimburse any officer covered by one of the Employer's insurance programs, any co-payment required for inoculation and/or immunization required due to the exposure to a contagious disease as a result of the officer carrying out his/her duties. This is subject to the review and approval of the Employer on the basis of documentation and verification presented by the employee to the Employer.[2]

[1] ***City of Lansing, Michigan and Fraternal Order of Police, Capitol City Lodge 141.***

[2] ***Albuquerque, New Mexico and Albuquerque Police Officers' Association.***

ARTICLE 63

LIABILITY INSURANCE

63.1 General.

63.1.1 Defense and Indemnification.

63.1.1.1 The Employer agrees to defend and hold harmless all employees covered by this Agreement against and from all civil claims, demands, causes of action suits or proceedings, regardless of the merits of the same, damages, liability or costs or expenses of every type, all or any part thereof which arises solely out of official performance of duty as a Law Enforcement Officer in the following instances: (a) Active duty; (b) rest duty; and (c) outside Law Enforcement Officer Employment.

63.1.1.2 Where an employee covered by terms of this Agreement works in the capacity of a law enforcement officer for a private employer on a regular or continuous basis, having first obtained Employer approval, based upon the recommendation of the Chief of Police, and consistent with the requirements of the Employer, and where the employee is not otherwise insured by the private employer.

63.1.1.3 Where an employee covered by the terms of this Agreement works in the capacity of a Law Enforcement Officer for a private employer on a short-term or intermittent basis, approved by the Employer and administered by the Community Services Division without requiring the approval by the Employer and where the employee is not otherwise insured by the private employer.

63.1.1.4 In all cases of outside Law Enforcement Officer employment, it shall be the responsibility of the Employer to determine whether or not the organization or individual hiring the employee(s) has appropriate liability insurance and to evaluate such employment on a case-by-case basis and discourage or deny such employment where it is determined that liability insurance does not exist or there is an unacceptable legal exposure to the Employer.[1]

63.2 Information on Settlement of Lawsuits.

63.2.1 In the event of settlement of any such civil suit, the Employer shall provide the officer with a copy of any release obtained.[2]

63.3 False Arrest and Liability Insurance.

63.3.1 Since employees of this Department are required by accepted tradition and policy to volunteer to suppress criminal acts and assume other law enforcement responsibilities at all times whether on regular duty assignment or not, and whether in the Township or not, the employer agrees to obtain such false arrest and liability insurance coverage in a contract of insurance which shall provide coverage to the employee for acts occurring in pursuit of this policy beyond regular duty assignment. In the event such insurance is not obtained, the employer agrees to provide legal defense for an employee against whom a civil claim or a suit is instituted and to indemnify the employee for any damage awarded to a claimant. Any policy of insurance obtained in accordance with this provision shall be delivered to the employee bargaining unit's Executive Committee for examination and approval.[3]

[1] ***Tucson, Arizona and Fraternal Order of Police.***

[2] ***Champaign, Illinois and Champaign Policemen's Benevolent and Protective Association.***

[3] ***Township of Middletown, New Jersey and Middletown Township Policemen's Benevolent Association, Inc., Local 124.***

63.4 Automobile Insurance.

63.4.1 The Employer shall provide liability insurance protection for each employee covered by this Agreement during authorized operation of a City vehicle or equipment. Any legal representative shall be provided by the insurer at no expense to the employee or pursuant to Section 2.62.100 et. seq. of the City Code.[1]

ARTICLE 64

INDUSTRIAL ACCIDENT AND ILLNESS

64.1 Workers' Compensation Supplemental Payment.

64.1.1 Each employee who is absent from duty because of an injury received or disability suffered in the performance of his duty shall receive full pay during the period of such disability.[2]

64.2 Emergency Ordinance Demolition Squad.

64.2.1 The Employer agrees to provide Accidental Death and Dismemberment Insurance in the principal amount of $200,000 to officers while they are performing the Emergency Ordinance Demolition (E.O.D.) duties.[3]

64.3 Acquired Immune Deficiency Syndrome (AIDS).

64.3.1 1. A bargaining unit employee who contracts AIDS after initial employment will be entitled to a rebuttable presump-

[1] ***City of Wichita, Kansas and Fraternal Order of Police, Lodge #5.***

[2] ***Bethlehem, Pennsylvania and Fraternal Order of Police.***

[3] ***City of Sacramento, California and Sacramento Police Officers Association.***

tion that she/he contracted AIDS in the line of duty and as a result of an accident if all of the following terms and conditions are strictly adhered to:

64.3.1.1 For all persons hired after the effective date of this Agreement, the employee agrees, prior to being employed, to submit to an AIDS test and the employee does not test positive; and

64.3.1.2 The employee has, while on duty and performing work for the Employer, been exposed to a patient who has AIDS and, further, this exposure was more than casual contact but instead involved the direct contact with blood or other bodily fluids; and

64.3.1.3 Said on-the-job exposure is reported by the employee by the way of a written incident or accident report which is completed and submitted to the Police Chief or his designee within thirty (30) days of said exposure or, within thirty (30) days of the employee receiving notification of exposure to AIDS, ARC or HIV pursuant to F.S. Sections 395.0147 or 796.08(5), whichever is later.

64.3.1.4 The employee who alleges to have contracted AIDS submits to a confirmatory AIDS test administered by the Employer, which test actually does confirm that the employee has contracted AIDS; and

64.3.1.5 The employee must immediately provide the Employer with a written medical authorization (on a form(s) approved by the Employer) which is sufficient to release any and all of the employee's medical records and which otherwise waives the physician-patient confidentiality and authorizes the employee's physician to discuss his/her medical condition(s) with the Employer; and

64.3.1.6 The employee otherwise cooperates with the Employer in administering this Article.

64.3.1.7 An employee who asserts and receives the above presumption may, in the Employer's sole and exclusive discretion, be required to:(1) continue performing his/her normal job duties; (2) perform some, but not all, of his/her normal job duties; (3) perform administrative or clerical work within the Police Department; or (4) take administrative leave. An employee who is claiming this rebuttable presumption and who refuses to perform work he/she is physically able to perform will lose this presumption and the AIDS condition or impairment will not then be presumed to have occurred accidentally or in the line of duty.[1]

64.4 Communicable Diseases.

64.4.1 Any officer who shall suffer from a serious communicable disease shall be treated with a rebuttable presumption that the disease was contracted on the job. Incident reports may be used to validate such claims.[2]

64.4.2 The parties agree that where a sworn police officer has been approved by the Civil Service Board to reside outside the jurisdictional limits of the City and the said officer is injured going to or coming from work within a reasonable period of time from the commencement or termination of his tour of duty on a reasonably direct route of travel, said accident may be considered as occurring in the line of duty. This provision is not applicable if the officer is charged with reckless driving and/or

[1] ***City of Pompano Beach, Florida and Broward County Police Benevolent Association.***

[2] ***Township of Cherry Hill, New Jersey and Fraternal Order of Police, Lodge #28.***

driving under the influence in violation of the provisions of State law entitled "State Uniform Traffic Control."[1]

ARTICLE 65

VISION INSURANCE

65.1 Benefits.

65.1.1 Each full-time bargaining unit employee shall have the option of participating in a group vision care plan, on either an individual or family basis. The Employer shall be solely liable for the payment of the premiums necessary to provide either individual or family coverage for the employees of the bargaining unit, subject to the employees being solely liable for the payment of any deductibles or co-payments required under the plan.[2]

ARTICLE 66

DISABILITY INSURANCE

66.1 Unlimited Benefits.

66.1.1 In lieu of all existing or past practices concerning pay continuation and/or return to limited duty, the Employer will provide a monthly income disability insurance policy for each member. Employees will be considered for re-employment when certified as capable to return to the job previously occupied. If an employee whose disability resulted from an off-duty injury or illness is returned to work, at the option of the Employer, for

[1] *City of Miami, Florida and the Fraternal Order of Police, Lodge #20.*

[2] *The City of Euclid, Ohio and Euclid Fraternal Order of Police, Lodge #18.*

limited duty, he shall be compensated at his regular rate. The policy shall provide compensation at 66-2/3% of total monthly base salary after ninety (90) days and continuing until age sixty-five (65).[1]

ARTICLE 67

LIFE INSURANCE

67.1 Face Value of Insurance.

67.1.1 The Employer will provide a term life insurance policy which will allow a benefit of the individual's annual salary rounded up to the next $1,000.[2]

67.1.2 The Employer shall provide $75,000 of life insurance protection for each member of the bargaining unit. The Employer shall pay 100% of the premium. The policy will be reviewed continually by the Employer for the specific purpose of attempting to reduce premiums and increase benefits.

67.1.2.1 Each employee shall have the option, upon retirement, to continue to receive life insurance benefits. Any employee electing to continue life insurance benefits upon retirement shall be solely responsible for any and all associated expenses, including premiums and billing fees.[3]

67.2 Death Benefit.

67.2.1 In the event an employee dies because of a line-of-duty injury received during the actual and proper performance

[1] ***Beaverton, Oregon and Beaverton Police Officers Association.***

[2] ***Garden Grove Police Officers Association and the City of Garden Grove, California.***

[3] ***The City of Euclid, Ohio and Euclid Fraternal Order of Police, Lodge #18.***

of police service relating to the alleged or actual commission of an unlawful act, or directly resulting from a characteristic hazard of police duty, through no fault of the employee's, a payment of $25,000 shall be made from funds other than those of the Retirement System in addition to any other payment which may be made as a result of such death. Such payment shall be made to the beneficiary designated under the Retirement System or, if no beneficiary is so designated, to the estate of the deceased.[1]

67.2.2 In the event of the death of a regular permanent employee, while employed by the Employer, all accumulated sick days up to sixty-five (65) days, all accrued wages due, including allowances for unpaid holidays and vacation time, in addition to a $4,000 no-cost Death Benefit, are to be paid to the person entitled thereto as designated by the employee, or by law. In addition, the person entitled as designated by law will receive an amount equivalent to the employee's regular wages for one (1) month after the legally required deductions.[2]

ARTICLE 68

FUNERAL EXPENSES

68.1 General.

68.1.1 In the event an officer is killed in the line of duty, or dies from injuries sustained in the line of duty, the Employer shall pay the sum of $5,000.00 toward funeral and connected expenses to the officer's surviving spouse (or, if none, to the officer's heirs), regardless of amounts paid from other sources.[3]

[1] ***New York, New York and Patrolmen's Benevolent Association of the City of New York.***

[2] ***Memphis, Tennessee and Memphis Police Association.***

[3] ***City of Portland, Oregon and Portland Police Association.***

ARTICLE 69

EMPLOYEE ASSISTANCE PROGRAM

69.1 General.

69.1.1 Employer and the Association agree to continue the Employee Assistance Program to assist employees who are experiencing personal problems which the employee believes may be affecting his or her job performance. This program is available to all employees and employee participation in the Employee Assistance Program shall be voluntary, confidential, and not used for, or considered in matters relating to, performance evaluations, discipline or promotions. Employees are responsible and accountable for maintaining satisfactory, job-related standards throughout and following any participation in the Employee Assistance Program.[1]

69.1.2 The Employer will make available an Employee Assistance Program which will provide counseling by an outside confidential firm which includes drug abuse, alcoholism, and marriage counseling.[2]

69.2 Psychological Counseling Program.

69.2.1 The Employer shall provide counseling/psychotherapy to all sworn personnel. Free counseling will also be provided to the dependents of sworn personnel up to a maximum of three (3) sessions. The services provided do not include medical prescription or specialized services such as inpatient substance abuse treatment. Employees who are disabled or unable

[1] ***Sonoma County, California and Sonoma County Sheriff's Office Employees Association.***

[2] ***City of Salt Lake City, Utah and Salt Lake City Police Association.***

to work their regularly assigned duties are not eligible for these services.[1]

ARTICLE 70

OTHER INSURANCE

70.1 Medicare Coverage.

70.1.1 Employer to contribute 1.45% of the covered payroll toward Medicare coverage for employees hired after March 31, ____. A 1.45% deduction will be made from employees' earnings, up to $42,000. In compliance with H.R. 3128, all full-time, part-time, temporary, and seasonal employees hired after March 31, ____, must participate in the Medicare program.[2]

70.2 Cafeteria Plan.

70.2.1 Design of Plan.

70.2.1.1 Plan Options: Represented employees may elect to participate in either the health care plan offered by the Association or the Employer's "Flexible Benefit Program" (hereinafter referred to as the Flexible Benefit Program). Effective as of the signing of this Agreement, a new participating group under the Flexible Benefit Program will be established, consisting of those employees who elect to be covered by the Association health care plan. The options available to this participating group will consist of the Association's health care plan, catastrophic illness protection (if determined by Employer's legal counsel to be an appropriate non-taxable benefit within Section 125 of the Internal Revenue Code) and cash back option.

[1] ***City of Modesto, California and Modesto Police Officers Association.***

[2] ***Montclair and Montclair Police Officers' Association.***

70.2.1.2 Employer Contributions: Effective upon implementation of this agreement, the Employer shall contribute $90 per pay period on behalf of each employee enrolled in the Association's plan. The Employer will contribute $107.50 per pay period for each full-time employee enrolled in the Employer's Flexible Benefit Program.

70.2.1.3 Enrollment: An employee, once enrolled in a Flexible Benefit option, shall be required to remain in said plan option for the remainder of the plan's fiscal year or until an appropriate enrollment period is declared.

70.2.1.4 Continuation of Health Plan: Should an employee exhaust his or her sick leave or annual leave and go on medical or maternity leave of absence without pay, the Employer agrees to continue to make its contribution to the health insurance option in which the employee is enrolled, for 60 days. The number of hours of compensation upon which payment of this premium is based shall be the number of hours compensated in the bi-week immediately preceding the placement of the employee on medical or maternity leave. All Flexible Benefit options other than health insurance coverage are discontinued during any leave of absence without pay.

70.2.1.5 Association-Management Committee: The parties agree to the continuation of a joint management/labor health care cost containment committee. Such committee shall meet quarterly for the purpose of discussing cost containment alternatives and expansion of flexible benefit program options, reviewing financial progress of the health plans, and assisting in educational activities.

70.2.1.6 Employer Medical Indemnity Plan: The composite rates for the Employer's self-funded medical indemnity plans shall be established annually by the Employer on the basis of the total cost of the plan during the most recent twelve-month period for which data is available, increased by the Employer-expected medical plan inflation rate for the coming year, as determined by the Employer's benefit consultant in conformance with accepted industry standards, plus anticipated fees for administration, medical plan conversions, and stop-loss protection. During the term of this agreement, Employer shall be entitled to implement any cost containment provisions in its current plans which do not result in a direct cost transfer to employees.

70.2.1.7 Audit of Health Plan: Association agrees to allow the Employer to audit the books and records of the Association insurance plans at Employer's request.

70.2.1.8 Health Plan Information: Association agrees to provide Employer with the following information upon request by Employer: (a) Present health care costs for employee, employee plus one, and employee plus two or more with costs of dental plan listed separately if the plan contains such features; and (b) a copy of the current health care contract and a sheet or pamphlet summarizing such features.

70.2.1.9 Health Plan Review: Annually and upon any modification to existing benefits, Association shall submit a detailed report of the benefits provided under the Association's medical health plan to the Personnel Director for his review and approval. Authorization by the Board of Supervisors of the Employer contribution provided under Section 2 above shall be contingent upon the Personnel Director's certification of eligibility.

70.2.1.10 Within 30 days of receipt of the information required above, the Personnel Director shall either certify the plan, or advise the Association in writing of his denial of certification and the reasons thereof.

70.2.1.11 The Association plan shall be deemed eligible to receive the Employer contribution when benefits provided under said plan are at least comparable to those provided under the Employer-sponsored plan.[1]

70.3 Deferred Compensation.

70.3.1 The Employer will match an employee's deferred compensation contribution to a maximum Employer contribution of seven point six five percent (7.65%) of the base wage rate for "6" Step Police Patrol Officer rounded to the nearest dollar.[2]

70.4 Deceased Unit Employees – Widows/ Widowers and Dependents Benefits.

70.4.1 Medical and Dental Insurance Benefits. Effective August 1, ____, the Employer shall provide insurance or funds equal to the Employer's contribution for active unit employees for Medical and Dental Insurance for the qualified spouse and/ or qualified dependents, as currently covered by the Employer's Medical and Dental Insurance plans, of any unit employee who dies while on active duty from injuries incurred while performing his or her job duties or who dies as a direct cause of such injuries. The maximum amount of the subsidy shall not exceed the Employer's contribution for such insurance provided to active employees covered by this memorandum of understanding.

70.4.1.1 Eligibility.

70.4.1.2 Only a spouse and/or dependents covered as qualified dependents under an employee's Medical and Dental In-

[1] ***Ventura County, California and Ventura County Sheriff's Association.***

[2] ***City of Tacoma, Washington and Tacoma Police Union, Local #6.***

surance plans, at the time of death, shall be eligible for the insurance or subsidy.

70.4.1.3 Upon application by a spouse and/or dependents for this benefit, the Director of Personnel and Employee Relations shall make a determination of eligibility. Such determination shall be final and binding and not subject to further appeal.

70.4.1.4 Unborn children of the deceased unit employee will be eligible for dependent status upon birth.

70.4.1.5 Limitations.

70.4.1.6 Qualified spouses and dependents will receive benefits or payments not to exceed those benefits for which they otherwise would be independently qualified. (For example, spouse alone is eligible for the employee only benefits contribution. Spouse plus one dependent is eligible for the employee plus one benefit contribution, and spouse plus two dependents is eligible for family benefit contribution).

70.4.1.7 The qualified spouses and/or dependents as described are subject to all terms, conditions and limitations set forth in this memorandum of understanding, the Employer's Medical and Dental Insurance Plans.

70.4.1.8 Should qualified spouses and/or dependents lose eligibility to participate in the Employer's plans, the Employer may elect, at its choosing, to purchase similar insurance or substitute a cash payment not to exceed the Employer's portion of the active employee's contribution to which the qualified spouse and/or dependents are eligible to receive.

70.4.1.9 Should qualified spouses and/or dependents lose eligibility to participate in the Employer's plans, the Employer may elect to reimburse the qualified spouse and/or dependents for other insurance purchased up to the maximum benefit said spouse and/or dependents are eligible to receive.

70.4.1.10 When a qualified spouse and/or dependents are covered by medical and dental insurance polices provided by a subsequent employer, the qualified spouse and/or dependents shall receive a supplemental reimbursement not to exceed the difference between that portion of premiums paid for by the subsequent employer and the total premiums for such insurance. The amount of each supplemental reimbursement shall not exceed the maximum benefit the spouse and/or dependents are eligible to receive.

70.4.1.11 The Employer shall have the right to request documentation and proof of payment of any reimbursed insurance premiums.

70.4.1.12 The benefits or subsidy to the spouse shall cease upon remarriage of the spouse or upon attaining the age of 65, whichever comes first.

70.4.1.13 The benefits or subsidy to the qualified dependents shall cease upon remarriage of spouse or as defined in the Employer's Medical and Dental plans.

70.4.1.14 These provisions and benefits are not applicable to members who were not on duty at the time of injury which resulted in their deaths.

70.4.1.15 Unit employees in the classification of Police Officer Recruit are not eligible for this benefit.

70.4.1.16 Funeral Expenses.

70.4.1.17 Effective August 1, ____, the Employer shall expend a sum not to exceed $7,500 for funeral expense to the heirs of any unit employee covered by this Memorandum of Understanding who dies while on active duty from injuries. This benefit is not applicable to members who were not on duty at the time of injury which resulted in their death. Unit employees who are in the classification of Police Officer recruit are not eligible for this benefit. To be eligible for such benefits, such employee's death must occur on or after August 1, ____. This amount includes the amount of $5,000 already available for this purpose in accordance with State law.[1]

70.5 Family Assistance Officer.

70.5.1 The Chief shall appoint a Family Assistance Officer. The Family Assistance Officer will be relieved of regular duty on a case-by-case basis in order to assist the families of officers who die or are seriously injured while on active duty, or suffer a catastrophic illness in making appropriate arrangements and completing necessary paperwork.[2]

ARTICLE 71

DEFENSE OF CIVIL CLAIMS

71.1 Legal Defense.

71.1.1 Whenever any claims are made or any civil action is commenced against the employee for damages caused by acts of the employee within the scope of the employee's authority and while in the course of employment, the Employer will pay for, or engage or furnish the services of, an attorney to advise the officer as to the claim and to appear for and represent the employee in the action.

[1] ***City of Glendale and Glendale Police Officers' Association.***

[2] ***City of San Antonio, Texas and San Antonio Police Officers' Association.***

71.1.2 The Employer may compromise, settle and pay such claims before or after the commencement of any civil action.

71.1.3 Whatever judgment for damages is awarded against an employee as the result of any civil action or damages caused by the employee while in the course of employment, the Employer will indemnify the officer or will pay, settle or compromise the judgment. The Employer's obligation under this section shall be contingent upon the employee giving prompt notice of the commencement of any action, and upon the employee cooperating in the preparation, defense and settlement of such action.[1]

71.2 Indemnification.

71.2.1 Except in cases of malfeasance in office or willful or wanton neglect of duty, Employer shall defend, save harmless and indemnify an Employee and/or his estate against any claim or demand, whether groundless or otherwise, arising out of an alleged act or omission occurring in the performance and scope of Employee's duties.[2]

71.3 Legal Protection.

71.3.1 The officer shall have the right to consult the attorney of the officer's choice regarding a lawsuit to which the officer is a party at Employer expense up to seventy-five dollars ($75) per lawsuit.[3]

71.3.2 In the event an employee desires the presence of an attorney to discuss a controversy with representatives of the

[1] ***City of Lansing, Michigan and Fraternal Order of Police, Capitol City Lodge 141.***

[2] ***Saint Paul and Saint Paul Police Federation.***

[3] ***City of Albuquerque, New Mexico and Albuquerque Police Officers' Association.***

Claims Division of the City, the parties agree that the attorney shall receive a token fee for his presence of $75.00 per hour, not to exceed $150.00.[1]

ARTICLE 72

CRIMINAL DEFENSE

72.1 General.

72.1.1 Employer shall, at the Employer's expense, defend any officer against any criminal charges brought against such employee for acts committed by the officer in the line of duty. If the Employer does not provide for such defense, the Employer shall reimburse the officer his cost of defense. If an outside attorney is hired to provide such defense, the Employer shall be notified of the identity of such attorney, and an agreement with the Employer shall be reached concerning the fees to be charged by such outside attorney prior to the time that he is retained.[2]

ARTICLE 73

RETIREMENT

73.1 Local Retirement Plan.

73.1.1 Retirement Benefits.

73.1.1.1 All present retirement and survivor benefits shall remain in effect except as follows: (a) The employee contribution to the pension fund will be 8% of total earnings; (b) service retirements for those employees hired before July 1, ____ will

[1] ***City of Miami, Florida and the Fraternal Order of Police, Lodge #20.***

[2] ***Yakima, Washington and Yakima Police Patrolman's Association.***

be based on 2.5% of final average pay for each whole year of service for the first 20 years of continuous service and 2.0% of final average pay for each whole year of service thereafter; (c) normal retirement for employees hired before July 1, ____ shall be after 20 years' continuous service. Employee pension benefits vest after 10 years of continuous service.

73.1.1.2 An employee who vests his or her pension and leaves the service of the Employer will be entitled to collect a pension benefit commencing on the date he or she would have reached his or her normal retirement date.

73.1.1.3 Employees hired on or after July 1, ____ will be entitled to a service pension identical to employees hired before July 1, ____ with the following exceptions: (a) Normal retirement after 20 years of continuous service or at age 45, whichever is later; (b) retirement benefit based on 2.5% of final average pay for each whole year of service for the first 20 years of continuous service and 2.0% of final average pay for each whole year of service thereafter to a maximum of 70% of final average pay; (c) final average pay will be computed on the basis of the employee's highest five of the last ten years of regular earnings, exclusive of overtime and private duty pay, added to a figure for overtime and private duty which is based on the employee's total overtime and private duty hours averaged over the employee's last 20 years of service or actual years of service, whichever is less.

73.1.1.4 An employee with less than 15 years of continuous service who suffers a permanent partial disability arising out of and in the course of employment as defined in the Workers' Compensation Act and who is eligible for a special disability allowance as provided for in the Municipal Employees Retirement Fund will have such special disability allowance reduced by any income from gainful employment which, together with the special disability allowance, exceeds 100% of the current rate of pay for an employee of the same or corresponding job classification held by the employee at the time of such retirement.[1]

73.2 Sworn Employees Retirement Plan.

73.2.1 Sergeants, Senior Police Officers, and Police Officers retiring from service after January 1, ____, shall be entitled to an annual benefit at retirement (eligible at 50 with five or more years of service) of two and one-half percent (2.5%) of the single highest year's salary for each year of service under the plan, which sum shall be paid over a twelve-month period. Employee shall become fifty percent (50%) vested in said retirement benefits upon successful completion of the probationary period. Such vested interest shall increase annually thereafter at the rate of five (5) percent to a total of one hundred percent (100%), and in the event that an eligible employee continues to work beyond the age of fifty that employee shall receive retirement benefits in an annual amount equal to the following schedule:

Retirement Age	Percentage of Earnings
50	2.50%
51	2.60%
52	2.70%
53	2.80%
54	2.90%
55 or higher	3.00%

73.2.1.1 Effective July 1, ____, the Professional Achievement Bonuses set forth in Article XV shall be included in the

[1] ***Hartford, Connecticut and Hartford Police Union.***

base compensation upon which retirement benefits and contributions are calculated. In addition, eligible employees retiring from the City during the ____ calendar year who qualified for one of the enhanced Professional Achievement Bonuses that became effective July 1, ____ (5% and 10% respectively), or would have so qualified but for their earlier retirement, shall receive the full value of the applicable enhanced bonus and shall be regarded as having received the enhanced bonus when calculating their highest annual base compensation under the Defined Benefit Pension Plan.

73.2.1.2 Effective the first payroll period of the Fiscal Year beginning July 1, ____, the Employer shall contribute up to 29.50% of base pay towards the retirement benefit.

73.2.1.3 Said plan shall further provide employees covered by this contract an opportunity to receive retirement benefits in a monthly amount equal to at least fifty percent (50%) of the employee's single highest year's base salary compensation, excluding overtime, bonus, incentive pay, etc., while employed with the Employer in each and every case where the employee is incapacitated from performance of his/her duties as a result of an illness or injury incurred during the course and scope of employment with such benefits to extend from the date of retirement for life.

73.2.1.4 An employee who has five years of service as a sworn employee and who is incapacitated from performance of his/her duties as a result of an illness or injury incurred outside the course and scope of employment, shall have the opportunity to receive retirement benefits in a monthly amount equal to at least 50% of the average of the employee's twelve highest months' base wages from the date of retirement for life.

73.2.1.5 Retirement allowances paid to retirees who retire after July 1, ____ shall be increased annually based upon increases in the National Consumer Price Index for All Urban Consumers for the twelve months ending October 31, up to a maximum of 2%. Those retiring employees who elect a lump sum distribution of their retirement funds forego any cost-of-living adjustments.

73.2.1.6 It is the understanding and intent of the parties that the Employee's contribution of up to 29.50% will pay the entire cost of such a retirement program for the period of this contract. It is further understood that such benefit may have increased costs after that time; and if it is the desire of the parties to continue such a benefit, the obligation to pay such increased costs shall be subject to the meet and confer process.[1]

73.3 Requirements of Plan.

73.3.1 The Employer Pension Ordinance applies to members of this bargaining unit. The rate of contribution by the employee shall be that which is specified in the pension ordinance.

73.3.1.1 The pension benefits for police personnel in the Employer Pension Plan are calculated for 0 to 25 years of service on the basis of 2.25% for each year of pension service credit times final average compensation as defined in pension ordinance Article II or Article VI where applicable. 1.0% is granted for each completed year of service after twenty-five (25) years of service to a maximum of thirty-five (35) completed years of service as defined in pension ordinance Article II and Article VI where applicable.

73.3.1.2 In no event shall the retirement allowance of any member exceed sixty-six and twenty-five one-hundredth per-

[1] ***City of Irvine, California and Irvine Police Association.***

cent (66.25%) of his final average compensation after thirty-five (35) years of creditable service.[1]

73.4 Purchase Service Credits.

73.4.1 Employees covered by this agreement may meet with City Human Resources/Risk Management Staff to discuss buy-back of up to four years' active duty military time and full-time sworn police experience not to exceed two years. Service credit buy-back shall be calculated pursuant to the Retirement Plan. The full cost of such buy-back time shall be assumed by the employee, with there being no cost to the retirement plan.[2]

ARTICLE 74

RETIREMENT PICKUP

74.1 General

74.1.1 The Employer will continue to "pick up" a six percent (6%) average employee contribution to the Public Employees Retirement Fund for the employee members participating in the Public Employees Retirement System. Such state "pick up" or payment of employee member monthly contributions to the System shall continue for the life of this Agreement. The full amount of required employee contributions "picked up" or paid by the state on behalf of employees pursuant to this agreement shall be considered as "salary" within the meaning of State law for the purposes of computing an employee member's "final average salary" within the meaning of State law but shall not be considered as "salary" for the purposes of determining the amount of employee contributions required to be contributed pursuant to State law. Such state "pick up" or paid employee contribu-

[1] ***Memphis, Tennessee and Memphis Police Association.***

[2] ***City of Irvine, California and Irvine Police Association.***

tion shall be credited to the employee's account pursuant to State law. If, by reason of a change in law, valid ballot measure, constitutional amendment, or a final, non-appealable judgement from a court of competent jurisdiction, the Employer must discontinue the 6% "pickup" of the employee's contributions to the PERS fund, the Employer shall increase by 6% the base salary rates for each classification in the salary schedules. This transition shall be done in a manner to assume continuous payment of either the 6% pickup or a 6% salary increase. For the reasons indicated above, or by mutual agreement, should the Employer cease paying the 6% pickup and provide a salary increase for eligible bargaining unit employees during the term of the Agreement, bargaining unit employees' 6% contributions to their PERS accounts shall be treated as "pre-tax" contributions pursuant to Internal Revenue Service Code, Section 414(h)(2).[1]

74.1.2 Effective September 1, ____, employees with at least twenty (20) years of service as a police officer and at least ten (10) years with the Employer, shall be allowed the option to convert their 9% Employer-paid PERS member contribution to 9% salary for retirement purposes. The higher salary resulting in this option will only apply to employees who take a service retirement. Disability retirement and industrial disability retirement are excluded from this option, unless the work-related disability occurs after this conversion is taken. Employees wishing to exercise this option must do so in writing.

74.1.2.1 This retirement conversion is a one-time option and cannot be revoked, once it is opted for, without specific written approval by the City Administrator.

[1] ***State of Oregon and Oregon State Police Officers' Association.***

74.1.2.2 The higher salary resulting from exercising this option shall not be applied to any vacation leave payoff, compensatory leave payoff, sick leave payoff, sick leave buy-back or sick leave conversion plan for which the affected employee may be eligible.

74.1.2.3 The Employer recognizes the benefit of maintaining a uniform application of the conditions and procedures of the Retirement Conversion benefit among the various safety service units; in response to this recognition and notwithstanding the foregoing provisions, the conditions and procedures applicable to an affected Police employee who seeks to exercise this benefit shall be uniform with and among the conditions and procedures applicable to employees in the other safety service units.[1]

74.2 Retirement Counseling.

74.2.1 Employees within fifteen (15) years of retirement shall be granted up to three and one-half (3-1/2) days off with pay once during their careers to investigate retirement programs. Such days off must be approved in advance by the Employer.[2]

74.3 Pre-Retirement Planning.

74.3.1 The Employer shall provide a regularly-scheduled pre-retirement advisory program covering benefits and rights of retired employees. Those employees who are contemplating retirement may attend this program.[3]

[1] ***City of Pomona, California and Pomona Police Officers' Relief Association.***

[2] ***State of Oregon and Oregon State Police Officers' Association.***

[3] ***State of Hawaii and Hawaii Organization of Police Officers.***

74.4 Separation Incentive Plan.

74.4.1 Incentive.

74.4.1.1 Employer to provide a self-funded retirement supplement plan enhancing retiree's pension by $50 per month, not to exceed a maximum benefit of $1,250 per month, for each year of service with the Employer.

74.4.1.2 Effective date for this plan shall be January 1, ____.

74.4.1.3 Program implementation date shall be not later than July 1, ____. Employees who qualify for retirement after the effective date shall be eligible to retire under this plan.

74.4.1.4 To qualify, employees must take a regular service retirement and work until age 50 if classified as police public safety, if classified as miscellaneous age 55.

74.4.1.5 Employees shall qualify for this plan at a rate of $50 per month for each full year of full-time service with the Employer, up to a maximum monthly qualified amount of $1,250.

74.4.1.6 The combined annual benefit from this plan and PERS shall not exceed 75% of employee's salary according to PERS retirement criteria.

74.4.1.7 Employees who retire under medical disability shall be eligible for a lump sum payment equivalent to 50% of the accrued annualized benefit up to a maximum of $7,500.

74.4.1.8 A surviving beneficiary shall be entitled to a lump sum payment of $5,000.

74.4.1.9 The parties recognize the relationship and dependency of this program on funding generated by reduced personnel costs agreed to in this Memorandum of Understanding. Fu-

[1] ***City of Westminster, California and Westminster Police Association.***

ture modifications which negatively impact said savings to the Employer may serve to allow the Employer to discontinue or modify the program for future retirees.[1]

74.5 Retirement Severance Pay.

74.5.1 Any employee who retires and immediately upon such retirement becomes eligible for regular retirement benefits under the provisions of the Police Retirement System, or resigns as a vested member under the provisions of the Police Retirement System, shall receive retirement severance pay at the rate of three (3) days' pay for each full twelve (12) months' service with the Employer at the time of retirement or resignation.

74.5.1.1 Computation of such retirement severance pay shall be on the basis of the employee's regular rate of pay at the time of termination, including longevity pay.[1]

74.6 Furnishing of Badges to Retirees.

74.6.1 The Employer shall provide each member who retires under one of the following conditions with his/her badge at no cost to the member: (a) Superannuation retirement (age 50); (b) retirement with 25 years of service; (c) service-connected disability retirement.[2]

74.7 Gun Purchase for Retirees.

74.7.1 Beginning with the twentieth (20th) year of service, including military service, and at any time thereafter, a patrol officer on active duty may purchase his .38 caliber revolver when issued a new weapon, or as long as such guns are in storage, at an agreed fair market value of ten dollars ($10.00) out of his clothing allowance and keep it when he retires; a patrol officer

[1] ***City of Sioux City, Iowa and Sioux City Police Officers' Association.***

[2] ***Commonwealth of Pennsylvania and Fraternal Order of Police.***

with less than twenty (20) years' service, including military service, may purchase his .38 caliber revolver when issued a different type of weapon, such purchase to be made at the fair market value. In addition, those officers who have more than one weapon may purchase any or all of those additional weapons at the then-fair market value.

74.7.1.1 A member of the bargaining unit who has twenty-three (23) years of service in the Department and has reached the age of forty-six (46), may purchase his/her .9 mm handgun at the agreed upon fair market value. Said purchase may be made via cash or deducted from the member's annual clothing allowance.[1]

74.8 Award.

74.8.1 When an employee retires under any provision of the State retirement system, including medical disability retirement, the employee shall be presented one complete uniform including the badge worn by him or her, the employee's service revolver or pistol, if one had been issued as part of the employee's equipment, and an identification clearly marked "RETIRED" as provided in State law.[2]

[1] ***City of Cleveland, Ohio and Cleveland Police Patrolmen's Association.***

[2] ***State of Florida and Florida Police Benevolent Association.***

CHAPTER 9

GRIEVANCE PROCEDURE AND PERSONNEL MATTERS

The grievance procedure is the heart and soul of a law enforcement collective bargaining agreement. It provides the mechanism for resolving all disputes about the interpretation or application of the substantive provisions in the agreement. Almost always, grievance procedures culminate with a final and binding decision by a neutral arbitrator.

Grievance procedures exist in two basic forms: so-called "loser pays" clauses, where the losing party in arbitration pays all of the arbitrator's fees, and the more traditional type of arbitration clause which calls for the fees of the arbitrator to be divided evenly no matter what the result in the case. Examples of both types of clauses are included in this chapter.

As well, this chapter includes a number of contract provisions dealing with other personnel issues, including the following:

- Access to Personnel Files
- Promotional Procedures and Standards
- Resignations From Employment
- Physical Examinations
- Outside Employment
- Non- Discrimination

Recognizing recent trends, this chapter also includes a lengthy drug-testing clause. The clause calls for drug testing only upon reasonable suspicion of drug use, and contains numerous chain of custody and procedural safeguards to insure the reliability of drug tests.

ARTICLE 75

GRIEVANCE PROCEDURE

75.1 Definition of Grievance.

75.1.1 Grievance Procedure. A grievance is any complaint arising with respect to wages, hours of work, or other conditions of employment. In order to provide for the expedition and mutually satisfactory settlement of grievances, the procedure hereinafter set forth shall be as follows.[1]

75.2 Early Steps of Grievance Procedure.

75.2.1 Processing of Grievances. An alleged grievance shall be taken up with the employee's immediate supervisor and shift commander within ten (10) working days of its alleged occurrence. The parties agree to make every effort to settle the grievance promptly at this level.

75.2.1.1 In the event the grievance is unresolved, the Association and employee shall determine whether to appeal the grievance through the Civil Service Commission or process the grievance to Step 2 of the Grievance procedure contained herein within five (5) days of the meeting with the employee's immediate supervisor. Should the employee choose to file an appeal with the Civil Service Commission, the Association and the employee shall provide the Employer with written notice of such election.

75.2.1.2 The grievance shall be reduced to written form by the aggrieved employee stating the section of the Agreement violated and explaining the grievance in detail and remedy sought. The employee and the Association representative shall present

[1] ***Township of Brick, New Jersey and Brick Township Policeman's Benevolent Association, Local 230.***

the written grievance to the Division Commander, Personnel Director, and the Chief of Police who will conduct a meeting within five (5) working days of receipt of the written grievance. The Chief of Police shall make a decision on the matter in writing within ten (10) working days from such meeting. Copies of the Chief's decision will be furnished the aggrieved Association representative and the Mayor.

75.2.1.3 A grievance remaining unresolved after the decision has been rendered in Step 2 shall be transmitted to the Mayor in writing within ten (10) working days whereupon the Mayor shall conduct an investigatory hearing within five (5) working days of the receipt of the written grievance. The Mayor shall render a decision within five (5) working days of such hearing.

75.2.1.4 Should the grievance not be resolved in Step 3 and should further consideration be desired by the grievant, a written notification requesting arbitration must be filed with the Mayor within ten (10) working days. The parties shall mutually select a disinterested third party to serve as Arbitrator. In the event the Employer and Association are unable to agree on an Arbitrator, the Arbitrator shall be selected by the process of elimination from a panel of seven (7) Arbitrators furnished by the Public Employment Relations Commission (PERC) or Federal Mediation and Conciliation Services (FMCS). If the parties cannot agree on PERC or FMCS, the disagreement shall be resolved by a flip of a coin.[1]

75.2.2 Any grievance that has been processed in accordance with provisions of this Section of this contract, but not satisfactorily settled shall, upon proper appeal, be submitted to arbitration before an impartial arbitrator to be selected by mu-

[1] ***Auburn, Washington and Auburn Police Guild.***

tual agreement of the parties. If, at any time within twenty (20) days (or longer period if mutually agreed upon) after receipt of such written appeal, the parties are unable to agree upon an arbitrator, the Iowa Public Employment Relations Board shall be requested to submit the names of five (5) disinterested persons qualified and willing to act as impartial arbitrators. From such list, the Employer and the Association shall each alternately strike one (1) name until four (4) names have been eliminated and the person whose name remains on the list shall be selected to act as the impartial arbitrator. A coin toss shall determine who shall strike the first name. In order to be considered timely, a hearing regarding a grievance which is appealed to arbitration must be scheduled no later than 60 days from the date the grievance was appealed to arbitration. This timeline may be extended by mutual agreement.[1]

75.3 Arbitrator's Authority.

75.3.1 The Arbitrator's decision shall be final and binding upon both parties, but he shall have no power to alter in any way the terms of this Agreement and he shall be requested to issue his decision within 30 days after the conclusion of the proceedings.[2]

75.4 Split of Arbitrator's Fees.

75.4.1 The arbitrators shall consider only the specific issues presented to them and shall have no power to add to, subtract from, or modify in any way the terms of this agreement. The decision shall be rendered within 30 days of the close of the hearing or submission of written briefs by the parties, whichever

[1] ***City of Sioux City, Iowa and Sioux City Police Officers' Association.***

[2] ***Clatsop County, Oregon and Clatsop County Employees Union.***

is later. Said decision shall be in writing, signed by at least two of the three arbitrators. It is understood by the parties hereto that:

75.4.1.1 The cost of the arbitrators shall be paid equally by the Employer and the Association.

75.4.1.2 Each party shall pay the cost of its witnesses, legal fees, and representatives.

75.4.1.3 To the extent provided by the state laws, the decision of the arbitrator shall be final and binding.[1]

75.5 Loser Pays.

75.5.1 Each party shall be responsible for paying the costs of presenting its own case in arbitration, including the payment of witness fees, if any. The costs by the arbitrator, court reporter (if any), and the hearing room shall be borne by the losing party. Following the rendering of the arbitrator's decision, the parties shall meet and attempt to agree which is the "losing party." If the parties are unable to so agree, the question of who the "losing party" is shall be submitted to the arbitrator who rendered the decision in question. The arbitrator's subsequent designation of the "losing party" shall be final and binding. If the arbitrator cannot designate which party is the loser, each party will pay one-half (1/2) the cost of the arbitration.[2]

75.5.2 Letters of counseling and documented oral reprimands shall remain part of the employee's personnel file, but shall be considered stale after one year after the incident which caused the reprimand to be issued unless the employee receives subsequent discipline within that time period. Written reprimands

[1] ***Olmsted County, Minnesota and Olmsted County Deputy Sheriffs' Association.***

[2] ***Portland, Oregon and Portland Police Association.***

shall be deemed stale after two years from the incident in question unless the employee receives subsequent discipline of a like nature within that time period. Suspensions without pay shall be deemed stale after five years from the incident in question unless the employee receives subsequent discipline of a like nature within that time period.[1]

75.6 Time Limits.

75.6.1 In the event that the Employer fails to answer a grievance within the time required at any step of the grievance procedure, or if the Association fails to appeal the answer given to the next step of the grievance procedure within the time allowed, then the grievance will be considered settled against the side which has defaulted. However, any of the time limits in the grievance procedure may be extended by mutual agreement. Grievances settled by default cannot be the basis of establishing precedent for the settlement of any other grievances.[2]

75.7 Class Action Grievances.

75.7.1 The Association may file a group grievance without mutual agreement at Step 3 of the Grievance Procedure within fifteen (15) calendar days after the grievants become aware of its occurrence. Such grievance shall identify the class of employees covered by the grievance, the contract Article alleged to be violated, the facts of the grievance available, and the remedy sought. The Employer's obligation to respond to the grievance shall not begin to run until the Association submits to the Employer a list of the employees covered by the grievance. If the Association does not submit this information within sixty (60) calendar days of the filing of the grievance, the grievance is

[1] ***City of Salem, Oregon and Salem Police Employees' Union.***

[2] ***Toledo, Ohio and Toledo Police Patrolmen's Association.***

deemed to be withdrawn. The Employer's potential liability extends only to the named class. Failure to identify the facts of an employee's grievance constitutes withdrawal from the group grievance of that employee. A group shall be defined as five (5) or more employees. The Employer and the Association shall fully cooperate on the identification of the individual members of the class. Only one person from the group may attend in paid status unless more than one individual is necessary in order to completely present the facts through the Group Grievance Process, and then only long enough to present their testimony.[1]

75.8 Expedited Grievance Procedure.

75.8.1 Procedures.

75.8.1.1 The Employer and the Association shall jointly establish a list which will be defined as an Expedited Labor Arbitration Panel. All grievances referred to this Panel will be by mutual agreement.

75.8.1.2 The Panel of Labor Arbitrators will be comprised of ten (10) persons and shall be selected from a panel of twenty-five (25) arbitrators as forwarded by the Federal Mediation and Conciliation Service. The list shall be put in random order as selected by the parties after a coin toss determines the first selector. An Arbitrator, upon rendering a decision, shall be placed in the tenth (10) position and the person originally listed as second will become the next Arbitrator so assigned.

75.8.1.3 The hearing shall be conducted by the Arbitrator in whatever manner will most expeditiously permit a full presentation of the evidence and arguments of the parties. There shall be no stenographic record of the proceedings, but the Arbitrator

[1] ***State of Washington and Washington State Patrol Troopers Association.***

shall make an appropriate record of the proceedings. Normally, the hearing shall be completed in one (1) day. In unusual circumstances and for good cause shown, the Arbitrator may extend the hearing beyond one (1) day, and schedule an additional hearing, within five (5) workdays.

75.8.1.4 There shall be no post-hearing briefs.

75.8.1.5 The arbitration may proceed in the absence of any party who, after due notice, fails to be present. An award shall not be made solely on the default of a party. The Arbitrator shall require the attending party to submit supporting evidence.

75.8.1.6 The Arbitrator shall be the sole judge of the relevancy and materiality of the evidence offered.

75.8.1.7 When both sides have completed their presentations, the Arbitrator shall ask whether either party has any further evidence to offer or witnesses to be heard. Upon receiving negative replies, the Arbitrator shall declare and note the hearing closed.

75.8.1.8 The award shall be rendered promptly by the Arbitrator and, unless otherwise agreed by the parties, not later than five (5) work days from the date of the close of the hearing.

75.8.1.9 The awards shall be in writing and shall be signed by the Arbitrator. If the Arbitrator determines that an opinion is necessary, it shall be in summary form.

75.8.1.10 The expenses of non-City employee witnesses for either side shall be paid by the party producing such witnesses. Employer employees called as witnesses shall be paid if called during normal working hours.

75.8.1.11 The Arbitrator shall interpret and apply these rules insofar as they relate to the Arbitrator's powers and duties.[1]

75.8.2 Grievance Procedure. Arbitration decision on grievances on a particular subject will be considered as a precedent and binding on both parties and shall be precedent in the resolution of future grievances involving substantially similar factual situations.[2]

75.9 Penalty Clause.

75.9.1 Procedures.

75.9.1.1 If either the Employer or the Association believe that the other party has violated any provisions of this agreement and that such violation was deliberate or intentional, the aggrieved party may bypass any or all steps in the grievance procedure, and may submit a grievance directly to the State Board of Mediation and Arbitration claiming that such violation was deliberate and intentional.

75.9.1.2 Said Board shall hear and act on such dispute and render a decision which shall be final and binding on all parties.

75.9.1.3 If the Board determines, in any case before it, that either party has deliberately or intentionally violated any provision of this agreement, in addition to the powers granted to it by the previous provisions of this Article and by the General Statutes, said Board is hereby authorized to award damages to the aggrieved party and impose penalties on such agreement violator in an amount or in a manner which, in the Board's judgment, will discourage further or future attempts to deliberately or intentionally violate any provisions of this agreement.

[1] ***Toledo, Ohio and Toledo Police Patrolmen's Association.***

[2] ***City of Sioux City, Iowa and Sioux City Police Officers' Association.***

75.9.1.4 Such damage awards may include, but are not limited to, monetary payments and such penalties may include, but are not limited to, withdrawal of recognition of the employee organization dues check-off.[1]

ARTICLE 76

BINDING ARBITRATION OF IMPASSE ISSUES

76.1 General.

76.1.1 Not less than ninety (90) days before the expiration of this Contract and any reopener provider herein, the Employer and the Association shall begin negotiation and shall negotiate for a period of at least sixty (60) days. After sixty (60) days, either party can demand final and binding arbitration, by written notice to the other, of all issues on which they are at impasse in accordance with the following procedures:

76.1.1.1 (a) Each party shall appoint an arbitrator and those two (2) arbitrators shall agree on a third arbitrator within five (5) days, or they shall select a third impartial arbitrator by the strike-off method from a list of seven (7) furnished by the American Arbitration Association.

76.1.1.2 (b) Five (5) days after the third impartial arbitrator has been selected, the parties shall submit their final offer on each issue which is at impasse to the arbitration panel.

76.1.1.3 (c) The arbitration panel may hold hearings, receive evidence or documentation, call witnesses in accordance with the arbitration rules of the American Arbitration Association.

76.1.1.4 (d) After receiving whatever evidence the parties wish to submit, the arbitration panel shall select the final offer of

[1] ***Bridgeport, Connecticut and Local 1159, AFSCME.***

one (1) of the parties on each of the impasse issues and shall issue an award incorporating all of these selected final offers, without modification.

76.1.1.5 (e) In reaching its decision, the arbitration panel shall give weight to the following factors:

76.1.1.6 (i) Past collectively bargained agreements, if any between the parties.

76.1.1.7 (ii) Comparison of the issues submitted to final offer settlement relative to the employees in the bargaining unit involved with those issues related to other public and private employees doing comparable work, giving consideration involved;

76.1.1.8 (iii) The interests and welfare of the public, the ability of the public employer to finance and administer the issues proposed, and the effect of the adjustments on the normal standard of public service;

76.1.1.9 (iv) The lawful authority of the public employer;

76.1.1.10 (v) The stipulations of the parties;

76.1.1.11 (vi) Such other factors, not confined to those listed in this section, which are normally or traditionally taken into consideration in the determination of the issues submitted to final offer settlement through voluntary collective bargaining, mediation, fact-finding, or other impasse resolution procedures in the public service or in private employment.

76.1.1.12 (f) Each party shall bear the expense of its own arbitrator and the parties shall split the expense of the third impartial arbitrator, and all other expenses of the arbitration proceeding, other than the expense of their own witnesses and/or counsel.[1]

[1] ***City of Cleveland, Ohio and Cleveland Police Patrolmen's Association.***

ARTICLE 77

DISCRIMINATION

77.1 General.

77.1.1 The Employer and the Association agree that each shall not discriminate in any aspect of employment or membership based on political affiliation, race, religious creed, color, national origin, ancestry, sex, marital status, sexual orientation, age (over 40), medical condition (cured or rehabilitated cancer) or physical disability.[1]

77.1.2 If a bargaining unit member pursues remedies for alleged unlawful discrimination through federal or state agencies charged with investigating such matters, or through the courts, then the decision of such agency, agencies, or court affecting that issue shall supercede any decisions, settlements, or agreements reached through the grievance procedure in this Agreement.[2]

77.2 Affirmative Action.

77.2.1 In the event a problem arises with respect to any Affirmative Action Program, the Employer and the Association will consult with each other in a sincere effort to resolve such problem.[3]

[1] ***City of Fremont, California and Fremont Police Association.***

[2] ***Washington State Patrol and Washington State Patrol Troopers Association.***

[3] ***Monroe County and Monroe County Deputy Sheriffs' Association, Inc.***

ARTICLE 78

PERSONNEL FILES

78.1 Employee Access.

78.1.1 Each employee shall, during normal business hours of the Employee Relations Department and the Police Chief's Office, have the right of access to his/her own personnel file.[1]

78.2 Employee Copies.

78.2.1 The contents of personnel records shall be made available to the employee for inspection and review at any reasonable time during the regular business hours of Employer. At his request, an employee shall be provided one copy of any document placed in the employee's file.[2]

78.3 Rebuttal Statement.

78.3.1 Before an adverse comment can be put into an employee's personnel file, or a completed staff inspection file, the employee must be made aware of the comment by having read the instrument containing the adverse comment and signing the instrument. The employee has the right to refuse to sign the comment after reading it, and the fact that the employee refused to sign the comment shall be noted in the document. The employee may file a written response to the adverse comment entered into his personnel file. Employer must attach the employee's written response to the adverse comment. All formal disciplinary actions, except oral admonitions, shall be recorded in the

[1] ***Sioux City, Iowa and Sioux City Policemen's Association.***

[2] ***Sonoma County, California and Sonoma County Sheriffs' Office Employees Association.***

employee's personnel file and shall constitute the official record to be utilized in disciplinary proceedings.[1]

78.4 Access by Others.

78.4.1 The only other persons permitted to have access to the contents of an employee's personnel folder, excluding background investigations and references from previous Employers, are a designated representative of the employee having the employee's signed authorization, and the Employer's authorized staff.[2]

78.4.2 The Employee's file shall not be made available to any person or organization other than the Employer and Employee without the Employee's express authorization, unless pursuant to Court order.[3]

78.5 Purging.

78.5.1 All disciplinary matters will be removed from the personnel file at the following times and under the following conditions:

78.5.1.1 Written Reprimand: One (1) year after the date of the imposition of the written reprimand;

78.5.1.2 Suspension, Demotion or Disciplinary Transfer: Two (2) years after the date of imposition of the suspension, demotion or disciplinary transfer.

78.5.1.3 Any similar violations occurring during the above time periods will cause the existing disciplinary action(s) to be

[1] ***Municipality of Anchorage and Anchorage Police Department Employees Association.***

[2] ***State of Oregon and Oregon State Police Officers' Association.***

[3] ***Macomb County, Georgia and Macomb County Deputy Sheriff's Association.***

maintained in the personnel file for an additional one (1) year period for written reprimands, or two (2) year period for a suspension, demotion or disciplinary transfer.

78.5.1.4 A record of an oral reprimand will not be maintained in the personnel file.[1]

78.5.2 Retention schedule shall be as follows in compliance with the State law. Material attached to and a part of any document identified below shall carry the same retention period as the document itself.

78.5.2.1 Permanent retention. The following materials shall be permanently retained in an employee's file:

Employment Application	Applicant Investigation
Pre-Appointment Interview	Medical History
Medical Examination	Oath of Office
Appointment Letter	Reports on Accidents
Summary Training Record	Employee Leave
Promotion Letters	Transfer Letters
Special Weapons Approval	Sick Leave Trade Form
Off-Duty Employment Approval	

78.5.2.2 Five-Year Retention. Notice of disciplinary action resulting in loss of time or pay.

78.5.2.3 Three-Year Retention. All reports, letters and other correspondence, including commendations and reports of discipline not included above.

[1] ***Municipality of Anchorage and Anchorage Police Department Employees Association.***

78.5.2.4 Records will be purged from an employee's personnel file in accordance with the above retention schedule.[1]

78.6 Notice of Placement of Item in File.

78.6.1 Officers shall be simultaneously notified in writing when anything other than of a routine nature is placed in their personnel files. In this same regard, a copy of any disciplinary action or material related to job performance which is placed in an officer's personnel files shall be made available to the officer prior to or at the same time that it is placed in the personnel files. Furthermore, no citizen complaint shall be placed in an officer's personnel files unless the complaint is accompanying a specific disciplinary action related to the complaint.[2]

78.7 No Secret Files.

78.7.1 Only one official personnel file shall be maintained on a bargaining unit member, though a copy of the file may be maintained at the district level. No secret personnel file will be kept on any bargaining unit member. This does not preclude a supervisor from maintaining notes on a bargaining unit member's job performance for the explicit purpose of preparing departmental employee performance evaluation reports.[3]

78.8 Information Contained in File.

78.8.1 Personnel investigations that result in "exonerated," "unfounded" or "not sustained" dispositions shall not be made a part of the employee's personnel file.[4]

[1] ***State of Oregon and Oregon State Police Officers Association.***

[2] ***Champaign, Illinois and Champaign Policemen's Benevolent and Protective Assocation.***

[3] ***Washington State Patrol and Washington State Patrol Troopers Association.***

[4] ***City of Sioux City, Iowa and Sioux City Police Officers' Association.***

78.9 Citizen Complaints.

78.9.1 It is recognized that the citizen's complaint against police officers must be investigated in order to preserve the integrity of the profession. Unsubstantiated unsigned citizen complaints shall not be placed in employee's personnel file. The investigation shall be carried out in an expeditious and professional manner. All record of citizen complaints shall be removed from the employee's personnel file after one (1) year from date of most recent complaint.[1]

78.9.2 All Internal Affairs Unit records shall be maintained for a period of five (5) years and one (1) month from the date of the occurrence of alleged conduct by an officer which conduct is the basis of an internal affairs complaint and/or investigation; However, they shall not be used as a basis for subsequent discipline of officers after two (2) years and one (1) month.[2]

ARTICLE 79

PROMOTION

79.1 Promotions.

79.1.1 Promotional Examinations – Example 1.

79.1.1.1 For the purposes of this Article, promotions will be defined as moving an employee from a position in one class in the bargaining unit to a different position in another class having a greater degree of responsibility and a higher maximum salary, which is at the first law enforcement level outside the bargaining unit.

[1] ***City of Southfield and Southfield Police Officers Association.***

[2] ***City of Kansas City, Kansas and Fraternal Order of Police, Lodge 4.***

79.1.1.2 The Employer will guarantee all bargaining unit employees the following:

79.1.1.3 Publication and dissemination of standards and criteria for promotion which permit all employees to adequately prepare for advancement.

79.1.1.4 Competitive promotional examinations that meet or exceed all legal requirements of validity and reliability and which are designed to assess the necessary knowledge, skills, and abilities to successfully perform the rank of Sergeant in the Police Department.

79.1.1.5 The Employer will announce the Sergeant's promotional examination at least ninety (90) days in advance of the test date. A list of the areas which the examination will cover as well as the sources from which the examination will be drawn will be posted by the Employer, and all such reference materials and sources will be made available to eligible candidates for study purposes. Candidates for the rank of Sergeant must meet the minimum eligibility requirements during the life of the eligibility list.[1]

79.1.2 Promotional Examinations – Example 2.

79.1.2.1 Study Materials Committee. On November 1 of each year, the Employer shall establish a committee(s) for the selection of study materials for the written promotional examination for each rank. Such materials which are selected shall be reviewed by the Employer who shall make the final selection subject to approval by the Civil Service Commission.

79.1.2.2 List of Study Materials. A listing of all potential materials from which promotional examination questions may

[1] ***City of Tallahassee, Florida and the Big Bend Benevolent Association, Inc.***

be taken shall be posted annually each January for examinations to be administered within the one-year period beginning the following April. Such material may not be used unless available from publishing companies more than sixty (60) days prior to the examination.

79.1.2.3 Reimbursement for Promotional Text Materials. The Employer shall reimburse to each officer attaining a passing score of seventy percent (70%) on the written examination for the cost of text materials announced for said examination. Payment is conditioned upon the officer providing the Employer with receipts for the purchase of said text(s).

79.1.2.4 Promotion to Detective Investigator and Sergeant. All eligible promotional candidates shall be given an identical examination in the presence of each other. The promotional examination shall be entirely in writing and no part of such examination shall be by oral interview. All of the questions asked on the examination must be prepared and composed in such a manner that the grading of all examination papers can be promptly completed immediately after the examination is held. All examination papers shall be graded as they are completed, at the place where the examination is given, and in the presence of any candidates who wish to remain during the grading. The Civil Service Director is charged with the responsibility for preparation and security of all promotional examinations. The fairness and validity of any competitive promotional examination is the responsibility of the Civil Service Commission, the Director, and any municipal employee involved in the preparation or administration of the examination. The written examination shall consist of questions relating to the duties of the classification of the position to be filled. The Commission shall announce all reading materials to be actually covered and the number of questions from each in the written promotional examination no more than one hundred twenty (120) calendar days and no less than sixty (60) calendar days prior to said examination. A score of 70% on the written examination shall be based upon a maximum score of 100 points, which shall be determined entirely by the correctness of the answers to the questions. In establishing the eligibility list from a promotional examination, the grade for each candidate taking the examination shall be computed by adding the candidate's points for seniority, not to exceed ten (10), to the written grade.

79.1.2.5 In the event that written examination scores are the same, the ranking of those shall be done on the basis of seniority in rank as defined in this Article.

79.1.2.6 Each eligible promotional candidate shall have the opportunity to examine test source materials, his examination, and his answers, together with the grading of that examination within five (5) working days after said examination. The candidate may see the above, but may not remove the examination or copy any question used. Matters which are appealable to the Commission shall continue to be appealable and the decision of the Commission shall be final. Candidates arriving after the appointed starting time of the examination will not be admitted or allowed to participate in the examination. The Commission shall announce the registration period for the examination to be given, and all candidates shall be required to register for said exam during the announced period, which period shall not be less than fifteen (15) days and no later registrations will be allowed.[1]

79.2 Internal Affairs Summary Sheet.

79.2.1 If a member is being considered for a promotion, he/she shall be provided a copy of the Internal Affairs summary

[1] City of San Antonio, Texas and San Antonio Police Officers' Association.

sheet that is forwarded to anyone considering the member's promotion.[1]

79.3 Promotional Salary Advancement.

79.3.1 When an officer or employee is promoted to a position in a higher classification from a position in a lower classification in the same occupational career ladder, he or she shall be reassigned to a Step "A" in the appropriate salary range for the higher classification; provided however, that if the base salary step currently being paid such officer or employee is already equal to or higher than said Step "A," he or she will be placed in the lowest step in the appropriate salary rate range as will grant that officer or employee an increase of one (1) salary step over his or her current case salary step including any additive or additives such as career development or educational incentive pay, but excluding shift differential, assignment pay and bilingual pay.[2]

ARTICLE 80

RESIGNATION

80.1 Basis for Resignation.

80.1.1 Any Police Officer whose removal from the service is sought may resign at any time prior to the decision of the Safety Director. The employee's work record as it pertains to the resignation shall show only that he resigned of his own accord. Upon request, a copy of the work record shall be furnished to the employee.[3]

[1] ***City of Columbus, Ohio and Fraternal Order of Police, Capital City Lodge 9.***

[2] ***City of Santa Ana and Santa Ana Police Officers Association.***

[3] ***City of Toledo, Ohio and Toledo Police Patrolman's Association, Local 10.***

80.2 Reinstatement After Resignation.

80.2.1 Procedures.

80.2.1.1 An employee who terminates his employment in good standing may be reinstated to a vacant position in his former job classification within three (3) years of his termination date without re-qualifying for employment by competitive processes.

80.2.1.2 An employee reinstated within thirty (30) days of his termination date shall be considered to have continuous service and shall be credited with the amount of accumulated sick leave he had at the time of termination. He shall be placed in his former salary step and shall retain his anniversary date for purposes of merit pay increases. If his anniversary date has occurred during the period of his absence, his new anniversary date shall be the first day of the next bi-weekly pay period following reinstatement.

80.2.1.3 An employee reinstated after thirty (30) days of his termination date may be considered to have broken service for purposes of salary step status, and shall be considered to have broken service for all other employee benefits.

80.2.1.4 An employee may be reinstated under the provisions of the Vocational Rehabilitation Administrative Regulation to any vacant position for which he/she meets the minimum qualifications.[1]

[1] ***Anaheim, California and Anaheim Police Association.***

ARTICLE 81

PHYSICAL EXAMINATIONS

81.1 Voluntary Examinations.

81.1.1 Procedures.

81.1.1.1 All employees covered by this Agreement shall be entitled to a physical examination. Sworn officers forty (40) years or older shall be provided an examination once each year, and each year thereafter on the anniversary date of the employee's first (1st) physical examination. Sworn officers under the age of forty (40) and non-sworn personnel are entitled to biennial examination.

81.1.1.2 Such examinations shall be performed by a licensed physician chosen by the Employer. Such examinations shall include the following tests for sworn personnel: (1) Medical History; (2) Complete Physical Examination; (3) X-Ray (chest - two views, L-S spine -one view); (4) Cardiovascular (ECG, blood pressure, pulse rate); (5) Spirometry (breath test); (6) Hearing Test; (7) Blood Test (CB and Chem 24); (8) Complete Urinalysis; (9) Vision Test (acuity and color); (10) Tonometry (glaucoma test); (11) Pap Smear and Breast Examination.

81.1.1.3 Examinations for non-sworn personnel shall consist of the above evaluation with x-ray limited to one view – chest.

81.1.1.4 Employees shall be allowed one (1) administrative leave day with full pay for said physical examination.

81.1.1.5 The Employer shall choose licensed physicians of the highest caliber to refer the employees to for their physical examinations.

81.1.1.6 All employees shall report to the examining physician and fill out all necessary forms before receiving their physical examinations.

81.1.1.7 The Employer agrees to pay for the complete physical examination as outlined in this Section, directly to the physician giving the physical examination to scheduled employees by check following receipt of billing by the attending physician.

81.1.1.8 All necessary forms when completed by the physician will be returned to the Employer who shall provide a copy to the employee upon request. If the annual physical examination results in any findings which the physician feels might affect the employee's ability to perform his duties, such findings shall be immediately communicated to the Employer and the employee. If the Employer requests the physician to develop a corrective plan, and the physician develops such a plan, the employee shall use his best efforts to follow it. However, the employee shall be allowed to seek a second medical opinion, at the Employer's expense, if he disagrees with the physician. Should the findings and recommendations of the two examining physicians significantly differ, a specialist, also at the expense of the Employer, will be requested to conduct a third party examination, in which case the specialist's findings shall be followed.

81.1.1.9 The designation of a physician by the Employer shall be for the sole purpose of performing said physical examination and shall not constitute interference with the employee's free choice of a physician for normal medical care thereafter.

81.1.1.10 It shall be mandatory that all employees covered by this Agreement shall receive a physical examination as required in this Article.

81.1.1.11 In the event the employee is required, by the Employer, for any reason, to submit to a physical examination on the employee's normal day off, the employee shall be granted one (1) day administrative leave to be selected by the employee subject to operational needs of the Department.[1]

81.2 Health and Safety Examinations.

81.2.1 In the interest of health, safety, or job performance, the Employer may require a medical or psychological examination of an employee. The Employer shall give reasons in writing to the employee for the required examination upon the employee's request. Any such examination shall be conducted by a licensed practitioner.

81.2.1.1 If, in the examiner's opinion, the employee's condition jeopardizes his health or safety, or that of another employee, or renders his job performance unsatisfactory, the Employer may relieve the employee from active employment, and he will be eligible to use his accrued sick leave.

81.2.1.2 Any Employer-required examinations shall be paid in full by the Employer. Any time spent by the employee traveling to, from, and during the examination will be work time, subject to any applicable call-in or overtime pay. Any other time necessarily lost by the employee awaiting examination or results will be treated as administrative leave. If the results of the examination are that the employee is properly relieved from duty, this will be charged instead to accrued sick leave. The employee will be provided complete copies of all reports, findings and recommendations of the examiner.

[1] ***Municipality of Anchorage and Anchorage Police Department Employees Association.***

81.2.1.3 At the employee's option, a "second opinion" medical or psychological examination may be conducted by a licensed practitioner of the employee's choice. Such examination will be paid for by the employee and time spent will not be subject to overtime provisions. Complete copies of all reports, findings and recommendations of the optional examination will be provided to the Employer.

81.2.1.4 If the opinions of the Employer's examiner and the employee's examiner are in conflict, either the Employer or the employee may appeal the determination to an examiner agreed upon by the first two. All relevant records and information will be made available to the third examiner, whose opinion shall be final as it relates to the specific issues originally prompting the first required examination. The cost of any third examination shall be shared equally between the Employer and the employee. Both the Employer and the employee shall receive complete copies of all reports, findings and recommendations of the third examiner.

81.2.1.5 If it is determined that the employee's medical or psychological condition did not jeopardize his health or safety, or that of other employees, or did not render his job performance unsatisfactory, all sick leave directed to be used will be reinstated to the employee and leave taken will be charged to paid administrative leave.

81.2.1.6 Employees returning from, or remaining on, leave of absence because of disability may be requested to participate in a medical or psychological examination subject to the above provisions and appeals. In such cases, the provision of reinstated sick leave provided in paragraph (d) of this article shall be in effect the date of the first required examination for any employee who was then fit for duty.[1]

81.3 Directed Care or Examination.

81.3.1 If the Employer directs a Patrol Officer to go to a doctor or other facility for treatment, the doctor or facility shall be agreeable to both the Officer and the Employer.[2]

ARTICLE 82

SUBSTANCE/ALCOHOL ABUSE TESTING AND POLICIES

82.1 Drug Testing.

82.1.1 Use of Alcohol and Drugs.

82.1.1.1 Policy: The Employer considers its employees to be its most valuable asset and is concerned about their safety, health and wellbeing. The misuse of alcohol and other drugs can impair employee performance and general physical and mental health, and may jeopardize the safety of co-workers and the general public. The Employer is committed to maintaining a safe and healthy work place for all employees by identifying the misuse of alcohol and drugs and assisting employees to overcome these problems through appropriate treatment and, if necessary, disciplinary action. The presence or treatment of a substance abuse problem will not excuse an employee from meeting performance, safety or attendance standards or following other Employer instructions.

[1] ***City of Kettering, Ohio and Fraternal Order of Police, Lodge #92.***

[2] ***City of Kettering, Ohio and Fraternal Order of Police, Lodge #92.***

82.1.1.2 Employee Assistance Program: The Employer will establish an Employee Assistance Program (EAP) at no cost to the employee. The general purpose of the EAP will be to reduce problems in the workforce and retain valued employees. The EAP will offer limited professional assistance to employees in dealing with problems of a personal nature, including alcohol and drug use, that may have an adverse effect on job performance.

82.1.1.3 Baseline Testing: Those employees who are or may be exposed to hazardous substances or health hazards, including dangerous drugs or dangerous chemicals used for the manufacture of drugs, at or above permissible exposure limits (as defined by OSHA regulations) in the course and scope of their employment shall be tested by the Employer for exposure to the hazardous substance as follows:

82.1.1.4 Baseline drug test prior to assignment to an area where employees will be or may be exposed to hazardous substances or health hazards.

82.1.1.5 At least once every 12 months thereafter unless the employee's attending physician believes a longer interval is appropriate, but not to exceed biannual exams.

82.1.1.6 At termination or reassignment to an area where exposure will not occur if the employee has not had an examination within the preceding six (6) months.

82.1.1.7 As soon as possible after the notification that signs or symptoms indicating possible overexposure have developed or, an injury has occurred, or exposure above the permissible exposure limits or published exposure levels has occurred in an emergency situation, and

82.1.1.8 Where the employee's attending physician determines that examinations on a basis more frequently than that outlined above are medically necessary.

82.1.1.9 The test will be done at Employer's expense and on Employer time.

82.1.1.10 Prohibited Conduct: The following conduct is prohibited:

82.1.1.11 A. The buying, selling, or providing, or possession for the purpose of buying, selling, or providing controlled substances, including marijuana, while on Employer property or in Employer vehicles or equipment, or during work hours, including paid rest and meal periods.

82.1.1.12 B. Being at work under the influence of alcohol intoxicants, or consuming alcoholic intoxicants while in Employer vehicles or equipment at any time, or on Employer property during work hours, including paid rest and meal periods.

82.1.1.13 C. Being at work with a blood alcohol content that reaches or exceeds .02% by weight of alcohol in the blood.

82.1.1.14 D. In the event that the Employer wishes to call out an employee to perform additional duties and the employee has consumed intoxicants, the employee will notify his or her supervisor as to the amount of intoxicants the employee has consumed, and the Employer will decide whether the employee will be called out to perform additional duties.

82.1.1.15 E. Possession of any controlled substance including marijuana (but excluding any substance lawfully prescribed for the employee's use which has not been obtained for the purpose of abuse) while on Employer property or in Employer vehicles or equipment at any time, during work hours, including paid rest and meal periods. However, this excludes substances that have been legally prescribed for an employee's own use.

82.1.1.16 F. Being at work under the influence of any controlled substance, including marijuana, or having such substances "present in the body" (excluding any substance lawfully prescribed for the employee's use which has not been obtained for the purpose of abuse) while on Employer property or in Employer vehicles or equipment at any time, during work hours, including paid rest and meal periods. An employee has a controlled substance "present in the body" when the employee tests "positive" in any blood or urine test administered. An employee shall be deemed to test "positive" for cannabinoids (marijuana or hashish) if his or her urine test indicates 50 or more nanograms THC metabolites/ml. However, this excludes substances that have been prescribed for an employee's own use.

82.1.1.17 G. Abusing any substance which is lawfully prescribed by regularly taking it in excessive quantities or by unlawfully obtaining it for purposes of abuse.

82.1.1.18 H. For purposes of this Article, the term "controlled substance" shall be defined in accordance with state law.

82.1.1.19 <u>Under The Influence</u>: The term "under the influence" of controlled substances including marijuana or alcoholic intoxicants covers not only the well-known and easily recognized conditions and degrees of impairment and intoxication, but any perceptible abnormal mental or physical condition which is the result of indulging to any degree in controlled substances, marijuana or alcoholic intoxicants which perceptibly tend to deprive the use of that clearness of intellect and control the employee would otherwise possess.

82.1.1.20 Mandatory Testing:

82.1.1.21 A. Where the Employer has a reasonable suspicion that an employee is under the influence of any alcoholic intoxicants or controlled substances, including marijuana, or has a controlled substance, including marijuana, present in the body, the Employer may require that the employee immediately consent and submit to field impairment tests, blood, urine or breathalyzer test. The Employer shall pay for the costs of the tests. A refusal to consent and submit to any of these tests shall subject an employee to immediate termination.

82.1.1.22 B. When the employee is notified that he or she is required to consent and submit to such tests, or searches as described in Section 10 of this Article, he or she may request the presence of an Association representative to witness the tests or searches. The test or searches may not be unduly delayed to wait for a representative. The absence of a representative shall not be grounds for the employee to refuse to consent and submit to such tests or searches. The presence of a representative shall not disrupt or interfere with the tests or searches.

82.1.1.23 C. Before a supervisor, acting on behalf of the Employer under this policy, may require an employee to consent and submit to any test(s) specified in this section, the supervisor must first obtain concurrence from the supervisor's department head or designee that the information available to the Employer about the subject employee is sufficient to determine reasonable suspicion that prohibited conduct will be established as a result of such test(s).

82.1.1.24 D. The employee shall give consent to a blood, urine or breathalyzer test by signing a consent form. The form shall contain the following information:

82.1.1.24 1. Employee's consent to release test results to Employer;

82.1.1.26 2. The procedure for confirming an initial positive test result for a controlled substance, including marijuana;

82.1.1.27 3. The consequences of a confirmed positive test result for a controlled substance, including marijuana;

82.1.1.28 4. The consequences of a positive test for alcohol, including one at or above .02%;

82.1.1.29 5. A listing provided by the employee of legally prescribed and over-the-counter medications which may be in the employee's body;

82.1.1.30 6. The right to explain a confirmed positive test result for a controlled substance, including marijuana, or a positive test for alcohol;

82.1.1.31 7. The consequences of refusing to consent to the blood, urine or breathalyzer test.

82.1.1.32 E. In the event that the blood or urine test results are positive for controlled substance(s), including marijuana, the Employer shall require that a second confirmatory test from the same sample be conducted, using gas chromatography mass spectrograph techniques or equivalent, which also must be positive before concluding the employee has such substance(s) present in their body.

82.1.1.33 F. If a blood or confirmed urine test is positive, the Employer will instruct the laboratory to retain the blood or urine sample for a period of not less than 30 calendar days from the date the tests are complete for the purpose of allowing the employee to conduct an independent test at his of her own expense at a laboratory approved by the Employer.

82.1.1.34 G. The procedure followed under this Article to obtain, handle and store blood and urine samples and to conduct laboratory test shall be documented to establish procedural integrity and chain of evidence. Such procedure shall be administered with due regard for the employee's privacy and the need to maintain the confidentiality of test results to an extent which is not inconsistent with the needs of this policy. The employee shall be notified of the results of all tests conducted pursuant to this policy.

82.1.1.35 Consequences of Test Results:

82.1.1.36 A. Test results which do not positively establish that the employee has engaged in prohibited conduct as described in this Article shall result in no further action against the employee related to an alleged violation of those sections. The employee shall be informed of such test results.

82.1.1.37 B. If an employee who has not previously committed prohibited conduct specified in this article as a direct result of undercover police assignments is found to have committed such prohibited conduct, the employee shall immediately submit to a medical evaluation by a doctor selected and paid by the Employer. The evaluation will determine the extent of the employee's use of, and dependence on, the applicable substance(s) and, if necessary, recommend an appropriate program of treatment, including but not limited to rehabilitation and counseling to prevent future use. If a program of treatment is recommended by the doctor, the employee shall enroll in it immediately. Failure by the employee to enroll in the recommended program or to complete it successfully shall result in his or her termination from employment.

82.1.1.38 C. If an employee has previously committed prohibited conduct as a direct result of undercover police work assignments, and subsequently is found to have committed such prohibited conduct a second time within three years, he or she shall be terminated. The level of discipline imposed for subsequent instances of such prohibited conduct beyond three years may be termination but shall be determined on a case by case basis.

82.1.1.39 Voluntary Rehabilitation:

82.1.1.40 A. The primary objectives of the Employer's drug and alcohol policy are to maintain employee performance and good health and a safe work environment. If, prior to a requirement by the Employer that the employee submit to any of the tests specified in this Article, the employee notifies a supervisor that he or she has drug or alcohol problems that require treatment, then in that event the employee shall immediately submit to a medical evaluation by a doctor selected and paid by the Employer and shall enroll in a treatment program recommended by the doctor.

82.1.1.41 B. If an employee has previously enrolled in voluntary rehabilitative treatment and subsequently again volunteers for such treatment in advance of being required to submit to any of the tests specified in this Article, then the employee shall immediately submit to a medical evaluation by a doctor selected and paid by the Employer and shall successfully complete the treatment program recommended by the doctor.

82.1.1.42 Supervisor Training: The Employer recognizes that, in order to administer the standards and procedures set forth in this Article fairly and to minimize the possibility of unwarranted testing and searches, supervisory personnel should receive training in how to recognize and deal effectively with substance abuse in the work place. Accordingly, the Employer will provide such training to supervisors before the requirements of this Article are implemented and enforced.[1]

[1] ***City of Salem, Oregon and Salem Police Employees' Union.***

82.2 Screening Standards.

82.2.1 The Employer and the Association in consultation with the Medical Provider have determined the type of screening to be used. The only substances to be tested for, and the threshold substance levels that should be considered a positive test result are as follows:

Drug	Initial Screening Level	Confirmation Level
Amphetamines	1000 ng/ml	500 ng/ml
Methamphetamine		
Barbiturates	300 ng/ml	500 ng/ml
Benzodiazepines	300ng/ml	300 ng/ml
Cannabinoids	50ng/ml	15 ng/ml
Cocaine Metabolite	300 ng/ml	150 ng/ml
Methadone	300 ng/ml	300 ng/ml
Methaqualone	300 ng/ml	300 ng/ml
Opiates	300 ng/ml*	300 ng/ml (Codeine) 300 ng/ml (Morphine)
	*25 ng/ml if immunoassay specific for free morphine	
Phencyclidine (PCP)	25 ng/ml	25 ng/ml
Propoxyphene	300 ng/ml	300ng/ml

82.2.1.1 Should NIDA add to or delete from the current panel of controlled substances or alter the initial screening or confirmation levels, this program will be modified to conform to NIDA standards. Employees will be notified, in writing, of such changes.

82.2.1.2 Screen Results.

82.2.1.3 Negative Results.

82.2.1.4 If the screen results are negative, the results will be reported in writing to the Medical Review Officer and the sample will be discarded.

82.2.1.5 Positive Results.

82.2.1.6 If the results of the first screen are positive, the Medical Provider will immediately conduct a second screening using a different methodology on a different portion of the original sample.

82.2.1.7 The Medical Provider will report the confirmation screen results, whether positive or negative, to the Medical Review Officer. Any adulterated sample, or samples otherwise tampered with, may be treated for disciplinary purposes as a positive result.

82.2.1.8 If the confirmation screen results are positive, employees may request an additional screening, beyond the confirmation screening, by any NIDA approved alternate laboratory. Employees will be responsible for the cost of any additional screenings. For chain of custody purposes, the sample will be transferred directly from the Medical Provider to the alternate laboratory, and the alternate laboratory will complete the Chain of Custody form.

82.2.1.9 If the confirmation screen results are positive, the Medical Provider will retain the sample for at least one (1) year to allow for additional screenings, and employee appeals.

82.3 Role of Medical Review Officer.

82.3.1 The Medical Review Officer (MRO) is a physician knowledgeable in the medical use of prescription drugs and the pharmacology and toxicology of illicit drugs. The MRO's primary responsibility is to review and interpret positive test results obtained through the DSP. In fulfilling these responsibilities, the MRO is to be guided by the U.S. Department of Health and Human Services (DHHS) Mandatory Guidelines.

82.3.1.1 If any question arises as to the accuracy or validity of a positive test result, the MRO should, in collaboration with the laboratory director and consultants, review the laboratory records to determine whether the required procedures were followed. The MRO then makes a determination as to whether the result is scientifically sufficient to take further action. If records from collection sites or laboratories raise doubts about the handling of samples, the MRO may deem the urinary evidence insufficient and no further actions relative to individual employees would occur.

82.3.1.2 The MRO must also assess and determine whether alternate <u>medical</u> explanations could account for any positive test result. In reviewing the laboratory results, the MRO may conduct a medical interview with the employee, review the employee's medical history, or review any other relevant biomedical factors. The MRO shall also review any information provided by an employee attempting to show legitimate use of a drug. The MRO may perform limited physical examinations, seeking, for example, needle tracks, in determining whether clinical signs of drug abuse are present.

82.3.1.3 The MRO must ultimately determine whether some reason other than illegal drug use explains a drug-positive urine. If the MRO verifies illegal drug use, the information related to the use of illegal drugs will be disclosed to the Chief or Acting Chief. Any medical information provided to the MRO that is not specifically related to use of illegal drugs will be treated as confidential and not disclosed. If it is determined with reasonable certainty that there is a legitimate medical or other reason to account for the positive laboratory findings, no information identifying the specific employee will be disclosed and the test results will be reported as negative.[1]

82.4 Duty Assignment After Treatment.

82.4.1 Once a member successfully completes rehabilitation, he/she shall be returned to his/her regular duty assignment, provided (1) the member is then in compliance with this Agreement, and (2) a member may not be returned to an assignment within five (5) years which poses an unusually high risk of exposure to a controlled substance or alcohol for which they have been treated (e.g., vice, narcotics).[2]

82.4.2 No officer shall be ordered to submit to a blood test, breathalyzer test, or any other test to determine the percentage of alcohol in the blood except as may be provided otherwise by specific statute.[3]

ARTICLE 83

OUTSIDE EMPLOYMENT

83.1 Standards.

83.1.1 The Employer reserves the right to restrict secondary employment for good cause.[4]

83.1.2 An employee may engage in outside business activity or outside employment provided it is not inconsistent or in-

[1] ***Akron, Ohio and Fraternal Order of Police Lodge #7.***

[2] ***City of Columbus, Ohio and Fraternal Order of Police, Capital City Lodge #9.***

[3] ***Akron, Ohio and Fraternal Order of Police Lodge #7.***

[4] ***Chicago, Illinois and Fraternal Order of Police .***

compatible with or does not interfere with the proper discharge of the employee's duties and responsibilities as a police officer.

83.1.2.1 Approval for outside business activity or outside employment must be obtained from the Chief of Police, and shall be for a period of one (1) year. The employee may request it be renewed after one (1) year.

83.1.2.2 Approval will not be granted for an outside business activity or for outside employment which would involve more than thirty (30) hours per week of work, or for work in private or personal security or in businesses that are regulated by the Employer, e.g., bars, adult movies or adult bookstores, etc.

83.1.2.3 Approval to engage in outside business activity or outside employment shall not be unreasonably withheld.[1]

83.2 Outside Employment Without Uniform.

83.2.1 Employees shall be entitled to engage in outside employment, including employment or service as an appointed officer for any public body, with full police authority, including powers of arrest, which does not require the use of the official uniform as defined in the Department's rules and regulations and which is not otherwise prohibited by the provisions of this Agreement, provided that the duties of the outside employment do not constitute a conflict of interest nor conflict with an employee's performance of his duties with the Employer. The provisions of this Section shall be enforced by the Department Head or his designated representative whose decision shall be final and binding and not subject to appeal or review by an arbitrator or Personnel Review Board.[2]

[1] ***Detroit, Michigan and Detroit Police Officers Association.***

[2] ***City of Omaha, Nebraska and Omaha Police Union, Local 101.***

83.3 Details.

83.3.1 Detail Pay. An employee who works a detail shall be paid at the rate of time and one-half a non-probationary patrolman's regular rate of pay as of July 1 of the current contract year and shall be guaranteed a minimum of four (4) hours pay at said rate.

83.3.1.1 In determining hours worked, any period of time worked in excess of fifteen (15) minutes, shall be considered as one (1) full hour.

83.3.1.2 Detail Manpower. In those details requiring three (3) or more employees, there shall be at least one superior officer assigned to the detail. In such case, that superior officer shall be paid at time and one-half a sergeant's regular rate of pay.

83.3.1.3 Unless otherwise agreed upon between the Association and the Employer, there shall be a minimum of one (1) employee for every seven hundred and fifty (750) persons in attendance or at the detail.

83.3.1.4 Assignment List And Proper Uniform. Details are to be assigned only to employees as defined herein and subject to the following conditions:

83.3.1.5 1. All details shall be first approved and authorized by the Chief of Police or his designee before any assignments are made.

83.3.1.6 2. Any employees assigned to a detail shall be required to wear the proper uniform as designated by the Chief of Police.

83.3.1.7 3. All employees assigned to a detail shall be subjected to all rules, regulations, policies, orders, instructions, and memoranda of the Police Division.

83.3.1.8 4. The Employer agrees to strictly enforce all ordinances dealing with the control of traffic during construction including but not limited to Chapter 1787 of the Ordinances of the City.

83.3.1.9 5. All requests for details must be made through the Police Division. Employees shall not be permitted to accept details unless the request has been made through the Police Division. All detail shall be made by the "Detail Officer" designated by the Chief of Police. Details shall be assigned on a rotating basis as far as practicable. The Detail Officer shall have control of the detail list and the responsibility of ensuring the proper operation of all details. At the start of each week, the Detail Officer shall submit to the Chief of Police a list of all details and the names of all members who are assigned to each detail. The authorized detail list shall also be posted once a week for details granted the previous week.

83.3.1.10 6. It shall be the Detail Officer's responsibility to maintain a Detail Book which shall include the following information for each detail: date, location of detail; scheduled hours of detail; officer assigned to the detail; officer actually working the detail; signature of officer who actually works the detail. Each employee assigned a detail shall be required to report to the police station prior to the assignment to complete the pertinent information in the Detail Book. At that time, the employee shall present himself to the platoon commander who shall confirm the accuracy of the information in the Detail Book and also the fact that the employee is properly attired for the detail.

83.3.1.11 7. Once an employee is assigned to and accepts a detail, he or she must work said detail, unless he or she obtains a replacement who will work the detail assignment. Any employee accepting a detail assignment who cannot obtain a replacement is responsible and must work that detail.

83.3.1.12 8. Employees shall not be eligible for assignment to detail while on injured-on-duty or light-duty status, while on suspension from the police department or while on suspension from the detail list.

83.3.1.13 Payment for Details. The Employer shall not be responsible for the payment or the collection of detail pay. Detail pay shall be made directly by the contractor or entity for whom the detail is worked to the employee who performed the detail, and the collection of detail pay shall be the responsibility of the employee who performs the detail.

83.3.1.14 Special Holiday Pay. Details on the following holidays and holiday eves shall be compensated at the rate of two (2) times a non-probationary patrolman's regular rate of pay as of July 1 of the current contract year. The holiday eves as set forth herein shall commence at 6:00 p.m.

New Year's Eve	Fourth of July
New Year's Day	Thanksgiving
Holy Saturday	Christmas Eve
Easter Sunday	Christmas

83.3.1.15 Notwithstanding the foregoing, Employer-paid details (e.g. PARE program) on holidays and holiday eves shall be compensated at the regular rate for detail pay.

83.3.1.16 Injuries on Details. Any employee who is injured on an Employer-approved detail, shall be entitled to the same rights, privileges and benefits as if he were injured while performing his duties for the Employer and shall be subject to all rules, regulations, policies, general orders, instructions, and memoranda of the Police Division.

83.3.1.17 Liquor Establishment Details. Employees shall only work Employer-approved liquor establishment details. Said details shall be worked in the uniform of the day as directed by the Chief of Police.

83.3.1.18 Removal Of Name From Detail List. Any member of the bargaining unit shall have the right to withdraw his/her name from the detail list at any time, but once withdrawn, an individual must wait a period of thirty (30) days before being placed back on the detail list.

83.3.1.19 No member's name shall be deleted from the detail list without his/her consent, unless the member has committed one of the following infractions, for which the penalties set forth below will be imposed:

83.3.1.20 A. OFFENSE: Failure to Appear at Detail Without Prior Notification to the Department.

PENALTY: First violation within a calendar year – 2 weeks' suspension from detail list. Second violation – 1-month suspension from detail list. Third violation within a calendar year – 6 months' suspension from detail list.

83.3.1.21 B. OFFENSE: Tardiness (Over 15 Minutes).

PENALTY: First violation within a calendar year - written warning. Second violation within a calendar year – 2 weeks' suspension from the detail list. Third violation within a calendar year – 3 months' suspension from the detail list.

83.3.1.22 C. OFFENSE: Failure to Sign Detail Book.

PENALTY: Same as "A."

83.3.1.23 D. OFFENSE: Leaving Detail Early Without Obtaining Permission.

PENALTY: Same as "B."

83.3.1.24 E. OFFENSE: Taking an Extended Lunch Break.

PENALTY: Same as "B."

83.3.1.25 F. OFFENSE: Assigning Detail to Another Employee Without Permission of Detail Officer.

PENALTY: Same as "B."

83.3.1.26 G. OFFENSE: Violation of Departmental Regulation While on Detail.

PENALTY: Same as "A."

83.3.1.27 H. OFFENSE: Accepting a Detail While Suspended From the Detail List or Performing Unauthorized Detail or Providing False Information in the Detail Book.

PENALTY: First violation – 4 weeks' suspension from the detail list. Second violation – 4 months' suspension from detail list. Third violation – permanent removal from detail list.

83.3.1.28 The above-described penalties are intended as a control factor for the detail list. In that context, any of the offenses and penalties described above shall not be considered disciplinary action as covered under the Law Enforcement Officers' Bill of Rights nor shall said offenses and penalties appear in any personnel files of the employee. In the event there is a violation of a departmental regulation while on a detail, the employee shall not be subject to both (1) the imposition of the penalties set forth above and (2) the punishment or penalties that the Chief may attempt to impose by bringing departmental charges. The Chief shall decide the manner in which he feels the employee shall be punished or penalized. If the Chief decides to punish/penalize the employee under the provisions of this section of the Agreement for a violation of a departmental regulation while on a detail (as set forth above), then said punishment is subject to the grievance procedure. If the Chief decides to recommend punishment under the Bill of Rights for a violation of a departmental regulation, then the employee shall be entitled to a hearing under the Bill of Rights.

83.3.1.29 Any "B" type violations shall be cumulative for future "B" type violations. Any "A" type violations shall be cumulative for future "A" and "B" type violations. "B" type violations shall not be cumulative for "A" type violations.[1]

[1] ***City of Pawtucket, Rhode Island and Fraternal Order of Police, Lodge #4.***

CHAPTER 10

INCENTIVE PLANS AND PREMIUM PAY

Increasingly, simply looking at wages is not an accurate measure of the total compensation paid to law enforcement officers under a collective bargaining agreement. A seemingly ever expanding list of incentive pays, hazardous duty pays and premium pays will occasionally add as much as an additional 10% to the average compensation received by the members of a law enforcement agency. For example, this chapter contains 47 different types of incentive pay received by law enforcement officers.

This chapter includes examples of the variety of wage supplements which appear today in collective bargaining agreements. Included in the chapter are examples of the following types of provisions:

- Longevity
- Education Incentive
- Certification (P.O.S.T.) Incentive
- Hazardous Duty Pay
- Specialty Pay
- Physical Fitness Pay

Also included in this chapter are examples of "combination" incentive plans, which combine a number of different elements of a variety of incentive plans. Combination incentive plans, which are appearing more often in law enforcement collective bargaining agreements, typically include education, longevity, physical fitness and community service components. Increasingly, such incentive plans are known as "career enhancement programs" or "community police officer" programs.

ARTICLE 84

LONGEVITY

84.1 Monthly Premium.

84.1.1 Non-Patrol Longevity.

84.1.1.1 Longevity premiums based upon the top pay step of the classification, Police Officer, shall be added to salaries in accordance with the following schedules:

Longevity	Percentage
Completion of five (5) years of service	2%
Completion of ten (10) years of service	4%
Completion of fifteen (15) years of service	6%
Completion of twenty (20) years of service	8%
Completion of twenty-five (25) years of service	13%
Completion of thirty (30) years of service	15%

84.1.1.2 Patrol Longevity.

84.1.1.3 In order to encourage experienced officers to remain in or to transfer back to the Patrol Division, the parties have agreed to the following Patrol Longevity provision: Police Officers and Sergeants assigned to patrol duty (including those assigned to the City Center, the Mounted Patrol and the Harbor unit) will be eligible for longevity premium pay, based upon the top pay step of the classification Police Officer, in accordance with the following schedule:

Longevity	Percentage
Completion of five (5) years of service	2%
Completion of ten (10) years of service	6%
Completion of fifteen (15) years of service	11%
Completion of twenty (20) years of service	15%

84.1.1.4 Longevity premiums shall be paid beginning with the first full pay period following the completion of the eligibility requirements. For the purpose of determining eligibility for longevity premiums, service shall be limited to continuous time served in good standing as a uniformed member of the Department.[1]

84.1.2 The longevity pay for employees shall be paid on the following basis: Upon completion of five (5) consecutive years of employment, covered employees shall be paid the equivalent of an additional two and one-half percent (2.5%) of their bi-weekly base salary. For each continuing year of consecutive service thereafter, each employee shall receive an additional one-half of one percent (0.5%) increase of the base salary until a maximum of fifteen percent (15%) has been reached. Longevity pay shall become effective at the beginning of the first full pay period following the hiring anniversary date of the employee.[2]

84.2 Annual Bonus System.

84.2.1 An employee who has completed three (3) full years of service in the top salary step shall be entitled to premium pay of three and two tenths percent (3.2%) of his/her annual salary. An employee who has completed three (3) full years in the Sergeant of Police classification shall be entitled to premium pay of two and one-half percent (2.5%) of his/her annual salary.[3]

84.3 Leave Bonus for Longevity.

84.3.1 All employees completing twenty (20) years of service shall be granted one (1) additional day of annual leave per

[1] ***City of Seattle, Washington and Seattle Police Officers Guild.***

[2] ***Las Vegas, Nevada and Las Vegas Police Protective Association.***

[3] ***Oakland, California and Oakland Police Officers Association.***

year up to the time when said employee completes twenty-five (25) years of service.[1]

ARTICLE 85

EDUCATION INCENTIVE

85.1 Monthly Incentive.

85.1.1 Incentive Amounts.

85.1.1.1 The Employer is favorable toward the principle and approves of longevity pay and college incentive pay as part of its salary budget. 45 credits (one year), 2.0% per month additional; 90 credits (two years), 3.5% per month additional; 135 credits (three years), 5.5% per month additional; B.A. or B.S. Degree, 7.0% per month additional; Master's Degree, 9.0% per month additional.

85.1.1.2 College incentive pay will be based on transcripts or other reports from accredited colleges, universities or approved training schools provided by the officer. A joint committee of the Association and the Employer will approve the transcripts and reports and approve credits to be assigned for college incentive pay. A report of this committee shall be placed in each officer's personnel file.

85.1.1.3 College incentive pay may not be received during the initial twelve (12)-month probationary period.

85.1.1.4 College incentive pay will be calculated on the base pay of a First Class Police Officer and added to the base pay of those positions.[2]

[1] ***City of Brownsville, Texas and Brownsville Police Officers' Association.***

[2] ***Everett, Washington and Everett Police Officers Association.***

85.2 Education and Longevity Matrix.

Completed Years of Service	5	6	7	8	9	10	11	12	13	14	15	16	17	18
Premium for Dedicated Service	2	2	2	3	3	3	3	3	5	5	5	5		
Associate's Degree Premium	4	4	4	4	4	5	5	5	5	5	7	7	7	7
Bachelor's Degree Premium	5	5	5	5	5	6	6	6	6	6	8	8	8	10

ARTICLE 86

TUITION REIMBURSEMENT

86.1 Tuition and Books.

86.1.1 Tuition Refunds.

86.1.1.1 The Employer agrees to pay tuition and book expenses for all employees enrolled in accredited university courses or degree programs.[1]

86.2 Reimbursement.

86.2.1 The Employer shall reimburse an employee for the actual cost of all books, tuition and fees paid by an employee to an accredited college or university, provided that those expenses are incurred: (1) In a course leading to a law enforcement related undergraduate degree (A.A. or B.A.); (2) that the employee has received a grade of "C" or better or "pass" in a pass/fail grading system; and (3) that such reimbursement for tuition shall not exceed the prevailing rate for undergraduate tuition es-

[1] ***Municipality of Anchorage and Anchorage Police Department Employees Association.***

tablished by the state-funded university. All books shall become the property of the Department's Law Enforcement Library, provided that when in the determination of the Library Committee such books are not usable by the library because of duplication or subject matter, such books shall be returned to the employee.

86.2.1.1 Reimbursement shall be made only in the event no funds are available from other public funding sources to pay education costs.

86.2.1.2 A Library Committee shall be created and maintained. The committee shall be comprised of five (5) members and shall be constituted as follows: Two (2) members appointed by the Employer; two (2) members appointed by the Association; one (1) representative of the Municipal Library Staff.

86.2.1.3 At least three (3) members of the committee shall be commissioned members of the Police Department. All members shall serve for not less than two (2) years and shall be solely responsible for the administration of the Library Fund. Such committee shall receive a minimum of $250.00 per year from the Employer for the purpose of maintaining and improving a Law Enforcement Library within the Police Department.[1]

86.3 Tuition, Books and Time Off for Classes.

86.3.1 Payment for Current Educational Classes.

86.3.1.1 Officers may be eligible to receive time off from work to attend approved educational classes, and/or they may be eligible to receive full or partial reimbursement for certain expenses which they have incurred in conjunction with such approved educational classes.

[1] ***Renton, Washington and Renton Police Officers Guild.***

86.3.1.2 Eligible Educational Classes: Educational classes which may be approved would include those which it is determined would be relevant to an officer's present job or career path within the Police Department, or which would otherwise be in the interest of and beneficial to the Police Department or the Employer.

86.3.1.3 As a general rule, highest priority shall be given to those educational classes which are directly related to Police Science, Police Administration and Criminal Justice.

86.3.1.4 Requests for Educational Classes: Requests for educational classes shall be submitted, processed and, if approved, paid in the following manner:

86.3.1.5 Request Procedure: When officers are either planning to attend or already attending an educational class which they believe would meet the eligibility criteria referenced above, they may submit a written request to the Employer concerning such class. In this regard, a request which is submitted by an officer concerning an educational class which he or she has already completed shall be deemed ineligible, and shall not be considered or processed any further.

86.3.1.6 A written request which is submitted by an officer prior to or during his or her enrollment in an educational class must include a brief description or course outline of the class, and a statement concerning the benefit which will be derived by the officer, the Police Department, and/or the Employer because of the officer's attendance in the class.

86.3.1.7 In conjunction with their attendance in an educational class, officers may request any or all of the following, provided and to the extent that such are applicable:

86.3.1.8 Paid Time Off from Work: In the case of an educational class which is scheduled to be held during an officer's regularly-scheduled workday or duty shift, the officer may request paid time off from work to attend the class. Such requested time off shall be limited to a maximum of four (4) hours per week, but in no case shall it be greater than the actual time required in conjunction with the officer's travel to and from, and attendance in the educational class. Requests for paid time off from work may only be approved on the condition that the officer's temporary absences from duty will not adversely affect or unduly jeopardize the respective operations and services of the Police Department.

86.3.1.9 Reimbursement for Class-Related Expenses: Officers may request that they receive full or partial reimbursement for any of the following expenses, provided and to the extent that such expenses are actually incurred by them in conjunction with their travel to and from, and attendance in the educational class: (1) Tuition or registration; (2) books and other required class materials; and (3) mileage to and from an educational class which is held outside the area. An estimated cost must be provided for each expense reimbursement which is being requested for a particular educational class.

86.3.1.10 Review and Recommendation Procedure: An Officer's written request concerning an educational class shall be submitted by the Officer to the Police Chief, who shall review and forward it to the Personnel Services Director, along with his or her recommendation.

86.3.1.11 The Personnel Services Director shall review the request and determine whether or not the educational class is relevant to the officer's present job or career path within the Police Department. Following such review, the Personnel Services Director shall forward the request, along with both his or her recommendation and the recommendation of the Police Chief, to the Employer.

86.3.1.12 Approval and Authorization Procedure: The Employer shall review an officer's written request concerning an educational class, along with the recommendations prepared and submitted by the Police Chief and the Personnel Services Director. Provided and to the extent that the Employer determines that the officer's attendance in the educational class will be relevant to the officer's present job or career path within the Police Department, and/or in the interest of and beneficial to the Police Department or the Employer, he or she may approve it. In this regard, the Employer may authorize (including on a modified or reduced basis) the paid time off from work and/or the class related expense reimbursements requested in the officer's written request. Such approval and authorization shall be made by the Employer. In this regard, the Employer's decision concerning requests for educational reimbursement shall be final. Such requests shall not be arbitrarily denied.

86.3.1.13 Payment Procedure: Following the officer's completion of the approved educational class, he or she shall be reimbursed for those class-related expenses authorized by the Employer, subject to any limitations established by the Employer, and provided that the officer submits the following (as applicable): (1) Proof of satisfactory completion of the educational class. For the purpose of this Section, "satisfactory completion" is understood to be a grade of "C" or better in a graded course, or a "pass" in a pass/fail course; (2) receipts showing payment of tuition, registration, books and other required class materials; and (3) Mileage records.[1]

[1] ***Champaign, Illinois and Champaign Policemen's Benevolent and Protective Association.***

ARTICLE 87

CERTIFICATION (P.O.S.T.) INCENTIVE

87.1 General.

87.1.1 Incentive Levels.

87.1.1.1 Intermediate Incentive Bonus: Employees shall receive an education incentive bonus after completion of 7 years of service with the Employer and the achievement of the intermediate P.O.S.T. certificate of 15% of base monthly pay (exclusive of longevity or special compensation).

87.1.1.2 Advanced Certificate: Employees shall receive an education bonus after completion of 9 years of service with the Employer and the achievement of the Advanced P.O.S.T. certificate of 20% of base monthly pay (exclusive of longevity or special compensation).

87.1.1.3 The certification standards shall be the same as those presently in effect by Police Officer's Standards and Training Certification Program or as subsequently revised.

87.1.1.4 An employee must maintain these standards and retain the respective certification in order to continue to receive this educational incentive bonus.

87.1.1.5 Payments shall be made every two pay periods.

87.1.1.6 Such bonus shall not be paid during the original probationary period of an employee. Up to two years of the required service may be substituted on a one year for each two years of full time (paid) external experience in Police Patrol work as a sworn officer.[1]

[1] ***Torrance, California and Torrance Police Officers Association.***

ARTICLE 88

COMBINATION INCENTIVE

88.1 Combination Incentive Plan – Example 1.

88.1.1 Requirements.

88.1.1.1 In order to maintain and improve an officer's health and law enforcement skills, as well as to increase the participation of officers in the life of the community, the parties adopt the following achievement program for bargaining unit members:

88.1.1.2 Achievement Levels.

Incentive Level	Pay Step	Requirement Outline
I	2.5%	Intermediate Certification Health Examination Range Qualification
II	4.0%	Advanced Certification Health Examination Range Qualification
III	5.0%	Intermediate Certification Rating of "Good" on Fitness Test Health Examination Range Qualification Education, Training and Service, 30 Hours
IV	10.0%	Advanced Certification Rating of "Good" on Fitness Test Health Examination Range Qualification Education, Training and Service, 50 Hours

88.1.1.3 Annual Requirements. The officer must obtain or maintain Board on Police Standards and Training (B.P.S.T.) intermediate certificate, for Levels I and III, or advanced certificate, for Levels II and IV.

88.1.1.4 The semi-annual fitness test shall consist of the following exercises: (a) Thirty (30) sit-ups in one and one-half (1-1/2) minutes; (b) twenty (20) consecutive pushups (female members will do pushups from the knees); (c) one and one-half (1-1/2)-mile run as specified in *The New Aerobics* (Bantam Ed., 1970, p. 31), or its equivalent for walking, swimming, or bicycling as specified in *The Aerobics Way* (Bantam Ed., 1978, pp. 90-92). In addition to meeting the minimum standards contained therein, the officer must satisfy the appropriate age-graded aerobic standard for a 1.5 mile run specified above, or for the other exercises cited above, in order to be awarded a rating of "Fair" or "Excellent" on the fitness test. Should the officer fail to meet his intended level of achievement at the time of the physical fitness test, he shall be allowed to continue participation in the program only as provided for in this Article.

88.1.1.5 Health Examination. The health examination shall be conducted at the officer's own expense and shall determine if the officer is in sufficient physical and mental health to perform regularly-assigned functions, to include activities specified in the preceding paragraph. Following the initial examination, a maintenance health examination shall be conducted every three (3) years prior to the age of forty (40) and every two (2) years thereafter. Failure to pass such a health examination or to comply with the above schedule shall disqualify the officer from participation in the achievement program except as provided for in this Article.

88.1.1.6 Education, Training and Community Service. Only as approved in advance by the Employer utilizing reasonable criteria and totaling the number of hours annually as indicated in this Article.

88.1.1.7 Quarter Hours College Credit (converted at a ratio of ten (10) service hours for each quarter hour of college credit). Credit is limited to 30 hours and must be paid for by the employee or a funding source other than the Employer.

88.1.1.8 Law Enforcement Training on Off-Duty Time. Within the education, training, and service hours requirement, the Employer may establish a training hours minimum not to exceed twenty (20) hours based on his assessment of the availability of training hours to off-duty employees. Any minimum training requirement established by the Employer pursuant to this section may be satisfied by completion of training hours as defined in the "Achievement Program Guidelines" published by the Employer and the Achievement Pay Board in September 1980.

88.1.1.9 Minimum Fifteen (15) Hours' Community Service Within the Education, Training and Service Requirement. Such hours shall be awarded only for service within the county and shall be confined to substantial contributions to the community which, in the Employer's judgment, exceed the uncompensated participation characteristic of responsible citizens. Upon mutual agreement of the Employer and the Association, certain Division assignments may be performed and the hours applied to satisfaction of the Achievement Program community service hours requirement.

88.1.1.10 The Employer may devise on an experimental basis proficiency tests for certain Law Enforcement knowledge, skills, or abilities requiring study or practice on the officer's own time.

The standards for such tests and the hour credits which may be earned will be announced in advance by the Employer. The taking of tests eligible for credit under this sub-section shall be on a voluntary basis.

88.1.1.11 It is recognized by the parties that achievement of an "Excellent" rating on the fitness test requires additional physical fitness training time prior to testing. Such a rating is therefore credited with five (5) hours' credit toward the Education, Training, and Service Hours requirement. (An employee receiving an "Excellent" rating on both semi-annual tests shall therefore receive a total of ten (10) hours' credit toward the annual requirement).

88.1.1.12 Range Qualification. Each participating officer shall score at least seventy-five (75) with duty weapon during semi-annual department range qualifications held on his own time.

88.1.1.13 Participation in the achievement program in each fiscal year is contingent upon having fulfilled the previous fiscal year's annual requirements by June 1. Election of level of participation for each fiscal year shall be made no later than June 30 of the previous fiscal year and shall be limited to the level for which the employee has met the fitness requirement in the June fitness test.

88.1.1.14 Continuation of payments under the terms of this program during each fiscal year shall be subject to the following additional requirements: (1) Satisfactory evaluation in a mid-year review of progress being made to fulfill the education training and community service requirements; (2) continued satisfactory scores on range qualification tests with make-up tests allowed on the employee's own time within sixty (60) days of the scheduled test, and (3) maintenance of required fitness level at mid-year fitness test.

88.1.1.15 An employee wishing to continue participation on the achievement program at a higher level than that elected at the beginning of the fiscal year may do so following the mid-year fitness test provided he has fulfilled all mid-year requirements for the newly-elected level.

88.1.1.16 In the event that an officer complies with all requirements, appropriate incentive compensation shall commence with the next pay period after certification is received from B.P.S.T.; however, payment shall be retroactive to the date the officer submits a completed application for B.P.S.T. certification.

88.1.1.17 In the event of a disabling medical occurrence, not to include preexisting physical conditions, in which the employee's or Employer's physician certifies that the officer is physically prohibited from taking the running fitness test or any of the equivalencies for a specific period of recuperation time, the Employer may waive the fitness test and allow the officer to participate at the incentive level previously held until the recuperation period has elapsed or the next fitness test, to include any make-up test, is given, whichever is later. (Examples of disabling medical occurrences are gun shot wounds, injuries sustained in an automotive accident, and temporary illness.) An employee may receive only one (1) waiver of fitness testing requirements during the term of this Agreement.

88.1.1.18 An officer with a permanent injury may participate in this program only if able to participate in one (1) of the options provided in this article. In such cases, the Employer may, upon receipt of a physician's certificate of disability, waive the requirements of this Article.

88.1.1.19 The parties recognize that there have been misunderstandings regarding the eligibility for, and termination of, payments under the terms of this Article. To address these problems, the parties have constituted a Committee composed of the Chief of Services and an Association representative. The final product of this Committee shall be memorialized in a Memorandum of Understanding.[1]

88.2 Combination Incentive Plan – Example 2.

88.2.1 Educational Incentive Pay shall be granted to any career status employee below the rank of Sergeant as Police Officer or Corporal who meets the requirements of this Article.

88.2.1.1 A two percent (2%) pay incentive, based on the employee's current salary, who possess EITHER a minimum of forty-five (45) points calculated by the Board of Public Safety Standards and Training (B.P.S.S.T.) or a minimum of forty-five (45) credit hours of college course work which includes a basic liberal arts curriculum from an accredited college or university.

88.2.1.2 A four percent (4%) pay incentive, based on the employee's current salary, shall be paid to each employee who meets one (1) of the following standards:

88.2.1.3 1. Holds an Intermediate Certificate issued by the Board on Public Safety Standards and Training (B.P.S.S.T.).

88.2.1.4 2. Has completed a minimum of two (2) years' course work (90 credit hours) which includes a basic liberal arts curriculum from an accredited college or university.

88.2.1.5 3. Holds an Associate degree in Police Science or field related to police work.

88.2.1.6 4. Has a minimum of ninety (90) points as calculated by B.P.S.S.T. (For purposes of this Article, one (1) point equals twenty (20) classroom hours of B.P.S.S.T. approved training). Officers who received the four percent (4%) incentive pay

[1] ***Multnomah County, Oregon and Multnomah County Deputy Sheriffs Association.***

as of November 17, ____ shall continue receiving such pay throughout the term of this Agreement.

88.2.1.7 A five percent (5%) pay incentive, based on the employee's current salary, shall be paid to each employee who qualifies in both of the following categories:

88.2.1.8 1. Holds an Intermediate Certificate issued by B.P.S.S.T.

88.2.1.9 2. Has completed:

88.2.1.10 a. two (2) years of college with a minimum of forty-five (45) credit hours of course work in a police-related field (must be able to register in an accredited college as a Junior or higher); or

88.2.1.11 b. an Associate Degree in Police Science or a field related to police work; or

88.2.1.12 c. has a minimum of ninety (90) points as calculated by B.P.S.S.T.

88.2.1.13 A six percent (6%) pay incentive based on the employee's current salary shall be paid to each employee who qualifies in one (1) of the following categories:

88.2.1.14 1. Holds an Advanced Certificate issued by B.P.S.S.T.

88.2.1.15 2. Holds a degree based on four (4) years of acceptable college level work as determined by B.P.S.S.T.

88.2.1.16 3. Has a minimum of one hundred-ninety (190) points as calculated by B.P.S.S.T.

88.2.1.17 A ten percent (10%) pay incentive based on the employee's current salary, shall be paid to each employee who holds both:

88.2.1.18 1. An Advanced Certificate issued by B.P.S.S.T.

88.2.1.19 2. A degree based on four (4) years of acceptable college level work as determined by B.P.S.S.T., or has a minimum of one hundred ninety (190) points as calculated by B.P.S.S.T.

88.2.1.20 Educational Incentive Pay shall be paid upon satisfactory completion of the probationary period. Educational Incentive Pay shall be paid commencing the pay period following fulfillment of the above qualifications and shall continue unless the officer receives an unsatisfactory rating. An employee so disqualified shall resume Educational Incentive Pay upon receiving a satisfactory rating.[1]

88.3 Physical Fitness.

88.3.1 In order to receive incentive pay of 1.5%, an employee must accumulate nine (9) points, and must achieve at least one point in each of the four core areas.

88.3.1.1 Blood Pressure - In order to take the examination and qualify for incentive pay, the employee must have a blood pressure no higher than 160/100.

88.3.1.2 Core Area 1 - Body Fat Standards:

Percentage body fat will be calculated from skinfold caliper measurements. At the employee's request, the accuracy of the body fat percentage will be validated using dual-energy x-ray absorptiometry (DXA) testing.

3 Points	AGE	MEN	WOMEN
	20's	13%	19%
	30's	14%	20%
	40's	16%	21%
	50's	17%	22%

[1] ***City of Salem, Oregon and Salem Police Employees' Union.***

2 Points	AGE	MEN	WOMEN
	20's	17%	24%
	30's	18%	25%
	40's	20%	26%
	50's	21%	27%

1 Point	AGE	MEN	WOMEN
	20's	20%	28%
	30's	21%	29%
	40's	23%	30%
	50's	24%	31%

88.3.1.3 Core Area 2 - Abdominal Curl Standards (1 minute time limit): The employee lies flat on his/her back with knees bent (about 90 degrees). Shoulders must touch the floor. Hands must be touching the head and remain in contact with the head throughout each repetition. Feet are secured.

To do an abdominal curl, the employee must lift his/her head and shoulders off the floor so that the entire head breaks the horizontal plane created by the tops of the knees.

The employee may pause and rest and start again, but the clock does not stop. The shoulders should return to the floor each time, but the head can remain lifted.

The employee attempts to do as many repetitions as possible in one minute.

3 Points	AGE	MEN	WOMEN
	20's	50	45
	30's	45	40
	40's	40	36
	50's	35	30

2 Points	AGE	MEN	WOMEN
	20's	45	35
	30's	38	30
	40's	30	26
	50's	26	21

1 Point	AGE	MEN	WOMEN
	20's	37	32
	30's	30	27
	40's	28	23
	50's	24	18

88.3.1.4 Core Area 3 - Push-Ups Standards: The employee begins in the "up" position with hands slightly wider than shoulder width apart or in a comfortable position, and the feet together or up to 12 inches apart. When viewed from the side, the body should form a generally straight line from the shoulders to the ankles. To perform a push-up the employee will lower his/her body until the upper arms are parallel to the ground. The employee will then return to the starting position by raising the entire body until the arms are fully extended. If the employee fails to keep his/her body generally straight, to lower the entire body until the upper arms are parallel to the ground, or to extend the arms completely, that repetition will not count; the tester will repeat the number of the last correct repetition. The "up" position is the only acceptable rest position. During a rest interval, the employee may flex the back or sag in the middle, but must return to the correct starting position before continuing. A rest interval may last a maximum of 3 seconds.

88.3.1.5 If the employee fails to perform the first few push-ups correctly, the tester will tell the employee to go to his/her knees and will explain what the mistakes are. The employee will be given a maximum of 5 minutes rest prior to re-testing. The employee may reposition his/her hands or feet during the test if necessary.

3 Points	AGE	MEN	WOMEN
	20's	45	21
	30's	39	17
	40's	29	12
	50's	23	10
2 Points	AGE	MEN	WOMEN
	20's	40	16
	30's	33	14
	40's	26	12
	50's	16	9
1 Point	AGE	MEN	WOMEN
	20's	30	11
	30's	23	9
	40's	18	7
	50's	13	7

88.3.1.6 Core Area 4 - Aerobic Capacity Standards: Aerobic capacity will be measured using one of the following tests according to the employee's preference:

1) Submaximal test using a bike ergometer.

2) 1.5 mile timed run test to be simulated on a treadmill or Stairmaster PT 4000.

The submaximal test will take approximately 15 minutes, beginning with an easy workload and progressing in 2-3 minute stages to a submaximal endpoint no higher than 85% of the predicted maximum heart rate. The submaximal test is based on two premises: There is a linear relationship between heart rate and oxygen consumption. A fit individual will exhibit a lower heart rate at a given submaximal workload than an untrained person. Aerobic capacity is calculated from the employee's heart rate response to the test and workload achieved.

SUBMAXIMAL TEST

3 Points	AGE	MEN	WOMEN
	20's	52	44
	30's	48	42
	40's	44	41
	50's	40	37
2 Points	AGE	MEN	WOMEN
	20's	47	39
	30's	43	37
	40's	39	36
	50's	35	34
1 Point	AGE	MEN	WOMEN
	20's	44	35
	30's	40	34
	40's	36	32
	50's	32	29

A standard of error of 10% shall be applied to the above figures.

88.3.1.7 In the alternative, an employee can achieve points in Core Area 4 by demonstrating aerobic capacity through reaching the following equivalents to running 1.5 miles by using a flat treadmill test or Stairmaster test (including a non-timed warmup and cool-down period). The exercise must be performed without the heart rate exceeding 90% of predicted maximum heart rate.

FLAT TREADMILL TEST

MEN				
	AGE	TIME	MPH	MIN/MILE
3 POINTS 65%	20	12:07	7.4	8.0
	30	12:34	7.2	8.2
	40	13:36	6.6	8.9
	50	15:02	6	10
2 POINTS 55%	20	12:34	7.2	8.2
	30	13:22	6.7	8.7
	40	14:11	6.3	9.4
	50	15:46	5.7	10.3
1 POINT 45%	20	13:04	6.8	8.7
	30	14:11	6.4	9.4
	40	15:08	6	10
	50	16:52	5.4	11

WOMEN				
	AGE	TIME	MPH	MIN/MILE
3 POINTS 65%	20	15:08	6	10
	30	16:10	7.2	10.7
	40	17:33	6.6	11.6
	50	19:51	6	13
2 POINTS 55%	20	15:46	5.8	10.3
	30	16:59	5.4	11.1
	40	18:29	4.9	12.2
	50	20:47	4.4	13.7
1 POINT 45%	20	16:39	5.6	10.9
	30	17:56	5.2	11.7
	40	19:13	4.7	12.8
	50	21:28	4.3	14.1

88.3.1.8 The Stairmaster PT 4000 test will be conducted in the same manner as the treadmill test, using the following Stairmaster levels and times. To complete the test successfully an employee must keep up with the speed of the equipment while using correct form:

1. Employee cannot lean or support his/her weight on the handrails. The backs of the hands can be placed against the inside of the handrail or the fingertips placed lightly on the side handrails for balance.

2. Pedals should not touch the floor or the upper stop level.

3. Short, quick "baby steps" are not allowed.

STAIRMASTER PT 4000

MEN				
	AGE	TIME	RATE	METS
3 POINTS	20	12:07	13	16
	30	12:34	12	15
	40	13:36	11	14
	50	15:02	10	13
2 POINTS	20	12:34	12	15
	30	13:22	11	14
	40	14:11	10	13
	50	15:46	9	12
1 POINT	20	13:04	11	14
	30	14:11	10	13
	40	15:08	9	12
	50	16:52	8	11

WOMEN				
	AGE	TIME	RATE	METS
3 POINTS	20	15:08	11	14
	30	16:10	10	13
	40	17:33	9	12
	50	19:51	8	11
2 POINTS	20	15:46	10	13
	30	16:59	9	12
	40	18:29	8	11
	50	20:47	7	10
1 POINT	20	16:39	9	12
	30	17:56	8	11
	40	19:13	7	10
	50	21:28	6	9

88.3.1.9 If an employee fails to achieve 9 points, the employee may attempt to re-qualify for the incentive plan within a 120-day period following the initial qualification attempt provided the employee pays the administrative costs associated with re-qualification and does such testing on his/her own time.

88.3.1.10 Flexibility - To be a mandatory non-graded part of test. The flexibility evaluation will include a modified sit-and-reach (trunk flexion) test, back extension test, hamstring, quadriceps and calf range of motion (ROM) tests.[1]

ARTICLE 89

PHYSICAL FITNESS

89.1 Condition of Employment/Incentive Plan.

89.1.1 Requirements and Procedures.

89.1.1.1 The purpose of the physical fitness plan is to ensure that members of the Department are physically capable of meeting all of the physical demands inherent in a police officer's job. It is the intent of the parties that the elements of the plan be directed to establishing such job-related physical fitness. The parties further recognize that each member of the Department has individual physical characteristics which must be taken into account in assessing and applying the requirements of the plan.

89.1.1.2 The design of the physical fitness plan is not punitive in nature, but is instead that of promoting physical fitness among all commissioned members of the Department. Any discipline which may be issued for noncompliance with the plan must be corrective and progressive in nature, and must take into account the individual characteristics of the officer involved.

89.1.1.3 The basic requirements of the physical fitness plan consist of the following core areas: Core Area #1 consists of an examination of the aerobic capacity of members; Core Area #2 consists of an examination of the body composition, or body fat percentages, of members; Core Area #3 consists of an exami-

[1] ***City of Seattle, Washington and Seattle Police Officers Guild.***

nation of the upper body strength of members, and can be fulfilled by completion of either Core Area #3a or Core Area #3b. Core Area #3a consists of a test of the percentage of the member's weight which can be bench-pressed by the member. Core Area #3b consists of the number of pushups which the member can complete in a one minute span; Core Area #4 consists of an examination of the number of sit-ups which can be performed by the member within a one minute span; Core Area #5 consists of a flexibility test including measurements of hamstrings, back and shoulder flexibility.

89.1.1.4 The minimum standards for the core areas are set forth below:

REQUIREMENTS FOR WOMEN

Age	Core Area #1	Core Area #2	Core Area #3a	Core Area #3b	Core Area #4	Core Area #5
20-29	33.0 to 36.9	21.1 to 24.2	70 to 79	17 to 33	33 to 38	Hamstring Back Shoulder
30-39	31.5 to 35.6	22.4 to 25.5	70 to 79	12 to 24	25 to 30	Hamstring Back Shoulder
40-49	29.0 to 32.8	25.7 to 28.2	70 to 79	9 to 19	19 to 25	Hamstring Back Shoulder

REQUIREMENTS FOR MEN

Age	Core Area #1	Core Area #2	Core Area #3a	Core Area #3b	Core Area #4	Core Area #5
20-29	42.5 to 46.4	16.0 to 18.3	80 to 89	35 to 44	37 to 42	Hamstring Back Shoulder
30-39	41.0 to 44.9	18.5 to 20.8	80 to 89	25 to 34	29 to 34	Hamstring Back Shoulder
40-49	39.0 to 43.7	20.8 to 22.9	80 to 89	20 to 29	24 to 29	Hamstring Back Shoulder

89.1.1.5 Core Area #1 may be satisfied alternatively by meeting the standards for the 1.5 mile run as outlined in *The Aerobics Way*, written by Kenneth Cooper. The standards are as follows:

Age Grouping	Men	Women
20-29	10:46 - 12:00	13:31 - 15:54
30-39	11:01 - 12:30	14:31 - 16:30
40-49	11:31 - 13:00	15:56 - 17:30

89.1.1.6 The Employer shall offer hydrostatic and caliper testing alternatives for Core Area #2.

89.1.1.7 Members must demonstrate compliance with the plan during the ninety-day period ending thirty days before the member's anniversary date. Members shall be given at least three opportunities to satisfy each core area requirement during the testing period. Members shall also take the test approximately six months after their evaluation date for monitoring purposes (the results of the monitoring test shall not be used for disciplinary purposes).

89.1.1.8 Members shall be on on-duty status during the examination process.

89.1.1.9 A member must satisfy the requirements specified in each core area during a single three-month test period. Any member meeting the core requirements shall be graded "Competent." Any member that exceeds the range maximum for three or more of Core Areas #1 - 4 during a single test shall be graded "Distinguished."

89.1.1.10 Members shall not be required to sign waivers of liability for the examination, but members may be provided the opportunity for alternative testing procedures requiring a waiver.

89.1.1.11 An employee within three years of the next age bracket may not be disciplined or downgraded on evaluations if they are in compliance with the subsequent age bracket's standards; provided, however, that in order to receive the incentive pay called for by this article, the employee must meet the standards applicable for his/her age group.

89.1.1.12 The parties recognize the integral role of the member's physician in any physical fitness plan. Accordingly, the Employer agrees to bear the reasonable costs of the member's physician to give the member a physical examination on an annual basis (if the member is above the age of 40), or on a bi-annual basis (if the member is below the age of 40). The Employer's obligation to bear such costs shall exist only to the extent that such costs are not borne in whole or in part by the medical insurance provided by this agreement, and only to the extent the tests and charges are in accordance with the standards in the medical community.

89.1.1.13 The parties agree that employees with temporary physical limitations which prevent or substantially hinder compliance with any or all of the requirements of the plan should be granted an exemption from compliance with those requirements. To be eligible for such an exemption, a member must submit to the Employer a written statement from the member's physician establishing the condition or disability which prevents the member from meeting any or all of the requirements of the plan. If the Employer disagrees with the judgment of the employee's physician, then the Employer shall have the right to have the employee examined by a physician of his choice, and at his expense. If the physician utilized by the Employer disagrees with the employee's physician, then the two physicians shall select a third physician, who shall examine the employee at the Employer's expense. The judgment of the third physician as to the member's physical condition shall be binding, unless mutually agreed to the contrary by the parties. If a member granted such a temporary exemption meets the requirements for which the member was not granted an exemption, then the member shall be deemed to be in compliance with the plan.

89.1.1.14 To the extent shift scheduling allows, the Employer, in its reasonable discretion, will endeavor to grant three hours of compensatory time off per week to train for the physical fitness plan.

89.1.1.15 Where a member has at no time been in compliance with the plan, but has made significant progression towards compliance since the member's last examination, no negative discipline will be imposed, unless the member has been out of compliance for two (2) years or more.

89.1.1.16 Employer agrees to promote compliance with the plan through education, incentive plan, intra-department counseling and other positive approaches.

89.1.1.17 The Employer agrees that the Physical Fitness section of the Performance Evaluation will not affect the member's overall evaluation until after January 1, ____.

89.1.1.18 Employees who are rated competent under the requirements of the plan shall receive 1.5% incentive pay. Employees who receive a distinguished rating under the plan shall receive 2.5% incentive pay.

89.2 Health Club Membership.

89.2.1 The Employer shall continue to furnish individual Senior Membership for each employee, at no cost to the employee, in the YMCA or the Employer shall reimburse the employee for the equivalent cost of such membership in a private health club upon presentation of paid receipt.[1]

89.3 Physical Fitness/Wellness Program.

89.3.1 Effective for costs for calendar year ____, Employer will provide fifty percent (50%) reimbursement in January ____ to employees for actual costs of participation in health club memberships for employee only, subject to the following conditions:

- Health Club membership must be in the City.
- Reimbursement shall not exceed $500 per calendar year, per employee.
- Reimbursement shall be made once a year during the month of January and requires the submission of actual receipts.

[1] ***Aurora, Illinois and Association of Professional Police Officers.***

89.3.1.1 Effective for costs between January 1 through June 30, ____, reimbursement will be made in July ____. Thereafter reimbursement will be made in July of each year for cost incurred on a fiscal year basis (July 1 through June 30).

89.3.1.2 Employees not participating in the reimbursement program are eligible for a voluntary physical fitness incentive program. Employees must achieve a passing score on the City's Fitness Assessment Program (June 9, ____), administered through Hartnell College in June of each year. Payment of five hundred dollar ($500) fitness premium shall be made in July of each year in a check separate from the normal paycheck.[1]

89.4 Police Officers Association Physical Fitness Maintenance Program.

89.4.1 Effective with the adoption of this contract, a trial program, not to exceed one fiscal year (July 1, ____ through June 30, ____) will be developed to encourage the voluntary maintenance of represented employees' physical fitness. Funding for this program, with the exception of incidental assistance by City personnel for conducting the actual annual testing, will be provided by the Association. Represented employees who voluntarily choose to take part in the program by notification of the Chief of Police (or designee) and achieve the required level of fitness on an annual testing basis will be awarded 20 hours of Compensatory Time Off (CTO), eligible for use under the same terms as other departmental CTO is available for use. During the trial program the Employer and Association will evaluate the effectiveness of the program on the basis of level of participation, impact of sick leave usage and impact on workers' compensation injury and illness rates. Continuation of this trial pro-

[1] ***City of Salinas, California and Salinas Police Officers' Association, Local #3.***

gram beyond July 1, ____ for the duration of this contract will be at the discretion of the Employer, subject to continued funding by the Association.

89.4.1.1 Prior to July 1, ____, the Association and the Employer will agree to the content of the Police Officers Association Physical Fitness Program submitted by the Association. The Association will contract with a Certified Fitness Trainer to develop the elements of the program and to monitor the annual testing. The Certified Trainer will also develop the standards for each element of the testing program, adjusted for age group (29 years and under, 30 to 39 years, 40 to 49 years and 50 to 59 years) and sex. It is expected that the test elements will include measurement of a minimum of resting heart rate and blood pressure, body composition measurement, body strength, body flexibility and endurance. The adopted program will be attached to this contract as an Exhibit.[1]

ARTICLE 90

ASSIGNMENT PAY

90.1 Acting Shift Supervisor.

90.1.1 Police Corporals are required to exercise direction and control over subordinates, and those job functions are within a Corporal's normal job duties. However, after a Corporal works more than forty (40) consecutive hours as a Shift Supervisor, the Corporal shall receive premium pay of 5%. The premium pay will be paid beginning with the forty-first consecutive hour

[1] ***City of Santa Clara and Santa Clara Police Officers Association.***

in which a Corporal works as a Shift Supervisor. Premium pay will not be paid for the initial forty (40)-hour period.[1]

90.2 Administrative Services.

90.2.1 Sworn employees assigned to Administrative Services Bureau shall receive an additional seven percent (7%) of their regular base pay when assigned to such special assignment. If one sworn employee assigned to such a unit receives special assignment pay, all sworn employees in the unit receive special assignment pay.[2]

90.3 Bilingual.

90.3.1 Qualified employees who meet the following criteria shall receive an additional twenty (20) cents per hour (approximately thirty-five (35) dollars per month) for all hours actually paid. This will not apply to the class of Interpreter.

90.3.1.1 An employee must be assigned by department management to speak or translate a language in addition to English. This may include such specialized communication skills as sign language.

90.3.1.2 Employees must regularly and frequently speak and/or translate a second language; i.e., once daily.

90.3.1.3 To become qualified, employees must be certified as qualified by the Personnel Director.[3]

[1] ***City of Clovis, California and Clovis Police Officers Association.***

[2] ***City of Westminster, California and Westminster Police Association.***

[3] ***Orange County, California and Association of Orange County Deputy Sheriffs.***

90.4 Complex Level Proficiency in Spanish.

90.4.1 All employees in the classifications of Police Officer and Police Sergeant who successfully meet the "Complex Level Proficiency" requirements set out in the departmental Spanish training program shall be paid a bilingual pay differential in an amount equal to the product obtained by multiplying the Step "E" base salary rate of Police Officer by five percent (5.0%) (ten (10) salary rate ranges).[1]

90.5 Street Level Proficiency in Spanish.

90.5.1 Police Officer or Police Sergeant who successfully meets the "Street Level Proficiency" requirements set out in the departmental Spanish training program shall be paid a bilingual pay differential in an amount equal to the product obtained by multiplying the base salary rate being paid to an employee in the rank of Police Officer at Step "E" by two and one-half percent (2.5%) (five (5) salary rate ranges).

90.5.1.1 Employees receiving "Street Level Proficiency" incentives pay will be required, as a condition of continued eligibility to receive such incentive pay, to successfully complete an eight (8)-hour refresher course once every twelve months from the date of initial certification.

90.5.1.2 "Street Level Proficiency" is part of a pilot program and its success will be evaluated on an ongoing basis. If at any time it is clear to the City Manager that the program is not completely successful in delivering expected results, the program will cease to exist. However, the employees who had successfully completed the coursework and the qualifying examination will receive the bilingual pay for the duration of the current contract period, provided they meet the requirements as set forth above.

[1] ***City of Santa Ana and Santa Ana Police Officers Association.***

90.6 Breathalyzer Operator.

90.6.1 In addition to the wage rates established by this agreement, the Employer shall pay premium pay as follows for the following: Licensed breathalyzer operator (if the employee is engaged as a breathalyzer operator. No more than 30 employees shall be entitled to premium pay as breathalyzer operators during the term of this agreement); $10.00 per month.[1]

90.7 Canine Officer.

90.7.1 Officers shall receive a premium of 3.5% per month prorated on an hourly basis while so assigned.[2]

90.7.2 All Police Officers assigned to one of the following positions shall be paid an additional 5% of the salary for the term of their assignment: Canine Officer.[3]

90.8 CIRT (Critical Incident Response Team).

90.8.1 Employees assigned to CIRT will receive an additional ten percent (10%) when they are required to perform CIRT activities.[4]

90.9 Commendation Pay.

90.9.1 Each Officer of the Month who is selected by the Awards Committee, as currently constituted, shall receive a fifty dollar ($50) gift certificate. The Officer of the Year, who shall be selected by the Awards Committee from among those who have

[1] ***Beaumont, Texas and Beaumont Police Officers Association.***

[2] ***Torrance, California and Torrance Police Officers Association.***

[3] ***City of Fremont, California and Fremont Police Association.***

[4] ***Municipality of Anchorage and Anchorage Police Department Employees Association.***

been named Officer of the Month shall receive one (1) day off with pay.[1]

90.10 Communications.

90.10.1 An employee in the classification of Police Officer assigned to Communications 23 watch and assuming certain specific lead person responsibilities shall receive a premium of 5% of base pay for actual hours worked in such assignments.[2]

90.11 Community Relations.

90.11.1 Employees assigned to Community Relations shall receive a premium of 3.5% of base pay prorated on an hourly basis while so assigned, paid each pay period.[3]

90.12 Computer Support Officer.

90.12.1 All Police Officers assigned to one of the following positions shall be paid an additional 5% of the salary for the term of their assignment: Computer Support Officer.[4]

90.13 Court Liaison.

90.13.1 Employees assigned to Court Liaison duty shall receive a premium of 3.5% of base pay prorated on an hourly basis while so assigned, paid each pay period.[5]

[1] ***Fort Lauderdale, Florida and Fraternal Order of Police.***

[2] ***Torrance, California and Torrance Police Officers Association.***

[3] ***Torrance, California and Torrance Police Officers Association.***

[4] ***City of Fremont, California and Fremont Police Association.***

[5] ***Torrance, California and Torrance Police Officers Association.***

90.13.2 All Police Officers assigned to one of the following positions shall be paid an additional 5% of the salary for the term of their assignment: Court Liaison Officer.[1]

90.14 Crime Analysis.

90.14.1 Employees assigned to Crime Analysis duty shall receive a premium of 3.5% of base pay prorated on an hourly basis while so assigned, paid each pay period.[2]

90.15 Crime Scene Investigator.

90.15.1 Employees assigned to the position of Crime Scene investigator shall receive a premium of 3.5% of base pay per month prorated on an hourly basis while so assigned.[3]

90.15.2 Any sworn, safety-member Police Officer who attains the following educational and experience requirements and the approval as set out below shall be paid an additional five (5) salary rate ranges (2.5%) above his or her then current base monthly salary step. The criteria for such designation shall be as follows:

90.15.2.1 A. Completion of two (2) years of experience as a sworn Police Officer, at least one of which shall be in the Department.

90.15.2.2 B. Completion of at least thirty (30) educational and/or training units.

90.15.2.3 C. Assignment to and actual performance of the duties and responsibilities of a CSI.

[1] ***City of Fremont, California and Fremont Police Association.***

[2] ***Torrance, California and Torrance Police Officers Association.***

[3] ***Torrance, California and Torrance Police Officers Association.***

90.15.2.4 D. Completion of a special training course for Crime Scene Investigators as developed and administered by the Department or such alternative course as designated for such purpose by the Chief of Police.

90.15.2.5 E. Approval of the Chief of Police. The number of such designations as CSI shall be no larger than the requirements of the Department as determined by the Chief of Police.[1]

90.16 D.A.R.E.

90.16.1 Police Officers (excluding Corporals) assigned to DARE/SRO shall receive five percent (5%) above current step, subject to administrative direction.[2]

90.17 Detectives.

90.17.1 Those officers who have been assigned to the investigatory position with less than two years shall receive 3.5% of base pay per month prorated on an hourly basis while so assigned. This shall be in addition to any Agent I compensation to which they might be entitled. Commencing with year three (3) of investigative experience, employees shall receive 5% of base pay per month prorated on an hourly basis while so assigned. Experience need not be continuous.[3]

90.18 Distinguished Police Officer Premium Pay.

90.18.1 Distinguished Police Officer designation shall be made to signify outstanding uniformed Police Officer performance. Distinguished Police Officers shall be selected by a panel consisting of all patrol section commanders and two sworn panel

[1] ***City of Santa Ana and Santa Ana Police Officers Association.***

[2] ***City of Salinas, California and Salinas Police Officers' Association.***

[3] ***Torrance, California and Torrance Police Officers Association.***

members designated by the Chief of Police. Distinguished Police Officers shall be selected from the uniformed Patrol Division Police Officers with at least five years of service and who are regularly assigned to general patrol duties. Designation as a Distinguished Police Officer shall be for a one-year period based upon work performance during the previous fiscal year. The selection of Distinguished Police Officers shall not be grievable.

90.18.1.1 A minimum of ten percent (10%) of the eligible candidates shall be selected as Distinguished Police Officers annually.

90.18.1.2 Those officers selected and designated as Distinguished Police Officers shall receive a one-time payment of three and one-half percent (3.5%) of their annual base salary, to be paid by September 1 in the year they are so designated.

90.19 Dive Team.

90.19.1 This section establishes additional compensation for a properly qualified employee who performs diving operations in the performance of his/her duties. Only an employee who possesses the required clearances and certifications as an underwater diver may be assigned to perform duties as a member of the Sheriff's Underwater Search and Recovery Team; additional compensation of $4.40 per hour (pro rata for periods of less than an hour) upon arrival at the command post and until relieved. This premium is not applicable to diving training time.[1]

90.20 Driving Instructor.

90.20.1 All police officers who are assigned to Driving Instructor duties shall receive an additional twenty-three cents

[1] ***San Diego County, California and San Diego County Deputy Sheriffs' Association.***

($.23) per hour. This amount is to be paid along with regular pay on each regularly-scheduled pay period.[1]

90.21 Equestrian Pay.

90.21.1 Effective January 7, ____, officers assigned to the Equestrian Unit shall be compensated for two and eight-tenths (2.8) hours of equestrian care and exercise, paid at time and one-half, for each pay period. Additional equestrian care outside of regularly-scheduled duty hours shall be compensated at time and one-half when approved in advance by the Operations Bureau Commander. Work hours on regularly-scheduled duty days may be adjusted by the department to permit equestrian training on duty time.[2]

90.22 Field Evidence Technician Pay.

90.22.1 Effective January 8, ____, officers assigned as Field Evidence Technicians will be entitled to a premium pay of two and one-half percent (2.5%) while they are in that assignment. Premium pay will not apply to emergency callback or voluntary overtime work that does not require the officer to work as an Evidence Technician.[3]

90.23 Field Training Officer (FTO).

90.23.1 FTO will receive one (1) hour's pay at time and one-half for each day that they are assigned to a recruit. For regularly-scheduled monthly FTO meetings only, three (3) hours at time and one-half (1½) will be paid.[4]

[1] ***Everett, Washington and Everett Police Officers Association.***

[2] ***City of Modesto, California and Modesto Police Officers Association.***

[3] ***City of Santa Clara and Santa Clara Police Officers Association.***

[4] ***City of Aurora, Illinois and Association of Professional Police Officers, Inc.***

90.23.2 Any officer outside the Academy who is training a Police Cadet or police recruit who has not completed his/her probationary period, Community Service Officer, or Reserve Police Officer shall be paid the seven and one-half (7 1/2%) rate for such out-of-classification assignment for each shift he/she is actually training.[1]

90.23.3 Bargaining unit members chosen as field training officers shall receive two (2) hours of compensatory time for every five (5) tours of duty as a field training officer. To be eligible for the compensatory time, an individual must work a minimum of four (4) hours for each tour of duty.[2]

90.24 Fingerprint Analysis.

90.24.1 In addition to the wage rates established by this agreement, the Employer shall pay premium pay as follows for the following: Any employee qualifying as an expert latent fingerprint witness and who is currently assigned to the identification bureau, $20.00 per month.[3]

90.25 Firearms Proficiency.

90.25.1 Throughout the term of this Agreement all members of the bargaining unit that meet or exceed the State of Ohio Annual Certification (as departmentally adopted) for firearms qualification will be given a proficiency allowance paid by the Employer as follows:

1996 - $3,640.00 yearly

1997 - $3,640.00 yearly

1998 - $3,640.00 yearly

[1] ***City of Sacramento, California and Sacramento Police Officers Association.***

[2] ***Akron, Ohio and Fraternal Order of Police Lodge #7.***

[3] ***Beaumont, Texas and Beaumont Police Officers Association.***

Satisfactory qualification will be evidenced by a letter of qualification from the range officer or training officer to the employee or the Employer.[1]

90.26 Harbor Patrol.

90.26.1 All police officers who are assigned to Harbor Patrol duties shall receive an additional twenty-three cents ($.23) per hour. This amount is to be paid along with regular pay on each regularly-scheduled pay period.[2]

90.27 Hazardous Material.

90.27.1 Employees assigned to handle hazardous material during transport to disposal sites shall receive a premium of $5.00 per transport hour.[3]

90.28 Helicopter Pilot.

90.28.1 The Employer agrees to provide specialist premium compensation to employees who are assigned to a specialized unit of duty by the Employer. This specialist premium compensation shall be in lieu of any other payment for hazard pay and for any other payment for any and all hours of overtime worked while attending or participating in mandatory training in such specialty. No employee shall receive specialist premium compensation totaling more than 5.0% above the employee's base hourly rate, excepting specialist premium compensation for employees assigned as primary or relief shift helicopter pilots who shall receive specialist premium compensation totaling not more than 7.5% above the base hourly rate. Specialist premium com-

[1] ***The City of Euclid, Ohio and Euclid Fraternal Order of Police, Lodge #18.***

[2] ***Everett, Washington and Everett Police Officers Association.***

[3] ***State of Oregon and Oregon State Police Officers Association.***

pensation shall be added to the employee's base hourly rate for the purpose of calculating overtime pay.[1]

90.28.2 Employees assigned as pilots in an aircraft shall receive a $5.00 per flight hour premium.[2]

90.28.3 Purpose. The purpose of the Police Helicopter Operations Assignment is to provide observation, patrol, surveillance, and emergency flights in support of the Police Division services.

90.28.3.1 Unit employees selected for this assignment are required to attain and maintain specialized skills, in addition to those of Police Officers, which are unique to aircraft operations.

90.28.3.2 These specialized skills require the application of special tactics, operations and applications.

90.28.3.3 Each unit employee in this assignment must maintain a current knowledge of aircraft operations, flight rules, aircraft maintenance and safety.

90.28.3.4 Compensation. Unit employees in the classification of Police Officer or Police Sergeant who are assigned by Police management to pilot a helicopter shall receive extra compensation above their base salary in the amounts as follows:

Effective 8/1/96	Eff. 7/1/97	Eff. 7/1/98	Eff. 7/1/99
	(Incr. $10/mo)	(Incr. $10/mo)	(Incr. $10/mo)
$320/mo	$330/mo	$340/mo	$350/mo

[1] ***Sonoma County, California and Sonoma County Sheriff's Office Employees Association.***

[2] ***State of Oregon and Oregon State Police Officers Association.***

90.28.3.5 Limitations. This extra compensation shall be paid only during those periods or portions thereof when such employees are actually assigned as a helicopter pilot in their daily work assignment.

90.28.3.6 However, should a unit employee assigned to helicopter pilot duty be unable to perform that function due to a non-job-related illness or injury for a period of twenty-one (21) calendar days or more, this assignment compensation shall be suspended for all scheduled workdays not worked in excess of the first twenty-one (21) calendar days and until the day he/she returns to this full duty assignment.

90.28.3.7 Temporary Assignment. Helicopter Pilot assignment is a temporary assignment, not a separate job classification; it does not have Civil Service status and is not subject to Civil Service selection procedures, appeals, or seniority; it is not a property right and may be revoked by Police Management at any time for job-related reasons or operational necessity.[1]

90.29 Helicopter Observer.

90.29.1 The employee assigned to the duties of Helicopter Observer shall receive specialist premium compensation totaling 7.5% above the employee's base hourly rate. Such specialist premium compensation shall only be authorized during actual flight time and during the performance of service maintenance that is required for the day, and shall not be added to the employee's base hourly rate when calculating overtime pay.[2]

90.29.2 Purpose. The purpose of the Police Helicopter Observer assignment is to provide observation, patrol, surveil-

[1] ***City of Glendale, California and Glendale Police Officers' Association.***

[2] ***Sonoma County, California and Sonoma County Sheriff's Office Employees Association.***

lance, and emergency flights in support of the Police Division services.

90.29.2.1 Unit employees selected for this assignment are required to attain and maintain specialized skills, in addition to those of Police Officers, which are unique to aircraft operations.

90.29.2.2 These specialized skills require the application of special tactics, operations and applications.

90.29.2.3 Each unit employee in this assignment must maintain a current knowledge of aircraft operations, flight rules, aircraft maintenance and safety.

90.29.2.4 Compensation. Unit employees who are assigned by Police management as an observer in a Police helicopter shall receive extra compensation above their base salary in the amounts as follows:

Effective 8/1/96	Eff. 7/1/97	Eff. 7/1/98	Eff. 7/1/99
	(Incr. $10/mo)	(Incr. $10/mo)	(Incr. $10/mo)
$170/mo	$180/mo	$190/mo	$200/mo

91.29.2.5 Limitations. This extra compensation shall be paid only during those periods or portions thereof when such employees are actually assigned as a helicopter observer in their daily work assignment.

90.29.2.6 Unit employees regularly assigned as a helicopter observer should be trained and should be able to perform emergency landings and have a working knowledge of FAA air regulations within six (6) months of an initial assignment as a helicopter observer.

90.29.2.7 However, should a unit employee assigned to helicopter observer duty be unable to perform that function due to a non-job-related illness or injury for a period of twenty-one

(21) calendar days or more, this assignment compensation shall be suspended for all scheduled workdays not worked in excess of the first twenty-one (21) calendar days and until the day he/ she returns to this full duty assignment.

90.29.2.8 Temporary Assignment. Helicopter Observer assignment is a temporary assignment, not a separate job classification; it does not have Civil Service status and is not subject to Civil Service selection procedures, appeals, or seniority; it is not a property right and may be revoked by Police Management at any time for job-related reasons or operational necessity.[1]

90.29.3 For promotional purposes for the rank of Sergeant only, final eligibility list standing shall be posted to the nearest hundredth of a point. (e.g. 86.57, 86.33, 86.00, etc.) An eligibility list shall remain in effect for one (1) year from the date of validation.[2]

90.30 Hostage Negotiator.

90.30.1 All police officers who are assigned to Hostage Negotiator duties shall receive an additional twenty-three cents ($.23) per hour. This amount is to be paid along with regular pay on each regular scheduled pay period.[3]

[1] City of Glendale, California and Glendale Police Officers' Association.

[2] County of Volusia, Florida and Coastal Florida Police Benevolent Association.

[3] Everett, Washington and Everett Police Officers Association.

90.31 Motorcycle Pay.

90.31.1 An employee in the classification of Officer and Sergeant assigned to a 2-wheel motorcycle patrol duty shall receive a premium of 10% of base pay while so assigned.[1]

90.31.2 Motorcycle traffic patrol duty shall also include the time spent performing the duties and responsibilities associated with winter storage of the officer's assigned motorcycle. Such duties shall be prescribed by the Chief of Police, who may, from time to time, change them. The duties shall include, but not be limited to frequent visual inspection, periodic recharging of the motorcycle's battery, performing the prescribed shut down procedure at the beginning of winter storage, and start up procedure at the end of winter storage and washing and waxing the motorcycle. The duration of time spent by an employee in the performance of winter storage duties shall not exceed 1½ hours per month; no employee shall devote more time to such duties without obtaining prior authorization from the employee's commanding officer.

90.31.2.1 A motorcycle shall be stored only in a private storage area approved by the Employer. The period of winter storage shall be determined by the Employer.

90.31.2.2 For the duration of the winter storage period, an officer who maintains his/her assigned motorcycle in an approved private storage facility shall receive $20 biweekly in addition to base salary in lieu of any other compensation for the duties (and the expected amount of time devoted to those duties) described above.

90.31.2.3 Except as modified by sections 1 through 3, all heretofore existing administrative procedures associated with the $20

[1] ***Torrance, California and Torrance Police Officers Association.***

biweekly payments received by employees assigned to motorcycle traffic patrol duty shall remain unchanged.

90.31.2.4 Winter storage of City motorcycles and compensation therefor, as set forth in this Article, may be terminated at any time at the sole discretion of the Employer.[1]

90.32 Paramedic Allowance.

90.32.1 Employees who are State-Licensed Paramedics shall receive an allowance of $90.00 the last pay in June and the last pay in December, pro-rated on a monthly basis for each month they have State Licensure, but are not assigned to the Paramedic Division. Employees who are State-Licensed Paramedics shall receive an allowance of $600.00 the last pay in June and the last pay in December, pro-rated on a monthly basis for each full month they have State Licensure and are assigned to the Paramedic Division. The June payment will cover the months of January through June, and the December payment will cover the months of July through December. Any over payment will be deducted from the first possible subsequent payment. Under no circumstances will an employee receive both allowances for the same period of time.[2]

90.33 Patrol.

90.33.1 All patrol officers who have completed their probationary period and all patrol sergeants will be eligible for an additional 1.5% of the base monthly, top step salary for a police officer.[3]

[1] ***City of Milwaukee, Wisconsin and Milwaukee Police Association, Local 21.***

[2] ***Genesee County, Michigan and AFSCME Council 25.***

[3] ***Seattle, Washington and Seattle Police Officers Guild.***

90.33.2 An additional 1.5% of the base monthly, top-step salary for a Police Officer shall be paid as a premium to patrol officers and patrol sergeants, including those assigned to the City Center, the Mounted Patrol and the Harbor Unit. Police Officers and Sergeants assigned to the D.W.I. Squad and A.M./P.M. Enforcement Squads will also be eligible to receive patrol premium pay. (However, they will not be eligible for patrol longevity.)

90.33.2.1 Effective September 1, ____, new hires will not be eligible to receive patrol premium pay until they have completed 5 years of service. However, Police Officers and Sergeants hired prior to September 1, ____, will receive patrol premium pay once their probationary period has been completed.

90.33.2.2 The above premiums shall be in addition to the regular salary of officers as specified in Section 1. There will be no pyramiding of specialty pays.[1]

90.34 Patrol Specialist.

90.34.1 A Police Patrol Officer assigned as a Patrol Specialist shall receive an application rate of five percent (5%) above the top step rate of Police Patrol Officer.[2]

90.35 Personnel Officer.

90.35.1 All Police Officers assigned to one of the following positions shall be paid an additional 5% of the salary for the term of their assignment: Personnel Officer.[3]

[1] ***City of Seattle, Washington and Seattle Police Officers Guild.***

[2] ***City of Tacoma, Washington and Tacoma Police Union, Local #6.***

[3] ***City of Fremont, California and Fremont Police Association.***

90.36 Photo Lab Officer.

90.36.1 All police officers who are assigned to Photo Lab duties shall receive an additional twenty-three cents ($.23) per hour. This amount is to be paid along with regular pay on each regularly scheduled pay period.[1]

90.37 Polygraph Examiner.

90.37.1 In addition to the wage rates established by this agreement, the Employer shall pay premium pay as follows for the following: Licensed polygraph examiner (if actively engaged during the term of this agreement as a polygraph operator), $25.00 per month.[2]

90.38 Rangemaster.

90.38.1 Employees assigned to Rangemaster duties shall receive a premium of 3.5% of base pay prorated on an hourly basis while so assigned, to be paid each pay period.[3]

90.39 Red Cross Certification.

90.39.1 Each employee who is qualified in American Red Cross Advanced first aid shall be paid for such qualification the sum of One Hundred Twelve Dollars and Fifty Cents ($112.50) on or about December 1st of each year and One Hundred Twelve Dollars and Fifty Cents ($112.50) on or about June 1st of each year, provided that an employee who receives payment for certification as an Emergency Medical Technician shall not receive payment for qualification in American Red Cross Advanced first aid.[4]

[1] ***Everett, Washington and Everett Police Officers Association.***

[2] ***Beaumont, Texas and Beaumont Police Officers Association.***

[3] ***Torrance, California and Torrance Police Officers Association.***

[4] ***Greenwich, Connecticut and Silver Shield Association.***

90.40 Research Officer.

90.40.1 Employees assigned to Research Officer duty shall receive a premium of 3.5% of base pay prorated on an hourly basis while so assigned, paid each pay period.[1]

90.41 School Resource Officer Pay.

90.41.1 Employees assigned as School Resource Officers effective the first payroll period after October 1, ____, shall receive a special assignment pay of five percent (5%) of their base pay while assigned to the School Resource Unit.[2]

90.42 SERT/SWAT Team.

90.42.1 The intent of this program is to provide a timely response to requests for Investigative personnel and does not preclude the call-out of other specialized investigators. Those employees assigned to the Emergency Response Team shall receive standby pay equal to 8 hours (compensated at time and a half) per week of assignment. This pay shall be guaranteed regardless of the scheduling of the employee during the period. Employees assigned to the Emergency Response Team must be available on call during the week so assigned to respond to call-outs. In addition, at least one officer shall report on the in-custodies and daily work. Time spent in excess of routine review of daily work and in-custodies will be compensated at regular overtime rate. Management will provide a car and beeper to these employees assigned to the team. The operation of this program is subject to the direction and control of management and may be discontinued.[3]

[1] ***Torrance, California and Torrance Police Officers Association.***

[2] ***County of Volusia, Florida and Coastal Florida Police Benevolent Association.***

[3] ***Torrance, California and Torrance Police Officers Association.***

90.43 Special Investigator.

90.43.1 All Police Officers assigned to one of the following positions shall be paid an additional 5% of the salary for the term of their assignment: Special Investigator to the Chief of Police.[1]

90.44 Traffic Unit Deputy Pay.

90.44.1 Effective October 1, ____, an employee assigned as Traffic Unit Deputy (i.e., motorcycle squad) shall receive special assignment pay of five percent (5%) of his base pay.[2]

90.45 Training Officer.

90.45.1 Employees assigned to Training Officer duty shall receive a premium of 3.5% of base pay prorated on an hourly basis while so assigned, paid each pay period.[3]

ARTICLE 91

PARKING

91.1 Furnished By Employer.

91.1.1 The Employer shall provide, without cost to employees on duty, adequate parking space adjacent to Police Department facilities.[4]

91.1.2 The Employer shall continue to provide, without cost to employees on duty, adequate parking space, whether off-

[1] ***City of Fremont, California and Fremont Police Association.***

[2] ***County of Volusia, Florida and Coastal Florida Police Benevolent Association.***

[3] ***Torrance, California and Torrance Police Officers Association.***

[4] ***City of Beaumont, Texas and Beaumont Police Officers Association.***

street or on-street, adjacent to or within a reasonable distance from Police Department facilities. On each February 1st, the Employer shall contribute Sixteen Thousand Dollars ($16,000) to the Association for purposes of acquiring off-street parking for non-sworn employees as a safety matter.[1]

ARTICLE 92

TRAVEL EXPENSES

92.1 General.

92.1.1 Necessary and actual expenses incurred by an employee while attending to business of the Employer may be reimbursed with the approval and authorization of the Employer head. A statement of justification satisfactory to the Auditor shall be submitted with the claims. Such reimbursement, however, does not apply wherever the provisions in the law provide for payment of such expenses.[2]

92.2 Mileage.

92.2.1 An employee who is authorized to use a personal motor vehicle for travel required in the performance of Employer's work shall be reimbursed at the rate of 29 cents ($.29) per each mile driven. This mileage reimbursement rate shall be subject to a one cent ($.01) per mile increase for each 10 cents ($.10) per gallon increase over $1.70 per gallon price of unleaded gas. The current monthly price of unleaded gas shall be determined by a monthly survey performed by the Employer.[3]

[1] ***Municipality of Anchorage and Anchorage Police Department Employees Association.***

[2] ***Ventura County, California and Ventura County Sheriff's Association.***

[3] ***Sonoma County, California and Sonoma County Sheriff's Office Employees Association.***

92.3 Mileage for Travel to Temporary Assignments.

92.3.1 An employee who travels from his/her home to a temporary assignment rather than to his/her regularly-assigned office shall be allowed transportation expenses for the distance between his/her home and his/her temporary assignment or between his/her regularly assigned office and his/her temporary assignment, whichever is less.[1]

92.4 Travel Compensation While on Extradition Assignment.

92.4.1 Effective with this contract, employees who are required to travel for prisoner extradition outside the City, or who voluntarily accept such assignment, will be compensated as follows for such travel to the extradition site:

92.4.1.1 A. Authorized travel on a regularly-scheduled workday, outside scheduled work hours, will be compensated at the appropriate overtime rate for actual time spent travelling to the extradition site.

92.4.1.2 B. Authorized travel on a regularly-scheduled day off will be compensated at the appropriate overtime rate for actual time spent travelling to the extradition site or the regularly-scheduled number of hours of the employee's regular workday, whichever is less. For example, an employee who regularly works a 10-hour shift Monday through Thursday would be compensated for up to ten hours for travel that took place on Sunday, but would not be compensated for any travel that was more than ten (10) hours.

[1] ***Commonwealth of Massachusetts and State Police Association of Massachusetts.***

92.4.1.3 C. The normal work schedule for the employee may be adjusted by the Division Commander and/or the immediate supervisor in order to minimize the overtime impact of the assignment with a minimum of 14 hours' notice.

92.4.1.4 Employees performing work connected with the extradition of the prisoner will be compensated at the appropriate rate while performing such work.[1]

ARTICLE 93

CAREER ENHANCEMENT PROGRAM

93.1 Purpose.

93.1.1 The purpose of the Career Enhancement Program (CEP) is to provide the path to improve the skills, enhance productivity, evaluate performance, promote professional growth, as well as job satisfaction for Patrolmen. This concept is further designed to provide compensation for advanced education as well as certain designated skills or a combination of formal education and professional training. The CEP is an alternative career path which as designed will assist in retaining as well as creating highly motivated and skilled police officers. The net result will be an economic asset to the Employer.

93.2 The Program.

93.2.1 The Career Enhancement Program is a nine-level phased program; based upon the accumulation of point scores for education and achievement, as well as certain specified job assignments.

93.2.1.1 Level One (1) – Total accumulation of ten (10) points

[1] ***City of Santa Clara and Santa Clara Police Officers Association.***

II. Level Two (2) – fifteen (15) points

III. Level Three (3) – twenty (20) points

IV. Level Four (4) – twenty-five (25) points

V. Level Five (5) – thirty (30) points

VI. Level Six (6) – thirty-five (35) points

VII. Level Seven (7) – forty (40) points

VIII. Level Eight (8) – forty-five (45) points

IX. Level Nine (9) – fifty (50) points

93.2.1.2 Entry Into The Program – The Career Enhancement Program is open to any police officer who meets the following minimum entry qualifications:

93.2.1.3 A minimum of three (3) full years from the date of appointment to the Police Department.

93.2.1.4 Concurrence by the CEP Committee (defined herein).

93.2.1.5 All police officers who wish to be placed within the program must submit their respective application to the Captain of Personnel and Fiscal Affairs. Applications will be reviewed annually and shall be submitted on the Career Enhancement Application Form after November 1st and by November 30th of each year. Points shall be based upon achievement as of December 31. Movement of an officer into one of the CEP pay steps shall not be considered as a promotion under City Charter or Civil Service Rules.

93.2.1.6 It shall be the full responsibility of the officer to properly complete the application form (as established) as well as to provide such documentation/materials which will enable the CEP committee to make a determination. Documentation for specialty assignments shall include but not be limited to the following: Assignment record or supervisory memorandum showing service of three (3) months in the specialty assignment since the preceding January 1st. Provided, however, Field Training Officers shall be eligible for assignment points for any year in which they serve one day or more. No assignment points shall be provided in years they have not served at least one day as an FTO. Documentation for academic accomplishments shall be by diploma or certified transcript.

93.2.1.7 Compensation for Successful Completion. Compensation for the successful completion of any step contained in this program shall be defined in the Collective Bargaining Agreement and shall be automatic.

93.2.1.8 Payment shall be based upon the following conversion factor: Each five (5) points = one-half of a percent (.05%).

93.2.1.9 Payment for each year of eligibility will occur in January of the following year in a lump sum payment by special check based upon the appropriate percentage of the base annual full rate effective in January of the prior year. Payments shall be made in January of 1998, 1999 and 2000. Officers who leave the Employer in good standing during the year shall receive upon application a pro rata payment as part of their severance pay.

93.2.1.10 Application Criteria – An applicant should fill out the complete CEP application for consideration for entry into the program. The officer shall include the following point assessed value factors that have been achieved as of December 31st of each year.

93.2.1.11 College Degrees – Points are not cumulative for degrees and must be from a college/university accredited by an appropriate accrediting association of colleges and universities. The maximum points allowed for formal education shall be twenty (20) and shall apply at time of completion.

Associate Degree – 10 points Bachelor Degree – 15 points
Advanced Degree – 20 points

93.2.1.12 Specialty Assignments.

SPECIALTY ASSIGNMENT	POINTS
ISB Investigators	20
Sr. ISB Investigators (over 20 yrs. w/Dept.)	30
Sr. Vice-Metro Officers (over 20 yrs. w/Dept.; after 6 months)	30
Vice-Metro Officers (after 6 months)	10
Sr. Directed Patrol Officers (over 15 yrs. w/Dept.)	40
Directed Patrol Officers	20
Sr. Patrol Officers (over 15 yrs. w/Dept. assigned to FOD)	20
Sr. Patrol Officer (outside FOD with 20 or more years)	20
Sr. Officers (over 20 yrs. w/Dept. and assigned outside FOD or ISB, for life of the agreement)	20
Sr. Field Training Officers (in yrs served) (over 15 yrs. w/Dept.)	30
Field Training Officers (in yrs. served)	10
Accident Reconstructionist (assigned to FOD)	10
Sr. Accident Reconstructionist (over 15 yrs. w/Dept. Assigned to FOD)	30
Bomb Squad	40

93.2.1.13 Officers shall be limited to one specialty assignment or senior status category despite any overlap (e.g. Senior Accident Reconstructionist with 15 years seniority, assigned within FOD receives total of 30 points).

93.2.1.14 The combined assignment and education points eligible for conversion shall be capped at fifty (50) points.

93.2.1.15 CEP Committee – The committee shall be composed of six (6) representatives, three from the Association and three (3) from the administration. Any expansion of the committee shall be by agreement of the parties. The committee shall serve to review CEP applications and educational reimbursement requests under the terms set forth herein and in the collective bargaining agreement. If the committee is unable to agree upon a particular CEP Application or Educational Reimbursement Request, the matter shall be resolved by the Chief in conjunction with the Association President and a third party agreed upon by the parties. The committee shall undertake such other studies and activities as are agreed upon by the parties consistent with the purpose of the program. Any recommendation of the committee that affects wages, hours, terms and conditions of employment shall be subject to agreement by the Association and the Employer.

93.2.1.16 For purposes of rates of pay, the financial incentives established in the Step Program shall not be added to the officer's base wage rate.[1]

93.2.2 The Association may advise and consult with the Employer on the possible development, content and the format of career advancement programs, courses, and workshops to

[1] ***City of Toledo, Ohio and Toledo Police Patrolman's Association, Local 10.***

be made available to the bargaining unit employees at the regularly-scheduled labor/management meetings. In that connection, the Employer agrees to make available to the Association all literature and other types of information on training opportunities which is received by the Employer. Such endorsement shall serve to notify employees whether participation in such program will serve to enhance their career with the Employer.[1]

93.3 Senior Police Officer I.

93.3.1 Any sworn, safety member Police Officer, regardless of duty assignment, who fulfills the requirements established in this section shall be designated as a Senior Police Officer I and shall be paid at a rate set fifteen (15) salary rate ranges (7.5%) above his or her then-current base monthly salary step. The criteria for such designation shall be as follows:

93.3.1.1 A. Completion of five (5) years of municipal police experience and attainment of the "E" Step of the base salary rate range for the Police Officer classification.

93.3.1.2 B. Completion (acquisition) of at least sixty (60) educational and/or training units.

93.3.1.3 C. Approval of the Chief of Police.

93.4 Senior Police Officer II.

93.4.1 Any sworn, safety member Police Officer who fulfills the requirements established in this section shall be designated as a Senior Police Officer II and shall be eligible to receive career incentive pay differential set forth below:

93.4.1.1 A. The criteria for such designation shall be as follows:

[1] ***Stark County, Ohio Sheriff and Fraternal Order of Police, Ohio Labor Council, Inc.***

93.4.1.2 1. Completion of seven (7) years of municipal police experience and attainment of the "E" Step of the base salary rate for the Police Officer classification.

93.4.1.3 2. Completion (acquisition) of at least ninety (90) educational /training units; or possession of an Associate of Arts Degree from an accredited college with an additional thirty (30) or more educational/training units.

93.4.1.4 3. Approval of the Chief of Police.

93.4.1.5 B. Pay Differential: A Senior Police Officer II will be paid a career incentive pay differential at a rate of twenty-five (25) salary ranges (12.5%) set above his or her then-current base monthly step.[1]

93.5 Senior Police Officer III.

93.5.1 Any sworn, safety member Police Officer who fulfills the requirements established in this section shall be designated as a Senior Police Officer III and shall be eligible to receive career incentive pay differential set forth in Subsection "B" below.

93.5.1.1 A. The criteria for such designations shall be as follows:

93.5.1.2 1. Completion of nine (9) years of municipal police experience and attainment of the "E" Step of the base salary rate for the Police Officer classification.

93.5.1.3 2. Completion (acquisition) of at least one hundred twenty (120) educational/training units; or possession of an Associate of Arts Degree from an accredited college with an additional sixty (60) or more educational/training units.

[1] ***City of Santa Ana and Santa Ana Police Officers Association.***

93.5.1.4 3. Approval of the Chief of Police.

93.5.1.5 B. Pay Differential: A Senior Police Officer III will be paid a career incentive pay differential at a rate of thirty (30) salary rate ranges (15%) set above his or her then-current base monthly salary step.[1]

[1] ***City of Santa Ana and Santa Ana Police Officers Association.***

CHAPTER 11

MISCELLANEOUS TOPICS

The last chapter in this book includes a variety of topics which do not neatly fall in any of the major categories of subject matters in law enforcement collective bargaining agreements. The topics range over a wide number of areas, and include the following:

- Staffing Levels
- Residency
- Pay Levels on Promotion
- Political Activity by Police Officers
- Second-Year Wage Adjustments

Particularly in the area of miscellaneous contract provisions, it is important that the reader check local bargaining laws to determine which topics are mandatory for negotiations. For example, where staffing levels are negotiable in some states, in the vast majority of states staffing is considered a non-negotiable reserved management right. Similarly, in some locations shift selection by seniority can be freely negotiated by labor organizations, where in other areas shift assignment issues are not thought to be mandatorily negotiable.

Law enforcement collective bargaining agreements typically contain a wide variety of clauses relating to the residence of officers. Some contracts contain requirements that officers live within the jurisdictional limits of their employer. Other contracts forbid the employer from imposing any residency requirement. A newer development, such as that represented by the clause contained in this contract from Anaheim, California, gives employees a financial incentive to live within the employer's jurisdictional limits.

Of particular interest is the variety of ways that second-year wage adjustments are determined. This contract contains examples of employers who compute second-year wage adjustments based upon the average wages or total compensation in a pre-determined set of jurisdictions. Yet other employers compute second-year wage adjustments based upon whether the employer's revenues are received in accordance with predicted revenues, while other contract clauses call for the employer to pay the same wage increases to law enforcement officers which are received by other employees in the jurisdiction. Such so-called "parity" or "me too" clauses may be difficult to enforce under the laws of many states.

ARTICLE 94

MISCELLANEOUS PROVISIONS

94.1 Copies of Contract.

94.1.1 The Employer shall provide sufficient copies of this contract for distribution to all Association members.[1]

94.1.2 The Employer shall cause this Agreement to be printed and shall deliver to the Association 3,000 copies of this Agreement for distribution to members by the Association.[2]

94.2 Licensing.

94.2.1 The Employer will pay the cost of state-required licensing for certified officers (currently $15.00 for three years) and for any other employees in the unit for whom state licensing is required during the term of this agreement not to exceed the above amount.[3]

94.3 Veterans' Preference Claims.

94.3.1 It is the intent of the parties to this Agreement that its terms and provisions shall be applicable to all employees included within the bargaining unit. Accordingly, the parties hereby agree that any employees who may come within the provisions of any legislative enactment entitling a military veteran to a preference in employment or which establishes a procedure whereby the military veteran may challenge the Employer's determinations regarding the veteran's employment status will be required to, no later than Step 3 of the Grievance Procedure, elect in

[1] ***Lake County, State of California and Lake County Deputy Sheriffs' Association.***

[2] ***State of New York and Police Benevolent Association.***

[3] ***County of Stearns, Minnesota and Minnesota Teamsters Public and Law Enforcement Employees Union, Local 320.***

writing either the Grievance Procedure or his statutory remedy as his single means of challenging the Employer's determination. If the employee elects to pursue his statutory remedy, any grievance concerning the Employer's employment determination shall be considered withdrawn by the Association and, further, shall not thereafter be a subject of any arbitration proceeding.[1]

ARTICLE 95

RESIDENCY

95.1 Residency.

95.1.1 Residency shall not be a condition of employment for employees; each employee must be a legal resident of the United States and reside within its boundaries.[2]

95.1.2 Officers of the Department shall be permitted to live anywhere outside the Township so long as said officers are able to report for duty within one (1) hour of telephone contact under normal weather conditions.[3]

95.1.3 Employees of the department shall reside in the continental United States.[4]

95.1.4 There is no residency requirement for employees of the Department covered by the collective bargaining agreement.[5]

[1] ***Genesee County, Michigan and AFSCME Council 25.***

[2] ***City of Beaumont, Texas and Beaumont Police Officers Association.***

[3] ***Redford Township, Michigan and Police Officers Association of Michigan.***

[4] ***Nashua, New Hampshire Police Commission and International Brotherhood of Police Officers.***

[5] ***City of Bridgeport, Connecticut and Bridgeport Police Local 1159 and Council 15 AFSCME.***

95.2 Residence Incentive.

95.2.1 The Employer and the Association agree that the public interest is served and that public safety is enhanced by encouraging Police Officers to live within the City limits.

95.2.1.1 The Employer agrees to provide a no-interest loan of ten thousand dollars ($10,000) towards the purchase of the principal residence of any employee in a classification listed in this Memorandum of Understanding. Such principal residence must be within the City limits at the time of purchase.

95.2.1.2 The loan authorized under the provisions of this Article shall be secured by a Second Trust Deed held by the Employer.

95.2.1.3 The loan authorized under the provisions of this Article shall be forgiven at the rate of one thousand dollars ($1,000) per year for each full year the employee maintains the property as his principal residence and remains an active Police Officer in the employ of the Employer. At the conclusion of the ten (10) years, the Employer shall sign its ownership interest in the property over to the employee.[1]

ARTICLE 96

PAY PRACTICES

96.1 Monthly Pay Periods.

96.1.1 Employees shall be paid on a monthly basis, and shall receive the check on the last working day of the month. In the event the regular payday shall fall on a Saturday, Sunday, or an Employer-recognized holiday, the last preceding regular work-

[1] ***City of Anaheim and Anaheim Police Association.***

day shall be the regular payday in lieu of the last day of the month.[1]

96.2 Bi-Weekly Pay Periods.

96.2.1 Payment of salaries herein established shall be bi-weekly. Each pay period shall begin at 12:01 a.m. Sunday, up to and including 12:00 midnight Saturday two weeks following. Each payment shall be made not later than the Friday following the ending of each payroll period and shall include payment for all earnings during the previous payroll period.[2]

96.3 Itemization of Employee's Pay.

96.3.1 The Employer shall itemize employees' paychecks to reflect payment of wages, overtime, incentive pay, clothing allowance and longevity.[3]

96.4 Distribution of Paychecks.

96.4.1 Paychecks will be placed in individual envelopes before being distributed to employees.[4]

96.5 Direct Deposit.

96.5.1 An employee's paycheck shall be directly deposited in an approved bank, savings and loan or credit union upon written request.[5]

[1] *Deschutes County, Oregon and Deschutes County Sheriff Association.*

[2] *Berkeley, California and Berkeley Police Association.*

[3] *City of El Paso, Texas and El Paso Municipal Police Officers' Association.*

[4] *Oneida County, New York and Oneida County Deputy Sheriffs' Benevolent Association.*

[5] *City of Fairfield, California and Fairfield Police Association.*

96.6 Payroll Deductions.

96.6.1 The Employer agrees to deduct from the paychecks of employees giving written authorization, bi-weekly or monthly, any moneys for any authorized Credit Union and remit same to such authorized Credit Union by separate check. The Employer agrees to deduct from the paychecks of employees giving written authorization, any moneys for the U.S. Savings Bond Program and the United Appeal Payroll Deduction Program and remit such withholdings to proper authorities. The Employer agrees to continue to make deductions for group insurance to protect dependents of deceased Police Officers and to remit such withholdings to the Police Insurance Fund.[1]

96.7 Working Out of Class.

96.7.1 Any employee required to work out of the class he holds shall be paid at the rate of the next higher class above his rank during such excess.[2]

96.8 Step Increases.

96.8.1 Progression of employees from their current step to the next higher step in the appropriate labor grade for their classification shall be automatic and will become effective at the beginning of the pay period in which the employee's anniversary date of classification falls.[3]

96.9 Pay Upon Promotion.

96.9.1 Except as modified below, a regular, limited-term or probationary employee promoted to a position in a class with a higher salary range shall receive the recruiting salary for the

[1] ***Toledo, Ohio and Toledo Police Patrolmen's Association.***

[2] ***City of Monroe, Louisiana and International Union of Police Associations Local #81.***

[3] ***St. Petersburg, Florida and Pinellas County Police Benevolent Association, Inc., for Police Officers and Technicians.***

higher class or such higher amount as would be the closest to a two (2)-step increase on the range over the salary received prior to the promotion not to exceed the top step of the range. A new merit increase eligibility date shall be established which shall be the first day of the pay period following completion of the first twenty-six (26) weeks of service in the new class.

96.9.1.1 Any employee who is promoted to a class from which the employee was previously reduced without a salary decrease shall be placed at a salary step no higher than the step which the employee would have achieved if the employee had remained in the class to which he or she was promoted and had demonstrated at least standard performance. The employee's merit increase eligibility date shall be reestablished in order to credit the employee with any time formerly served in the higher class.[1]

96.10 Lateral Entry.

96.10.1 Original appointment shall be at the first step of a pay range. Initial compensation may be at a higher step in the range for the class based on the outstanding and unusual character of the employee's experience or educational ability over and above the qualification requirements specified for the class. Where a higher starting rate is required by a temporary shortage of applicants all current employees in the class involved who are receiving less than the new initial compensation rate shall have their rate of pay adjusted to such rate.[2]

[1] ***Orange County, California and Association of Orange County Deputy Sheriffs.***

[2] ***Torrance, California and Torrance Police Officers Association.***

96.11 Rounding Off of Salaries.

96.11.1 All salaries shall be rounded to the nearest whole dollar.[1]

ARTICLE 97

SECOND YEAR WAGE ADJUSTMENTS

97.1 Local Labor Market Wage Adjustment.

97.1.1 The ten (10) cities used for fixing the monthly salaries shall be those ten (10) cities remaining from an original and complete list of all California cities in the 100,000 to 250,000 population range based on the latest Annual Report of Financial Transactions of California Cities, published by the State Controller, after representatives of the Employer and the appropriate recognized employee organization have alternately struck the names from the list one at a time until the names of ten (10) cities remain. The representatives to strike the first name from the list shall be determined by lot. In the event one or more of the ten (10) cities does not have one or more of the comparable position classifications, the monthly salary for the particular classification shall be computed as the arithmetic average of the next highest and next lowest comparable position classification of that city.

97.1.1.1 The salaries paid in Step "A" shall be the same as the arithmetic average of the starting salaries of the comparable positions in the ten cities and the salaries paid comparable positions in the ten cities. The salaries paid in steps "B," "C," and "D" shall be fixed at amounts which will cause the local safety

[1] ***Glendale, California and Glendale Police Officers' Association.***

members in the Department to advance from the starting steps to the maximum pay steps in approximately equal salary advances.[1]

97.2 Total Compensation.

97.2.1 For the purpose of this agreement, total compensation is defined to include the following items:

1. Salary

2. Fringe Benefits:

    a. Retirement**
    b. Holiday Pay*
    c. Sick Leave Pay*
    d. Vacation Pay*
    e. Uniform Allowance
    f. Night Shift Differential
    g. Mandatory Health Ins**
    h. PERS Health Fund**
    i. Other Pay
    j. Retired Employee Medical Fund
    k. P.O.S.T. Certification Incentive Program

**Movement allowed only under the provisions agreed to in this or existing contracts.

*These elements are directly tied to salary and move as a function of salary.

No independent movement is allowed in these element areas.

3. Insurance

    a. Life
    b. Medical

[1] ***City of San Bernardino, California and San Bernardino Police Officers' Association.***

c. Dental
d. Psychological Counseling

97.2.1.1 Total compensation as defined above will be determined by computing the total compensation effective November 15th of each preceding year afforded similarly-represented classifications of Police Officer in comparable agencies of San Jose, Palo Alto, Santa Clara County (Deputy) and Mountain View (benchmark classifications) and obtaining the total compensation afforded those comparable agencies.

97.2.1.2 It will be a requirement of the Association to allocate each year in advance, in accordance with the attached tabular description, and consistent with this contract, the distribution of total compensation monies within the following element areas as noted in Section IB: (1) salary, (2) fringe benefits, and (3) insurance premiums counseling. Distribution of total compensation monies is to be made based upon: (1) the total compensation arrays for the related benchmark classifications, and (2) the maximum premiums payable by the Employer, and not actual premium to be paid by the Employer, except as noted elsewhere in this contract.

97.2.1.3 Effective with the adoption of this contract, the total compensation allocation currently in effect, including the Employer's mandatory contribution to the Public Employee's Retirement System (PERS), will be the total compensation allocation upon which subsequent adjustment of total compensation is to be based and will be referred to as Base Total Compensation. This replaces the practice that defined the Base Total Compensation as that which is in effect as of November 15th of any year.

97.2.1.4 Adjustment of Salaries and Fringe Benefits for ____, ____, ____, and ____.

97.2.1.5 For all classifications represented by the Association, the base total compensation allocation in effect on January 1, ____, with an additional 12 hours in Holiday Pay, shall be increased by 2.7% effective December 31, ____.

97.2.1.6 For each of calendar years ____, ____ and ___, for all classifications represented by the Association, the base total compensation allocation in effect for each of the preceding calendar years (December 31, 1995 for 1996; December 29, 1996 for 1998; and December 28, 1997 for 1998) shall be increased by the average benchmark movement for Mountain View, Palo Alto, San Jose and Santa Clara County or 3.0%, whichever is less. The effective dates for those increases to total compensation are December 29, 1996 for calendar year ____; December 28, ____ for calendar year ____; and December 27, ____ for calendar year ____.

97.2.1.7 Prior to February 1st of each year of this contract, if it is determined by the Association and representatives of Management of the City, that any of the classifications represented by the Association are 2.5% below the survey average in salary after the common salary adjustment afforded on the dates specified in this contract, the City shall adjust such classifications to the nearest salary step to bring them as close as possible to 2.5% above the survey average on the current salary schedule in effect for classified police. This adjustment will become effective the first day of the first full pay period in February of each year.

97.2.1.8 It will be the prerogative of the Association to allocate, during the term of this contract, total compensation monies among the element areas as defined in the foregoing. Specific retirement benefits, excluding the Employer's payment of all or part of the represented employee's share of PERS contributions, as may be allowed by the Public Employees Retirement System, may be added or deleted subject to the following conditions:

97.2.1.9 1. All such changes will have equal application to all public safety personnel, including eligible members of the Fire Department, if the modification will increase the Employer contribution.

97.2.1.10 2. The Association will assume the responsibility of coordinating with the eligible members of the Fire Bargaining Units and Police Management Unit any desired retirement modifications prior to submission to the Employer, and be prepared to ensure the Employer, in writing, that such modifications are consistent with the wishes of the majority of eligible personnel in each of the Public Safety Units.

97.2.1.11 3. A minimum of nine (9) calendar months' advance notice will be given the Employer, in writing, specifying the nature of the desired changes.

97.2.1.12 4. Any cost associated with obtaining the proposed retirement benefit, such as actuarial valuations or administrative expenses imposed by PERS, shall be paid by the Police and Fire Units. Before any such costs are incurred, representatives of one of the units must assume the responsibility of reimbursing the Employer for all related costs upon demand.

97.2.1.13 It is recognized by both parties to this agreement that it is their mutual responsibility to independently verify, to the extent possible, the accuracy of the information upon which total compensation adjustments are made. Should it be discovered by either party that adjustment(s) to salary and fringe benefits are based on erroneous information or has been erroneously computed, the necessary corrective action will be taken as soon as practical after the discovery and notice of the error has been given. It is the mutual responsibility of both parties to report any suspected error immediately upon discovery to the other party. However, the period for which there will be a right to recover any monies which are either overpaid by the Employer or underpaid to the employee shall be limited to amounts owed or owing during the prior 90 calendar days. The 90-calendar-day period will begin upon the date of written notification by personal service upon the other party.

97.2.1.14 Right of recovery by the Employer of overpayment shall be limited to recovery over the same time period as the overpayment was made. Said repayment will begin with the next paycheck following final determination of the amount to be repaid. Underpayment to the employee shall be made by the Employer in a lump sum of the amount owed on the next regular paycheck following final determination of the amount to be paid.

97.2.1.15 Definitions.

97.2.1.16 Top Step Salary – Maximum step in the monthly salary range for classification (excluding longevity steps).

97.2.1.17 Life, Medical, Dental and Other Insurance - Maximum agency monthly contribution per employee to insurance premium plus maximum agency monthly contribution to other fringe benefit insurance premiums.

97.2.1.18 Retirement - Maximum agency monthly contribution per employee to retirement.

97.2.1.19 Holiday Pay - Number of paid holiday hours allowed by agency per year times hourly salary rate of classification, divided by 12.

97.2.1.20 Vacation Pay - Maximum number of annual paid vacation hours allowed by agency per employee upon completion of five (5) years' service times hourly salary rate for classification divided by 12.

97.2.1.21 Sick Leave Pay - Maximum number of annual paid sick leave hours allowed by agency per employee times hourly rate for classification divided by 12.

97.2.1.22 Other - Monthly salary equivalent of or maximum agency contribution to other fringe benefits available to all full-time agency employees. To be eligible for inclusion in comparison data, such benefits of the comparing jurisdiction must be of a reoccurring nature to become part of their compensation base.

97.2.1.23 Psychological Counseling - Actual dollar amount paid for this service during the prior fiscal year divided by the number of budgeted employees divided by 12.

97.2.1.24 Total Compensation - The sum of items 97.2.1.16 through 2.1.23 above.

97.2.1.25 Hourly Salary Rate - Top step salary as defined above times 12 divided by total number of regular work hours per year.

97.2.1.26 Tabular Descriptions of Adjustment of Total Compensation.

97.2.1.27 November 15, ____; ____; ____; and ____ - Determine average total compensation as of the current November 15th afforded benchmark classifications specified in item IB in comparing agencies noted therein. By November 30, ____, ____ and ____ determine the percentage change in average monthly total compensation afforded said benchmark classifications in the comparing agencies and provide said information to Association.

97.2.1.28 Any comparing agency that is still in negotiations or subject to an arbitrator's decision which has not yet been rendered that will affect the total compensation of that agency's benchmark position as of November 15th will not be used for comparison purposes.

97.2.1.29 When a total compensation adjustment has been implemented in the affected agency, the Employer will recompute the total compensation array, either upward or downward, and such adjustment will be applied effective beginning the pay period following confirmation of the adjustment(s).

97.2.1.30 Any recalculations prompted by the foregoing provisions will not entitle the Association to make any change in allocations to the total compensation array as specified in this agreement.

97.2.1.31 December 10, ____; ____; and ____ - Association provides Employer with total compensation allocation to be in effect for the forthcoming calendar year.

97.2.1.32 December 29, ____; December 28, ____; and December 27, ____ - Employer adopts total compensation allocation as presented by Association and develops salary schedule to be in effect for the forthcoming calendar year.

97.2.1.33 Prior to February 1, ____; findings ____; and ____ - Association provides to the Employer that any represented classification is 2.5% or more below the survey average for that classification.

97.2.1.34 First pay period of February, ____; ____ and ____ - Employer verifies Association finding and adjusts the salary range for classifications which are found to be 2.5% below the survey average to the range on the salary schedule currently in effect which is closest to 2.5% above the survey average.[1]

97.3 Salaries.

97.3.1 During the term of this contract, the monthly salaries of local safety members of the Police Department shall be fixed annually effective August 1st, in accordance with the City Charter as follows: At the amount equal to the arithmetic average of the monthly salaries, paid or approved for payment to local safety members of like or most nearly comparable positions of ten (10) California cities with populations of between 100,000 and 250,000 as shown in the latest Annual Report of Financial Transactions of California Cities published by the State Controller.[2]

97.4 Compensation.

97.4.1 Effective 7/1/__, the salaries for top-step Police Officer will be adjusted to the average of survey cities. If any adjustment is necessary, the increased adjustment shall not be greater than five percent (5%) above the salary rate in effect. If the salary for top-step Police Officer is greater than the City survey average, that salary will be "Y" rated at the salary rate then in effect. Said survey will be conducted based on the top-step Police Officer salary of the survey cities as of June 30, _____.

97.4.1.1 If members' salaries are more than 5% below the average, the Employer shall adjust salaries based on the following schedule:

[1] ***City of Santa Clara, California and Santa Clara Police Officers Association.***

[2] ***City of San Bernardino, California and San Bernardino Police Officers' Association.***

7/1/__	Not to exceed 5%
7/1/__	50% of the difference between current salary and the average or 3%, which ever is greater.
1/1/__	The average of the agreed-upon survey.

97.4.1.2 Should the Employer have the ability to adjust salaries to the average prior to the dates so specified above, it may do so at its sole discretion.

97.4.1.3 Effective 10/1/__, and every October 1st thereafter except as stated below, once the salary for the top-step Police Officer has reached the average salary level of the survey cities, the salary level shall continue to be maintained at the average salary level of the survey cities. In the event that the Employer is unable to maintain the average salary levels due to economic conditions and a budget shortfall, which may result in the elimination of City positions and the layoff of City employees, the Employer agrees that it will meet and confer with the Association to develop a plan for implementing a phased program designed to accomplish the goal of maintaining salaries at the average of the survey cities for like positions.

97.4.1.4 The Employer shall maintain the salary alignment as follows:

Senior Police Officer	10% above Police Officer
Investigator	12% above Police Officer
Sergeant	15% above Investigator

97.4.1.5 The survey cities have been identified as San Bernardino, Orange, Inglewood, Ontario, Torrance, Glendale, Pasadena and Fullerton.[1]

[1] ***City of Pomona, California and Pomona Police Officers' Relief Association.***

97.5 Wage Adjustment Determined by Employer Revenue.

97.5.1 Effective the first payroll period beginning nearest July 1, ____, a four percent (4%) increase shall be applied to all steps in the pay plan. Effective the first payroll period beginning nearest January 1, ____, a three percent (3%) increase shall be applied to all steps in the pay plan.

97.5.1.1 The Employer and the Association agree upon the following formula for determining an across-the-board increase, if any, for the period January 1, ____ to September 30, ____.

97.5.1.2 For each one percent (1%) increase, or fraction thereof, rounded to the nearest one-hundredth of one percent (0.01%), in the preliminary certification in the assessed value for the City on June 30, ____, above the June 30, 1986 value ($3,040,002,699), there shall be an across-the-board increase for all pay steps in the pay plan of one-half of the percentage increase in the preliminary certification, rounded to the nearest one-hundredth of one percent (0.01%), not to exceed a total of five percent (5%).

97.5.1.3 In the event that the increase in preliminary certification in assessed value does not result in an across-the-board increase to the maximum percentage under Part I, then the following criteria in addition to Part I shall apply:

97.5.1.4 The Association and the Employer agree that a $4,200,000 unreserved general fund balance should be maintained. The Association and the Employer agree that for each $300,000 of unreserved general fund balance, as determined for September 30, ____, in excess of $4,200,000, all pay steps in the Pay Plan shall be increased across-the-board as follows:

1st 300,000	1.0%
2nd 300,000	1.0%
3rd 300,000	0.9%
4th 300,000	0.8%
5th 300,000	0.7%
6th 300,000	0.6%

97.5.1.5 The above increases are not to exceed a combined total of 5% from Part I and Part II. In the event that Part I results in an across-the-board increase, the above scale shall be adjusted by reducing the percentage for the 2nd through the 6th 300,000 increments by one-fifth of the amount the across-the-board increase produced from Part I, rounded to the nearest one hundredth of one percent.

97.5.1.6 The Association and the Employer agree that any surplus generated from the ____-____ fiscal year budget will first be applied to maintain the $4,200,000 unreserved general fund balance.

97.5.1.7 The Employer agrees that all available balances and/ or retained earnings contained in all non-general funds that may be transferred to the unreserved general fund balance will be so transferred by September 30, ____.

97.5.1.8 The Employer agrees to review all dormant, inactive, and over-budgeted appropriations and to transfer the unexpended balances of such budgeted funds to the unreserved general fund balance by September 30, ____.

97.5.1.9 The Employer agrees that any dollar savings resulting from the implementation of any program of cost-savings, reorganization, hiring freeze, or similar efforts to reduce expenditures, shall be credited to the unreserved fund balance, except where a reallocation of those dollar savings is necessary to ensure the health, safety, and welfare of the public for FY ____/ ____ only.

97.5.1.10 The Employer agrees that it will not create new reserves, liabilities or encumbrances or increase the amount of existing reserves, liabilities or encumbrances for the purpose of reducing the amount of the unreserved fund balances as of September 30, ____.

97.5.1.11 The Employer agrees that the Reserve for subsequent year's expenditures as of September 30, ____, will be determined only after the conditions found above have been fulfilled.[1]

97.6 Parity Clause.

97.6.1 If the Employer agrees to an across-the-board wage increase (COLA) with the firefighters' union, or with city employees not covered by a collective bargaining agreement, which exceeds that granted police officers in this Agreement for the year in question, the police officers covered by this Agreement shall be granted the same improvement.[2]

ARTICLE 98

SAVINGS CLAUSE

98.1 General.

98.1.1 If any Section of this Agreement or any addendum thereto should be held invalid or to conflict with applicable Federal or State law by any court of competent jurisdiction, the remainder of the Agreement and its addendums shall not be af-

[1] ***Miami Beach, Florida and Fraternal Order of Police.***

[2] ***City of El Paso, Texas and El Paso Municipal Police Officers' Association.***

fected thereby, and the parties shall enter into immediate collective bargaining negotiations for the purpose of arriving at a mutually satisfactory replacement for such Section.[1]

98.2 Waiver of Breach of Contract.

98.2.1 The waiver of any breach, term or condition of this Agreement by either party shall not constitute a precedent in the future enforcement of all its terms and conditions.[2]

ARTICLE 99

ENTIRE AGREEMENT/WAIVER

99.1 General.

99.1.1 The Agreement expressed herein in writing constitutes the entire Agreement between the parties and no oral statement shall add to or supersede any of its provisions.[3]

ARTICLE 100

DURATION

100.1 General.

100.1.1 The term of this Memorandum of Understanding shall commence on August 30, ____ and shall continue in full force and effect until June 30, ____.[4]

[1] ***Genesee County, Michigan and AFSCME Council 25.***

[2] ***Outagamie County, Wisconsin and Outagamie County Deputy Sheriff's Association.***

[3] ***Auburn, Washington and Auburn Police Guild.***

[4] ***Orange, California and City of Orange Police Association.***

ARTICLE 101

EVERGREEN CLAUSE

101.1 General.

101.1.1 This Agreement shall remain in full force and effect until a new Agreement is signed by the parties herein.[1]

ARTICLE 102

WAGES

102.1 Wage Differential Between Ranks.

102.1.1 There will be a five percent (5%) differential in the hourly rate between salary steps A, B, C, D, E and G. Salary step F will be the mid-point between salary steps E and G.[2]

102.1.2 There shall be maintained a minimum differential of fifteen percent (15%) between the ranks of officers.[3]

102.2 Merit Pay.

102.2.1 One (1) additional merit step of one percent (1%) above the maximum for the salary range shall be available to all Patrol Officers and Detectives who have been at the maximum salary for at least one (1) full year of uninterrupted service. All employees who have been at the maximum salary for one (1) full year shall be eligible to receive this merit increase. An employee shall be eligible to receive this increase based on individual performance, as determined by the Police Chief.[4]

[1] ***Nashua, New Hampshire and Nashua Patrolman's Benevolent Association.***

[2] ***City of Santa Clara and Santa Clara Police Officers Association.***

[3] ***Portland, Oregon and Portland Police Association.***

[4] ***Boulder, Colorado and Boulder Police Benefit Association.***

102.3 Pay Upon Reduction.

102.3.1 When a regular, limited-term or probationary employee is reduced as the result of a position reclassification, the applicable salary shall be determined as follows:

102.3.1.1 If the salary of the employee is the same or less than the maximum of the new class, the salary and merit increase eligibility date of the employee shall not change.

102.3.1.2 If the salary of the employee is greater than the maximum of the new range, the salary of the employee shall be designated as a Y-Rate and shall not change during continuous regular service until the maximum of the new range exceeds the salary of the employee or until the period of calendar time indicated in the schedule below has elapsed, whichever is sooner. If, at the end of the calendar period indicated below, the salary of the employee still exceeds the maximum of the new salary range, the salary of the employee shall be reduced to the maximum salary for the new class.

Y-RATE SCHEDULE

Years of Full-Time Continuous Service	Duration of Y-Rate
Less than 5 years	Two years from the date of reclassification
5 years but less than 10 years	Three years from the date of reclassification
10 years but less than 15 years	Four years from the date of reclassification
15 years but less than 20 years	Five years from the date of reclassification
20 years but less than 25 years	Six years from the date of reclassification
25 years or more	Seven years from the date of reclassification

102.3.1.3 When an employee on Y-Rate accepts a voluntary reduction, his or her salary shall be reduced by the amount of the difference between the maximum salary of the class from which the employee is being reduced and the maximum salary of the new class.[1]

102.4 Priority of Wage Increases.

102.4.1 Whenever a general increase, a merit salary increase, a higher salary range or salary range placement, a promotional salary increase, or any combination thereof are effective on the same date, the salary to which an employee is entitled shall be fixed as follows: To the salary received by the employee on the preceding payday shall first be added any general salary increase, then any higher salary range or salary range placement, then any anniversary merit increase, and then any promotional increase.[2]

102.5 Interest on Wage Adjustments.

102.5.1 Interest on wage increases shall accrue at the rate of three percent (3%) per annum from one hundred-twenty (120) days after execution of the Agreement or one hundred-twenty (120) days after the effective date of the increase, whichever is later, to the date of actual payment. Interest on longevity and step-up increments, differentials and holiday pay shall accrue at the rate of three percent (3%) per annum from one hundred-twenty (120) days following its earning or one hundred-twenty (120) days after the execution of this Agreement, whichever is later, to the date of actual payment. Interest on overtime pay shall accrue at the rate of three percent (3%) per annum from one hundred-twenty (120) days following the earning or one

[1] ***Orange County, California and Association of Orange County Deputy Sheriffs.***

[2] ***Ventura County, California and Ventura County Sheriff's Association.***

hundred-twenty (120) days following the employee's submission of an overtime report, whichever is later. Interest accrued pursuant to this paragraph shall be payable only if the amount of interest due to an individual employee exceeds five dollars ($5.00).[1]

102.6 CPI Reformulation.

102.6.1 In the event the specific Consumer Price Index relevant to this Agreement is reformulated by statute, the parties agree to disregard the changes caused in the Consumer Price Index by virtue of the statutory reformulation (for example, this would apply in the instance of passage of a statute which would reduce the Consumer Price Index by a fixed percentage. However, this would not apply to other reformulations of the Consumer Price Index made by the Bureau of Labor Statistics, such as adjusting the relevant weighting of market basket items or other statistical rebasing adjustments).[2]

102.6.2 In lieu of an across-the-board pay raise for fiscal year ____-____ and continuing thereafter, employees shall upon retirement (all kinds, including vesting), receive a retroactive salary increase of five percent (5%) for the employee's last or highest one (1) year's salary.[3]

[1] ***New York, New York and Patrolmen's Benevolent Association of the City of New York.***

[2] ***City of Seattle, Washington and Seattle Police Officers Guild.***

[3] ***City of Miami, Florida and the Fraternal Order of Police, Lodge #20.***

Index

A

B

C

D

E

F

G

H

O

P

T

U

V

W